W9-DDJ-007

OPPOSING
VIEWPOINTS®
SERIES

| Renewable Energy

Other Books of Related Interest:

Opposing Viewpoints Series

Eco-Architecture
Garbage and Recycling
Pollution

At Issue Series

Biofuels
Foreign Oil Dependence
Green Cities

Current Controversies Series

Gasoline

"Congress shall make no law ... abridging the freedom of speech, or of the press."

First Amendment to the US Constitution

The basic foundation of our democracy is the First Amendment guarantee of freedom of expression. The Opposing Viewpoints Series is dedicated to the concept of this basic freedom and the idea that it is more important to practice it than to enshrine it.

OPPOSING VIEWPOINTS® SERIES

| Renewable Energy

David M. Haugen and Susan Musser, Book Editors

GREENHAVEN PRESS
A part of Gale, Cengage Learning

GALE
CENGAGE Learning·

Detroit • New York • San Francisco • New Haven, Conn • Waterville, Maine • London

Elizabeth Des Chenes, *Director, Publishing Solutions*

© 2012 Greenhaven Press, a part of Gale, Cengage Learning

Gale and Greenhaven Press are registered trademarks used herein under license.

For more information, contact:
Greenhaven Press
27500 Drake Rd.
Farmington Hills, MI 48331-3535
Or you can visit our Internet site at gale.cengage.com.

For product information and technology assistance, contact us at:

Gale Customer Support, 1-800-877-4253.
For permission to use material from this text or product, submit all requests online at www.cengage.com/permissions.

Further permissions questions can be emailed to permissionrequest@cengage.com.

Articles in Greenhaven Press anthologies are often edited for length to meet page requirements. In addition, original titles of these works are changed to clearly present the main thesis and to explicitly indicate the author's opinion. Every effort is made to ensure that Greenhaven Press accurately reflects the original intent of the authors. Every effort has been made to trace the owners of copyrighted material.

Cover Image © GYRO PHOTOGRAPHY/amanaimagesRF/Getty Images

LIBRARY OF CONGRESS CATALOGING-IN-PUBLICATION DATA

Renewable energy / David M. Haugen and Susan Musser, book editors.
   p. cm. -- (Opposing viewpoints)
   Summary: "Renewable Energy: Opposing Viewpoints is the leading source for libraries and classrooms in need of current-issue materials. The viewpoints are selected from a wide range of highly respected sources and publications"-- Provided by publisher.
   Includes bibliographical references and index.
   ISBN 978-0-7377-6139-9 (hardback) -- ISBN 978-0-7377-6140-5 (paperback)
   1. Renewable energy sources--Juvenile literature. I. Haugen, David M., 1969- II. Musser, Susan.
   TJ808.2.R448 2012
   333.79'4--dc23
                              2011051842

Printed in the United States of America
1 2 3 4 5 6 7 16 15 14 13 12

Contents

Chapter 1: Will Renewable Energy Sources Help Resolve Global Problems?

Chapter 2: What Must Be Done to Transition from Nonrenewable to Renewable Energy?

Chapter 3: What Renewable Energy Sources Are Viable Parts of the World's Energy Future?

Chapter 4: What Should Be Government's Role in Promoting Renewable Energies?

Why Consider Opposing Viewpoints?

> *"The only way in which a human being can make some approach to knowing the whole of a subject is by hearing what can be said about it by persons of every variety of opinion and studying all modes in which it can be looked at by every character of mind. No wise man ever acquired his wisdom in any mode but this."*
>
> *John Stuart Mill*

In our media-intensive culture it is not difficult to find differing opinions. Thousands of newspapers and magazines and dozens of radio and television talk shows resound with differing points of view. The difficulty lies in deciding which opinion to agree with and which "experts" seem the most credible. The more inundated we become with differing opinions and claims, the more essential it is to hone critical reading and thinking skills to evaluate these ideas. Opposing Viewpoints books address this problem directly by presenting stimulating debates that can be used to enhance and teach these skills. The varied opinions contained in each book examine many different aspects of a single issue. While examining these conveniently edited opposing views, readers can develop critical thinking skills such as the ability to compare and contrast authors' credibility, facts, argumentation styles, use of persuasive techniques, and other stylistic tools. In short, the Opposing Viewpoints Series is an ideal way to attain the higher-level thinking and reading skills so essential in a culture of diverse and contradictory opinions.

In addition to providing a tool for critical thinking, Opposing Viewpoints books challenge readers to question their own strongly held opinions and assumptions. Most people form their opinions on the basis of upbringing, peer pressure, and personal, cultural, or professional bias. By reading carefully balanced opposing views, readers must directly confront new ideas as well as the opinions of those with whom they disagree. This is not to argue simplistically that everyone who reads opposing views will—or should—change his or her opinion. Instead, the series enhances readers' understanding of their own views by encouraging confrontation with opposing ideas. Careful examination of others' views can lead to the readers' understanding of the logical inconsistencies in their own opinions, perspective on why they hold an opinion, and the consideration of the possibility that their opinion requires further evaluation.

Evaluating Other Opinions

To ensure that this type of examination occurs, Opposing Viewpoints books present all types of opinions. Prominent spokespeople on different sides of each issue as well as well-known professionals from many disciplines challenge the reader. An additional goal of the series is to provide a forum for other, less known, or even unpopular viewpoints. The opinion of an ordinary person who has had to make the decision to cut off life support from a terminally ill relative, for example, may be just as valuable and provide just as much insight as a medical ethicist's professional opinion. The editors have two additional purposes in including these less known views. One, the editors encourage readers to respect others' opinions—even when not enhanced by professional credibility. It is only by reading or listening to and objectively evaluating others' ideas that one can determine whether they are worthy of consideration. Two, the inclusion of such viewpoints encourages the important critical thinking skill of objectively evaluating an author's credentials and bias. This evaluation will illuminate an author's reasons for taking a particular stance on an issue and will aid in readers' evaluation of the author's ideas.

It is our hope that these books will give readers a deeper understanding of the issues debated and an appreciation of the complexity of even seemingly simple issues when good and honest people disagree. This awareness is particularly important in a democratic society such as ours in which people enter into public debate to determine the common good. Those with whom one disagrees should not be regarded as enemies but rather as people whose views deserve careful examination and may shed light on one's own.

Thomas Jefferson once said that "difference of opinion leads to inquiry, and inquiry to truth." Jefferson, a broadly educated man, argued that "if a nation expects to be ignorant and free . . . it expects what never was and never will be." As individuals and as a nation, it is imperative that we consider the opinions of others and examine them with skill and discernment. The Opposing Viewpoints Series is intended to help readers achieve this goal.

David L. Bender and Bruno Leone,
Founders

Introduction

> *"If we hope to continue leading the*
> *global economy, America must place*
> *first in [the clean energy] race. That's*
> *why we're making the most significant*
> *investment in clean energy in history,*
> *offering grants to companies that*
> *produce wind turbines and solar*
> *panels, helping us double renewable*
> *energy production in the coming years."*
>
>

Barack Obama, Smithsonian,
July–August 2010
>

> *"A radical, government-mandated,*
> *expensive conversion to renewable*
> *resources will create many more*
> *problems than it pretends to solve."*
>
>

Daniel Holler, Human Events,
May 4, 2009
>

Since the passage of the Energy Policy Act of 2005, the US Department of Energy (DOE) has been authorized to issue loan guarantees for business projects that reduce greenhouse gas emissions or implement new energy-saving technologies. The government does not necessarily fund these projects, but it does guarantee repayment of loans to any bank or lending institution that arranges the financing. In 2009, in the wake of the global recession, the DOE began soliciting alternative energy projects in earnest. Flush with money provided through the economic stimulus package, the DOE backed roughly forty ventures that included the construction of the world's largest wind farm, several large solar power facilities, an ethanol manufacturing center using cellulose as its prime resource, and the first new nuclear power plant built in the United States in the last three decades. The stimulus funding allocated for these projects ceased on September 30, 2011, when the program's official deadline had been reached. Advocates and critics of this $2.5 billion spending package (which through market subsidy rates actually supports 10 to 16 times its value in debt) were left to debate whether the investment in renewable energy was worth the expense to taxpayers.

Those who questioned the objectives and costs of this spending plan found a rallying point for their arguments when Solyndra Inc., a California-based, solar energy startup that produced cylindrical, rooftop solar panels, filed for bankruptcy on August 31, 2011. Solyndra received $535 million in government-backed loans in September 2009, but executives claimed the money was not enough to make them competitive with foreign manufacturers. The company closed its doors in August and laid off more than one thousand employees. The day after the bankruptcy filing, House Energy and Commerce Committee Chairman Fred Upton told ABC News, "This is just a classic case of fraud and abuse and waste."

On September 23, 2011, facing Upton and other members of the committee at a hearing, Solyndra's top two officers invoked their Fifth Amendment rights and refused to answer questions about how the loan money was used and how the company planned to pay it back. According to former employees, Solyndra's executives spent big sums in anticipation of a boom in the renewables market. In interviews with the *Washington Post* for a September 22, 2011, article, Peter M. Kohlstadt, a research engineer, stated, "Obviously their forecasts weren't correct. We just didn't have the sales we thought we had." Writing in a September 17, 2011, piece for *National Review* Online, Andrew C. McCarthy claimed, "The chance that Solyndra would ever become profitable was essentially nonexistent, particularly given that solar-panel competitors backed by China produce energy at drastically lower prices."

While some critics are content to chastise President Obama for backing the wrong company, others insist the administration's support for green technology is wrongheaded. "This whole idea that the president is going to create jobs from this green technology is suspect," remarked Cliff Stearns, chairman of the House Energy and Commerce Oversight and Investigations Subcommittee. In a September 13, 2011, article for the Internet newsmagazine *Slate*, columnist David Weigel quotes Stearns saying, "I think the president is unwise to spend the government's money on industries that are not viable." In Stearns' view—and the views of other naysayers—renewable resources will not provide the solution to the country's energy needs because of their high cost and low performance.

President Obama, however, was quick to challenge such claims. In an ABC News television interview on October 3, 2011, the president said, "Hindsight is always 20/20. [The backing of Solyndra] went through the regular review process and people felt this was a good bet." Diverting this public conversation toward the larger issue, Obama made it clear that he believes the nation must continue to support companies that want to compete in a marketplace that he feels is imperative to America's future. Three days after his appearance on ABC, the president declared during a White House press conference that he did not believe American companies could not compete with China and other foreign interests in the field of renewable energies. "I'm not going to surrender to other countries technological leads that could end up determining whether or not we're building a strong middle class in this country," he argued. "And so . . . we're going to have to keep on pushing hard to make sure that manufacturing's located here, new businesses are located here and new technologies are developed here."

Obama puts faith in Secretary of Energy Steven Chu, whose department anticipates that the government loan program will create sixty thousand US jobs while jumpstarting a green industry—through replication of the initial forty projects—that could potentially lead to far more employment opportunities for Americans. Like Obama, Chu has stated many times that the United States has to remain competitive in the renewable energy market and be a leader in the fight against climate change. In an October 3, congratulatory speech at the 2011 Solar Decathlon (a competition to design energy efficient dwellings), Chu dismissed critics by stating, "Others say this is a race America shouldn't even be in. They say we can't afford to invest in clean energy. I say we can't afford *not* to." This is the view the Obama administration has pushed since its inception. The White House's March 2011 *Blueprint for a Secure Energy Future* concisely reiterates the position. "Maintaining our leadership in research and development is critical to winning the future and deploying innovative technologies that will create quality jobs and move towards clean energy economy that reduces our reliance on oil," the *Blueprint* contends. Only through such leadership and innovation does the administration believe that Americans, working in support of renewable energies, will "leave this generation and future generations with a country that is stronger, healthier, and more prosperous."

With official financial and rhetorical backing for renewable energy projects, it would seem the die has been cast in favor of a "greener" America. However, as the Solyndra controversy and the difficulties to date in successfully scaling up solar, wind, geothermal, and alternative fuel programs have illustrated, the green future is far from assured. In *Opposing Viewpoints: Renewable Energy*, the debate over the practicality of renewable energy solutions as well as the demand for and the costs of their implementation belie any unity regarding the correct course for the nation—even the world—to pursue. In the following chapters: Will Renewable Energy Sources Help Resolve Global Problems? What Must Be Done to Transition from Nonrenewable to Renewable Energy? What Renewable Energy

Sources Are Viable Parts of the World's Energy Future? and What Should Be Government's Role in Promoting Renewable Energies? the authors assembled in this anthology dispute the strengths and drawbacks of renewable energies and the political, environmental, and financial reasons they should or should not be part of the national and global energy outlook.

Will Renewable Energy Sources Help Resolve Global Problems?

Chapter Preface

The belief that the world must find the means to provide power through renewable energy resources in order to stave off serious environmental and climate disasters has been trumpeted for decades. However, not all observers and analysts concur that this vision is practical or even feasible. Most critics, for example, insist that wind power is too intermittent to handle base-load power supply for large regions and solar energy is simply too expensive to implement on a large scale. In an editorial in the *Washington Post* on February 3, 2010, William O'Keefe, the CEO for the George C. Marshall Institute, a science and public policy think tank, rejects the idea that renewables can provide enough viable power for the United States alone. He states flatly, "The notion that so called green technologies can significantly replace fossil energy in a large way is a fiction and pursuing that illusion will only waste more taxpayer dollars."

Other countries, though, have bowled over such skepticism and invested in the widespread use of solar, wind, and other green technologies. In 2000 Germany began a massive subsidy (one billion euros per month) of solar energy production that quickly led to a boon in the industry and an increase in renewable energy supply. According to a September 30, 2011, SustainableBusiness .com news piece, "Renewable energy supplied a record 20.8% of its electricity in the first half of 2011, from wind, solar, biomass and hydro." These figures are quite a startling jump from the roughly 6 percent of Germany's energy needs that were being met by renewables in 2000. The same article boasts that the price of energy in Germany is decreasing as the contribution of green energy rises.

China is another foreign power that has ramped up its renewable energy portfolio. Flush with capital from its financial growth over the past several decades, China has launched an ambitious wind project, building onshore and offshore turbines in key areas. Like Germany, China has feed-in tariffs that demand the country's utilities purchase renewable energy at a higher rate than conventional resources, thus ensuring that producers have a price incentive to expand supply. According to senior writer Steve Hargreaves of CNN/Money, China's incentives have encouraged more local and foreign investors to fund these projects, edging the United States out of the top spot in 2010 for renewable energy investment. In his September 23, 2010, article, Hargreaves explains, "Most analysts feel the investment money is flowing to China because that country has stable policies that encourage the construction of renewable energy power projects." Although Hargreaves points out that the United States still produces more gigawatts of energy from renewables than China, he believes the uniform government policies in China are helping it to expand at a faster rate.

In the following chapter, various authors put forth their beliefs on whether renewable technologies can meet global energy demands and whether the consequences of making the transition away from fossil-fuel energy production will alleviate or exacerbate environmental and climate concerns. Despite the supposed successes in countries such as Germany and China, forecasters like O'Keefe maintain that the costs of these projects are untenable for taxpayers and unjustified when compared to the growing energy demands of the planet. Others insist the global community cannot shy away from exploring and expanding these energy resources without bringing greater harm to populations and ecosystems.

"If Governments were serious about combating climate change, the focus would be on supporting the massive uptake and deployment of existing, market-ready renewable energy and energy efficiency technologies."

Renewable Energies Will Halt Climate Change

Greenpeace

Renewable energy resources are already supplying electricity to millions of people throughout the globe. In the viewpoint that follows, Greenpeace argues that these resources need to be expanded to meet growing energy demand and to counteract climate change. According to Greenpeace, fossil-fuel-based energy production cannot be the solution to rising energy demands because the carbon emissions from the burning of these resources contribute to climate change. The organization also contends that nuclear power is too hazardous and expensive to be an effective remedy. Instead, Greenpeace maintains that the wind and solar energy industries are already improving technologies and gearing up to provide the carbon-free energy the world needs. Greenpeace insists that governments should invest in these industries to prove their commitment to fighting global climate change. Greenpeace is an international environmental and wildlife protection advocacy organization.

As you read, consider the following questions:

1. Total global installed electrical generation capacity of renewable energies passed what wattage at the end of 2005, according to Greenpeace?
2. According to the cited *Global Wind Energy Outlook of 2006*, what percentage of the world's electricity needs is expected to be met by wind power by 2050?
3. Why does Greenpeace claim that carbon capture and storage practices are an "unwise" solution to the problems of climate change?

It is a truism that we cannot continue forever consuming the earth's finite energy resources. In the long term, the world's energy system will be supplied completely by renewable energy sources. Unfortunately 'in the long term' isn't good enough. Although the renewable energy sector is growing rapidly, the climate change imperative dictates that we begin the wholesale transformation of our energy system now, if we are to have any possibility of avoiding the worst of dangerous climate change by keeping global mean temperature rise well below 2°C above pre-industrial levels.

In today's world, there are many other reasons to support a massive uptake of renewable energy and to move away from conventional fossil fuel and nuclear sources:

- Air pollution from the transport and power sectors has made our cities hazardous to our health, particularly to our children's;

- A distributed system of generation from a variety of renewable sources provides a much more robust energy system much less susceptible to interruptions of supply;

• Relying on largely indigenous renewable sources of energy can protect local economies from the massive economic disruptions caused by speculation-driven swings on global commodities markets;

• A dispersed system of renewable generating systems is much more physically secure from attack;

• As the growing renewable energy industry has demonstrated, the sector is a fast-growing supplier of high quality jobs, much more so than the capital-intensive conventional energy sector.

The renewable energy industry is booming worldwide, attracting almost 40 billion USD [US dollars] in investment in 2005, with most technologies growing at double-digit rates. Total installed electrical generation capacity passed 180 GW [gigawatts] by the end of 2005, with nearly half of that in the developing world. The [2005] REN21 [Renewable Energy Policy Network for the 21st Century] Global Status Report estimates that at least 85 renewable energy companies or divisions have market valuations greater than USD 40 million, up from 60 companies or divisions in 2004.

Renewable Energies Can Meet Electricity Demands

Wind—Greenpeace has been working with the renewable energy industry for many years, seeking to promote the benefits of the technology in both ecological and economic terms. The wind industry has been the leading success story to date, with a global industry now worth more than € [euro] 13 billion (2006), employing about 150,000 people. Greenpeace and the Global Wind Energy Council's latest scenario, the Global Wind Energy Outlook [2006], foresees continued rapid growth of the industry. After a record year in 2005 during which 11,531 MW [megawatts] of new capacity was installed, total wind power capacity worldwide was at 59,084 MW. The report outlines 3 scenarios for installed capacity against two different projections of future electricity demand. While well on target to meet our previous projections of providing 12% of global electricity supply by 2020, the report goes on to outline future scenarios where wind's contribution tops out between 17 and 34% of global electricity supply by 2050, saving up to almost 5 billion tons of CO_2 [carbon dioxide] annually by that date.

Solar Photovoltaics—There is enough energy from the sun reaching the earth to supply total global energy needs many thousand times over. Learning to harness this energy efficiently and economically, however, has taken some time. The solar photovoltaic industry (solar PV—converting sunlight into electricity) continues to grow at about 35% per year, even faster than the wind industry, with grid-connected PV growing at 55% last year. It now represents a €5 billion/year industry in Europe alone. As detailed in our [2005] joint report with the European Photovoltaic Industry Association, "The Solar Generation", solar PV can supply more than 1% of total global electricity supply by 2020, and as much as 24% by 2040. There really is no limit to the growth of this technology.

Greenpeace and the German Aerospace Center (DLR) have developed a scenario which shows how energy efficiency and renewable energy technologies can be employed to help us meet rigorous climate targets, reaching an 80% reduction in fossil-fuel related CO_2 emissions for the EU-25 [European Union of 25 nations] by 2050. The 'Energy Revolution' Scenario achieves these targets while at the same time phasing out nuclear power.

Improved Technologies for a Sustainable Energy Future

Renewable energy is not the whole solution to the climate change problem. Energy efficiency measures have extraordinary potential to reduce our greenhouse gas emissions in the energy sector, and much of this could be achieved at a net negative cost, i.e., we would save money. Renewable energy will not stop deforestation, nor stop emissions of methane or industrial greenhouse gases.

President Obama Commits America to Clean and Renewable Energy

We are making our government's largest ever investment in renewable energy—an investment aimed at doubling the generating capacity from wind and other renewable resources in three years. Across America, entrepreneurs are constructing wind turbines and solar panels and batteries for hybrid cars with the help of loan guarantees and tax credits—projects that are creating new jobs and new industries. We're investing billions to cut energy waste in our homes, our buildings, and appliances—helping American families save money on energy bills in the process.

We've proposed the very first national policy aimed at both increasing fuel economy and reducing greenhouse gas pollution for all new cars and trucks—a standard that will also save consumers money and our nation oil. We're moving forward with our nation's first offshore wind energy projects. We're investing billions to capture carbon pollution so that we can clean up our coal plants. And just this week, we announced that for the first time ever, we'll begin tracking how much greenhouse gas pollution is being emitted throughout the country.

Later this week, I will work with my colleagues at the G20 [group of 20 nations and finance institutions leading global economic growth] to phase out fossil fuel subsidies so that we can better address our climate challenge. And already, we know that the recent drop in overall U.S. emissions is due in part to steps that promote greater efficiency and greater use of renewable energy.

Barack Obama, Remarks by the President
at United Nations Secretary-General Ban Ki-
Moon's Climate Change Summit, New York,
September 22, 2009.

But it can and must play the major role in combating climate change. Renewable energy and energy efficiency technologies are ready now—existing industries with proven technologies, which with the right support can move us rapidly towards a sustainable energy future.

Some Governments and industry keep talking about how we need 'new technologies' with which we can meet the climate challenge, usually some combination of 'clean coal' with carbon capture and storage, nuclear power, and hydrogen. New technologies are certainly needed and welcome, but the climate will not wait.

Carbon capture and storage (CCS): The pursuit of CCS as a 'solution' is unwise given its lack of technological maturity and the absence of commercial viability. The construction of 'capture ready' power plants places hope in an end-of-pipe solution that may or may not be realised in time to effectively reduce CO_2 emissions from the power sector. Reliance on CCS is veiled in uncertainty as to whether CO_2 can be permanently stored in an environmentally-sound manner. Even if CCS could significantly reduce CO_2 emissions, it would not solve other problems which are inherent to the combustion of dirty fuels.

Nuclear: After having received untold billions in direct government subsidies, nuclear power remains very expensive, [and] presents both proliferation risks and health hazards, not to mention the radioactive waste problem, which the industry has been unsuccessfully trying to 'solve' for at least four decades. The long lead times needed for nuclear plant construction mean that it is unlikely that nuclear will play any substantial role in the coming two or three decades in meeting the climate challenge.

Hydrogen: Hydrogen is an energy carrier, not an energy source, and commercially viable and robust fuel cells remain many years off, assuming we had sufficient renewably generated electricity which needed to be stored as hydrogen.

If Governments were serious about combating climate change, the focus would be on supporting the massive uptake and deployment of existing, market-ready renewable energy and energy efficiency technologies. They would not be chasing future technological rainbows supported by massive R&D [research and development] budgets while continuing to spend hundreds of billions per year subsidizing conventional energy technologies.

Energy Security for All

We urgently need a clean energy system based on the efficient use of renewable energy sources, that has at its heart protecting us from climate change, the protection of the environment and the delivery of sustainable development. We need an energy system, which does not render our cities uninhabitable; increases the radioactive burden for future generations; and which does not lead to the proliferation of nuclear weapons.

We seek a world in which the manifest benefits of energy services, such as light, heat, power and transport are equitably available for all: north and south, rich and poor. Only in this way can we create true energy security, as well as the conditions for true human security.

> *"The state of renewable technology means we just can't get to a level of carbon in the atmosphere that will stop major climate changes from occurring this century."*

Renewable Energies Will Not Halt Climate Change

Jason Harrow

In the viewpoint that follows, Jason Harrow asserts that the global emphasis on renewable energies replacing fossil-fuel-based energies is wrongheaded. Harrow claims the drive to make this change is based on the assumption that renewables will help arrest climate change; however, he insists that renewables cannot hope to offset carbon emissions because they are not cheap enough to widely adopt and they will not make a significant dent in the problem. Harrow believes climate change is already a certainty that cannot be undone after decades of carbon pollution and environmental abuse. He advocates forgetting about climate change and drafting short-term energy policies that will not sacrifice jobs or precious funding on the impractical "renewables" solution. Jason Harrow is a law student at Harvard University and the former president of the school's chapter of the American Constitution Society.

Jason Harrow, "Moore's Law and the Future of Renewable Energy: Part 4," *Harvard Law and Policy Review Blog*, February 25, 2011. Reproduced by permission.

As you read, consider the following questions:

1. Why does Harrow believe the problem of stopping climate change is akin to trying to stop a runaway train?

2. Why does the author think that investing in renewable energy solutions will not likely lead to job growth in the United States?

3. What solution does Harrow propose may be a necessary project the world may have to invent and adopt in order to mitigate the problems of climate change?

Before turning to how policymakers should act given what we can expect of renewable technology for the next few decades, let me first summarize the upshot of my [previous writings on this subject]. As Freeman Dyson recently wrote in the *New York Review of Books* [March 10, 2011], since 1965, the price of electronic computer equipment "has decreased and the numbers have increased by a factor of a billion, nine powers of ten." In 1965, practically no one had computers. Now, most people encounter dozens of things with computer chips every single day. That's because "nine powers of ten are enough to turn a trickle into a flood."

But the astonishing speed of adoption in the computer industry cannot be replicated in the renewable energy field. It is unlikely that the current trickle of renewables will turn into a flood by 2035. To be sure, it will be a larger trickle, and maybe there will be a major breakthrough. The good money says that the trickle won't turn into a flood, though.

Few policymakers want to admit this, because it would make life much easier if a bunch of smart engineers could solve the nasty little problem of climate change. And so the President [Barack Obama] has offered a goal of getting to 80% "clean" energy by 2035. Yet that goal is likely unattainable, and even if we do get there, we'll be relying more on natural gas and less on renewables than the President cared to admit publicly. That's because renewables probably will not be cheap enough in 10 or 20 years for universal deployment by 2035 in America, let alone the developing world. If that's the case, then we need to seriously rethink what our policy should look like.

Ignoring Climate Change for Now

I want to argue in this post something that most liberals won't like to hear: we should do nothing about climate change in the short term. Squadoosh. Zero. We should pretend the problem doesn't exist. Honestly.

A quick disclaimer: I think the problem of climate change is exceedingly serious. I agree with leading climate scientists, like Dan Shrag, who think that the situation is "dire" and that, in fact, "our predictions may be conservative." I believe that the climate will drastically change in ways that will have major effects on human society in the span of a few decades. As Cal Tech's Nate Lewis says, "this is not changing a few lightbulbs in Fresno." This is upending our entire energy infrastructure, and soon—because real disaster looms.

We have to start admitting to ourselves, though, that we can't stave off disaster by reducing carbon emissions over the next several decades. It won't happen because of politics, so technology is our only hope. I've argued over the last several weeks that this last hope is unlikely to bear fruit in the next few decades, though. Ultimately, we are too far down the line, and we can't throw a switch and turn off the carbon emissions any time soon.

We have to think about the problem of stopping climate change as akin to trying to stop a runaway train: once you've passed the critical distance needed to break the train, it's just over. You can't stop the train in time any more—you just try to contain the damage. You can cross your fingers that it'll stop, and you can pretend like there's still hope because a crash hasn't happened yet (and maybe, just maybe, Denzel Washington will be on board). But if the train is 50 feet away from the wall and it takes 100 feet to break, it's a matter of if, not when. That hope is false hope.

Likewise, the state of renewable technology means we just can't get to a level of carbon in the atmosphere that will stop major climate changes from occurring this century. We emitted too much carbon before we knew that doing so would cause a problem, and renewable technologies won't be good enough in the near future to put the genie back in the bottle.

Unfortunately, if technology won't do the job, then the next best solution is politically impossible. We need a really high price on carbon, and we need it yesterday—that's the only way to flip the carbon emissions switch from on to off. But much less drastic measures have failed to attain sufficient political support. The failed Waxman-Markey Bill would have required electricity providers to satisfy 20% of demand "from a combination of electricity savings and renewable electricity" in 2039. I'm sorry, but as far as the climate's concerned, that's closer to turning off a lightbulb in Fresno than turning off every coal plant in America, let alone all the new ones that China builds every year. And even that bill couldn't pass.

A Misguided Energy Policy Will Cost Jobs

Actually, both Waxman-Markey and the President's 80% clean energy goal are the equivalents of throwing a small glass of water on a five-alarm blaze (especially once you realize that the "clean energy" goal is really a "natural gas" goal plus a blind wish that renewables will somehow start getting a lot cheaper a lot faster than they are). We need the fire department, not a glass of water. Sadly, the Fire Department doesn't seem to be forthcoming.

Some readers may agree with that proposition, but I think most would then say "but something must be better than nothing." I don't think that's true. Rather, doing basically nothing—for now—is preferable to the ineffectual and unrealistic proposals that represent the only steps that could be politically feasible. How could this be?

The main reason is that there will almost certainly be fewer American jobs and lower economic growth in the near and medium term if we have some middling green energy policy than with no green energy policy. That's because there's no such thing as "green jobs"—there are only "jobs" and "unemployment." Given that, why must it be the case that a country powered by wind and solar—especially when those technologies are more expensive than the alternatives—would have more jobs in it than a country powered by gas and coal?

In fact, as reported recently in *Slate* [February 13, 2011], an important new study on this topic concluded that "the number of jobs that these policies create is likely to be offset—or worse— by the number of jobs that they destroy." Worse, even the jobs that are created will not necessarily be American jobs, because "China tops the world in solar panel manufacturing." Moreover, our cost of electricity would be higher if we had a policy that artificially incented companies to build solar facilities, and those higher prices simply have to slow short-term economic growth. Such costs in terms of lost jobs, higher energy prices, and slower growth could be worth it if we were making any headway on the climate change problem with these policies. We're not.

Second, a middling policy will let us pretend that we are doing something about the problem. This possibility looms large because the climate change problem is not like traditional governmental problems that operate on individuals. Consider that for problems like providing healthcare or eliminating segregation or alleviating poverty, the government might be validly criticized from the left for not doing "enough." But everyone would concede that for the people helped by the government program, "something" is better than "nothing." For instance, I wish more children participated in Head Start, but surely a program that includes some children is better than not having the program at all.

Pushing Renewables at the Expense of Better Solutions to Climate Change

We should ask ourselves what our aim is [in the climate change debate]. Is it to stop climate breakdown, or is it to engineer the maximum roll-out of renewable power? Sometimes it seems to me that greens are putting renewables first, climate change second. We have no obligation to support the renewables industry—or any other industry—against its competitors. Our obligation is to persuade policy makers to bring down emissions and reduce other environmental impacts as quickly and effectively as possible. The moment we start saying we won't accept one technology under any circumstances, or we must use another technology whether it's appropriate or not is the moment at which we make that aim harder to achieve.

George Monbiot, *"The Moral Case for Nuclear Power," August 8, 2011. www .monbiot.com.*

Climate change is not like that. It's much more like an on-off switch: either we do something major, from a global perspective, or we're cooked. It's not the case that "every little bit helps"— actually, only really big changes help. Pretending we're doing something may stop us from thinking bigger sometime down the line when the political winds have changed.

New Energy Policy Should Focus on Short-Term Problems

I think we should therefore free ourselves from the strictures of thinking about climate change when we design energy policy this decade. We should recognize that down the line we will need to mitigate the problem and likely even engage in geoengineering to cool the planet. That is scary but inevitable, and we should get used to it. But we don't have to do it today or tomorrow, and we can't do much about it now anyway.

So let's make good energy policy based on other factors in the short and medium term instead of pursuing the ineffectual and incoherent course we are now pursuing. Some of that may of course mean renewable energy sources, because there are other good reasons to pursue them—reducing dependence on oil for national security reasons first among them. But, if it's inevitable that we're not going to make a dent in carbon emissions this decade by radically altering our energy sources, let's at least not artificially slow economic growth while we're at it. One mistake is more than enough.

| "By setting up wind and wave farms, we convert part of the sun's useful energy into unusable heat."

Relying on Renewable Energies Would Damage the Earth

Mark Buchanan

Mark Buchanan is an American physicist who writes a column for Nature Physics. *He was formerly an editor for* Nature *and wrote for* New Scientist. *In the following viewpoint, Buchanan remarks on the work of geoscience professor Axel Kleidon of the Max Planck Institute for Biogeochemistry in Germany. According to Kleidon, renewable energies—such as wind, wave, and solar power—may have unintended consequences if put to greater use. In Kleidon's view, the world has only so much "free energy" to be used by all systems on the earth. If wind farms and solar panels co-opt more and more of that free energy, then less will reach the earth to stabilize the planet's natural systems, Kleidon argues. He goes on to say that the removal of that energy from nature could drastically alter wind and precipitation patterns. He also claims that, because renewable energy conversion is not perfect, energy lost in the system is turned into heat, and enough heat produced by ever-expanding solar, wave, and wind projects will be vented into the atmosphere, creating significant climate change.*

Mark Buchanan, "The Fantasy of Renewable Energy," *New Scientist*, vol. 210, April 2, 2011, pp. 8–9. Copyright © 2011 Reed Business Information–UK. All Rights Reserved. Distributed by Tribune Media Services. Reproduced by permission.

As you read, consider the following questions:

1. As Buchanan writes, what fraction of the sun's energy does humankind currently use?

2. As Buchanan notes, how many terawatts of energy will humanity have to currently replace if fossil fuel generators are sacrificed for renewables?

3. What two solutions does Buchanan propose to increase the amount of free energy within the earth's systems?

Witness a howling gale or an ocean storm, and it's hard to believe that humans could make a dent in the awesome natural forces that created them. Yet that is the provocative suggestion of one physicist who has done the sums.

He concludes that it is a mistake to assume that energy sources like wind and waves are truly renewable. Build enough wind farms to replace fossil fuels, he says, and we could seriously deplete the energy available in the atmosphere, with consequences as dire as severe climate change.

Axel Kleidon of the Max Planck Institute for Biogeochemistry in Jena, Germany, says that efforts to satisfy a large proportion of our energy needs from the wind and waves will sap a significant proportion of the usable energy available from the sun. In effect, he says, we will be depleting green energy sources. His logic rests on the laws of thermodynamics, which point inescapably to the fact that only a fraction of the solar energy reaching Earth can be exploited to generate energy we can use.

Depleting the Earth's Free Energy

When energy from the sun reaches our atmosphere, some of it drives the winds and ocean currents, and evaporates water from the ground, raising it high into the air. Much of the rest is dissipated as heat, which we cannot harness.

At present, humans use only about 1 part in 10,000 of the total energy that comes to Earth from the sun. But this ratio is misleading, Kleidon says. Instead, we should be looking at how much useful energy—called "free" energy in the parlance of thermodynamics—is available from the global system, and our impact on that.

Humans currently use energy at the rate of 47 terawatts (TW) or trillions of watts, mostly by burning fossil fuels and harvesting farmed plants, Kleidon calculates in a paper to be published in *Philosophical Transactions of the Royal Society*. This corresponds to roughly 5 to 10 per cent of the free energy generated by the global system.

"It's hard to put a precise number on the fraction," he says, "but we certainly use more of the free energy than [is used by] all geological processes." In other words, we have a greater effect on Earth's energy balance than all the earthquakes, volcanoes and tectonic plate movements put together.

Radical as his thesis sounds, it is being taken seriously. "Kleidon is at the forefront of a new wave of research, and the potential prize is huge," says Peter Cox, who studies climate system dynamics at the University of Exeter, UK. "A theory of the thermodynamics of the Earth system could help us understand the constraints on humankind's sustainable use of resources." Indeed, Kleidon's calculations have profound implications for attempts to transform our energy supply.

Of the 47 TW of energy that we use, about 17 TW comes from burning fossil fuels. So to replace this, we would need to build enough sustainable energy installations to generate at least 17 TW. And because no technology can ever be perfectly efficient, some of the free energy harnessed by wind and wave generators will be lost as heat. So by setting up wind and wave farms, we convert part of the sun's useful energy into unusable heat.

"Large-scale exploitation of wind energy will inevitably leave an imprint in the atmosphere," says Kleidon. "Because we use so much free energy, and more every year, we'll deplete the reservoir of energy." He says this would probably show up first in wind farms themselves, where the gains expected from massive facilities just won't pan out as the energy of the Earth system is depleted.

Using a model of global circulation, Kleidon found that the amount of energy which we can expect to harness from the wind is reduced by a factor of 100 if you take into account the depletion of free energy by wind farms. It remains theoretically possible to extract up to 70 TW globally, but doing so would have serious consequences.

Altering Weather Systems and Producing Heat

Although the winds will not die, sucking that much energy out of the atmosphere in Kleidon's model changed precipitation, turbulence and the amount of solar radiation reaching the Earth's surface. The magnitude of the changes was comparable to the changes to the climate caused by doubling atmospheric concentrations of carbon dioxide.

"This is an intriguing point of view and potentially very important," says meteorologist Maarten Ambaum of the University of Reading, UK. "Human consumption of energy is substantial when compared to free energy production in the Earth system. If we don't think in terms of free energy, we may be a bit misled by the potential for using natural energy resources."

This by no means spells the end for renewable energy, however. Photosynthesis also generates free energy, but without producing waste heat. Increasing the fraction of the Earth covered by light-harvesting vegetation—for example, through projects aimed at "greening the deserts"—would mean more free energy would get stored. Photovoltaic solar cells can also increase the amount of free energy gathered from incoming radiation, though there are still major obstacles to doing this sustainably.

In any event, says Kleidon, we are going to need to think about these fundamental principles much more clearly than we have in the past. "We have a hard time convincing engineers working on wind power that the ultimate limitation isn't how efficient an engine or wind farm is, but how much useful energy nature can generate." As Kleidon sees it, the idea that we can harvest unlimited amounts of renewable energy from our environment is as much of a fantasy as a perpetual motion machine.

> "*The truth is that in addition to cutting pollution and reducing our dependence on oil imports, renewable energy has a major advantage over fossil fuels: sharply declining prices over time.*"

Renewable Energies Will Stabilize Energy Prices

Jorge Madrid, Bracken Hendricks, and Kate Gordon

In the following viewpoint, Jorge Madrid, Bracken Hendricks, and Kate Gordon dispute arguments that renewable energy will lead to higher energy prices and gouge poor Americans. Madrid, Hendricks, and Gordon maintain that several states and the US government are adopting renewable energy standards that call upon energy producers to adopt more renewable energy resources. By promoting this policy, the authors claim, the United States will achieve greater energy security because of the decreased dependence on fossil fuels. In addition, Madrid, Hendricks, and Gordon argue that greater security will stabilize energy markets and lead to lower energy bills for all Americans. Jorge Madrid is a research associate for the Energy Policy Team at the Center for American Progress (CAP), a progressive public policy research and advocacy organization. Bracken Hendricks is a senior fellow working

Jorge Madrid, Bracken Hendricks, and Kate Gordon, "Renewable Energy Standards: The Health, Security, and Competitiveness Benefits," ThinkProgress.org, March 6, 2011. This material was created by the Center for American Progress. www.americanprogress.org.

on climate change and economic development issues at CAP, and Kate Gordon is the organization's vice president for energy policy.

As you read, consider the following questions:

1. According to the authors, what is the target year that the Center for American Progress hopes the country can and will achieve 35 percent renewable energy use?
2. As Madrid, Hendricks, and Gordon state, what did Southern California Edison deem one of the cheapest ways for its company to produce new electricity?
3. Besides increased energy costs, what other burden do the authors claim poor Americans bear from burning fossil fuels for power?

It has become quite the trend lately for conservatives and their media cronies to come out with attacks on "clean energy" and "green jobs." These attacks run the gamut from debates about exactly how many jobs have been created to broad jabs at the very notion that America needs to move to a cleaner, more efficient clean energy economy. While the attacks range widely in their scope and focus, they all miss a critical point: greening our economy is an environmental and energy security imperative, and one that also happens to provide the opportunity for the U.S. to compete in the huge emerging global clean tech marketplace.

A recent *New York Post* article by Shikha Dalmia, "Green Boondoggles" (3/1/2011), is a great example of just how misguided these attacks can be.

While attacking the President's [Barack Obama's] clean energy investment in general, Ms. Dalmia also focuses in on—and utterly mischaracterizes—a national renewable energy standard (RES).

First, a quick explanation: a national RES, or a similar policy called a Clean Energy Standard or CES, would require U.S. utilities to produce a percent of their electricity from renewable energy or low-carbon energy sources. Twenty-nine states already have such policies in place, as do China, the E.U. [European Union] nations, and a host of other countries.

Contrary to Ms. Dalmia's article, which asserts that a national RES is simply a smoke screen for an "anti-warming" agenda, there are a number of strong reasons beyond greenhouse gas reduction (which, by the way, should be enough of a reason on its own) why the U.S. should embrace this type of policy.

Diversifying to Promote Energy Security

The only way the U.S. can end our current energy insecurity is to diversify our use of energy away from our dependence on fossil fuels—and in fact away from dependence on any one technology or magic bullet energy solution. That means investing now in home grown American renewable energy and energy efficiency. Growing global energy demand, particularly from rapidly industrializing countries like China and India, will increase competition for the earth's finite resources; this is already increasing scarcity and driving up prices. Unrest in places like Egypt, Libya, and the Middle East only serves to further drive price volatility, sending shockwaves throughout our economy and down to consumers. A renewable energy standard represents an insurance policy for the economy against these gyrations in global energy markets. Indeed, failing to free our economy from volatile fossil fuels is one of the greatest risks to our energy security—not to mention the risks to our public health and national security.

Competing in a Greener Global Marketplace

Throughout Europe and Asia, countries are not only setting renewable standards but they are surpassing their original goals in favor of stricter pollution controls and stronger economies. As other countries continue to invest in renewable energy, supported by a strong energy policy, not only is the United States falling farther behind, but investments will continue to leave this country in search of stronger, more reliable markets overseas. In the last few years, China has invested a large percentage of total GDP [gross domestic product] into clean energy R&D [research and development] and deployment and it outpaced the world in manufacturing, being the world's leading supplier of solar PV [photovoltaic] panels and solar hot water heaters. China's huge success has not been because of their historical strengths of efficiency and cost cutting in its manufacturing sector but because of its development of stringent renewable energy policies.

Cheaper Energy Costs

The Center for American Progress [CAP] recently came out with a Clean Energy Standard [in February 2011] that includes a specific goal of reaching 35 percent renewable energy use by 2025. Ms. Dalmia attacks this standard, calling it a "guarantee for higher prices." But her basis for this absurd claim is a thoroughly debunked "study" by the hard-right (and oil-funded) Heritage Foundation.

For starters, CAP calls for ten percent of the "35" to be achieved with energy efficiency measures, a low cost way to reduce electricity use in homes and businesses, thus leading to lower electricity bills. Efficiency investments beyond 10 percent will only further reduce costs, and both President Obama's and CAP's plan support this.

The even greater weakness in Ms. Dalmia's argument, however, is that renewable energy standards in individual states, and abroad, have successfully demonstrated that an aggressive RES will not drive up prices. Moreover, we know that as we move these technologies to scale, renewable energy will be cheaper to deploy than traditional fossil fuels.

In the State of Michigan, for example, utility contracts for renewable electricity under their 2008 renewable energy standard have come in at prices below the cost of power generated from new coal plants, and consumers continue to pay below the national average for their electricity. In fact, a [February 2011] report from the Michigan government clearly states that there is "no indication" that their clean energy standards "have had any impact on electricity prices in Michigan." While a report done by Bernstein Research found that wind generation in Texas (complimented with an aggressive RES of 5880 MW [megawatts] of installed renewable capacity by 2015) actually lowered the cost of power for utilities by $2 and $4 per megawatt-hour in 2008. This experience is borne out by other countries as well, with wind prices reaching cost competitiveness with coal in a number of regional electricity markets in countries as diverse as Mexico, Sweden, and Brazil.

The truth is that in addition to cutting pollution and reducing our dependence on oil imports, renewable energy has a major advantage over fossil fuels: sharply declining prices over time. The price of solar energy production, for example, has fallen dramatically as the industry has gained new economies of scale. A recent request [in January 2011] for proposals by Southern California Edison (one of the largest investor-owned utilities in the country) found that solar power is already among the cheapest ways for them to generate new electricity. And to understand where this technology is headed as the industry scales to meet new markets, you need look only to the experience of semi-conductors and computing power which followed "Moore's Law"[1] of a continuous declining cost curve every time the market grew.

Colorado is another state that has successfully pursued an aggressive a renewable energy standard. In November of 2004, Colorado passed a renewable energy standard for the first time. The original standard required that the state's three largest utilities acquire 3 percent of their electricity from renewable energy sources by 2007 and 10 percent by 2015. Colorado's program has been extremely successful with the first 1,000 megawatts of wind power generating enough electricity to power almost 250,000 homes, creating 1,700 full-time jobs during construction and 300 permanent jobs thereafter plus multiple other benefits. In

April of last year [2010], the Colorado State Senate passed a bill to increase the renewable energy standard to 30 percent by 2020. Currently, a study of the Xcel system, a utility in Colorado, found that the wind already on their system would save Colorado ratepayers over $251 million.

Colorado is one of 29 states plus Washington D.C. and Puerto Rico (7 more have goals to implement), that have an established a renewable energy standard. Each state's goal varies, from 8% by 2020 in Pennsylvania to 33% by 2030 in California. Nevertheless, these laws will encourage utilities and businesses to invest in clean energy resources by creating certainty through guaranteed markets.

Likewise, benefits from established renewable energy standards are being felt abroad as well. Recent data released [in March 2011] by the Irish Wind Energy Association states, "11.5% reduction in wholesale electricity prices will be achieved through delivering 45% of the overall generation mix from wind by 2020."

Clearly Dalmia fails to realize that renewable energy stabilizes energy costs because, unlike fossil fuels, renewable fuels (wind, sun, etc) are 100% free. Administrators of the University of Minnesota understand this; their newly installed wind turbines will allow campus officials to "predict what energy costs will be for the next 15 years." That is a level of economic security you can't get from OPEC.

High Prices and Unstable Markets
Adversely Affect the Poor

Ms. Dalmia next pivots her argument to say that low-income families will suffer the most from a renewable energy standard. What Ms. Dalmia fails to recognize is that price spikes in energy are significantly caused by volatility in the unstable fossil fuels market, and that diversifying our energy portfolio would actually even out prices and give consumers more options. Not to mention the fact that low-income families bear the worst of the health impacts caused by burning fossil fuels. An aggressive

Renewables Are Less Volatile and Sometimes Less Expensive than Fossil Fuels

The point is often made that renewables, while price stable, are more expensive than conventional power. Therefore, renewable power may be less volatile, but consistently more expensive, than conventional power—resulting in a hedge that guarantees you always pay more. In practice, this gap does not always exist and is quite geographically and/or temporally specific. There are a number of case studies demonstrating how renewables are in some regions price-competitive with conventional power, and even Integrated Resource Plans that have identified renewables as least-cost in all-source bidding. Moreover . . . there are other monetizable values of renewables that may bridge the cost gap between renewables and conventional sources in cases where renewables are "more expensive."

Commission for Environmental Cooperation, "Renewable Energy as a Hedge Against Fuel Price Fluctuation," CEC Backgrounder Paper, September 2008.

clean energy standard coupled with strong targets for renewable energy and energy efficiency would help stabilize and reduce prices for working families. The real enemy of the poor is our current "do nothing" energy plan.

Exhibit A can be found in our recent experience. Throughout the G.W. Bush administration (and without a RES), energy prices were high and unstable. In the years leading up to the recession beginning in December of 2007, American households began spending significantly more on energy. During this time, the typical annual American household expenditure on electricity increased more than $170, and the typical annual American expenditure on gasoline increased more than $960 (in 2007 dollars). This kind of increase is certainly felt most by low-income families. In contrast, a renewable energy standard would lower American household energy bills.

With no coherent energy policy in place, America continues to remain vulnerable to price spikes for imported energy, while we allow ourselves to be exposed to unnecessary costs from inefficiency and the real impacts of pollution. Instead, America will be stronger, healthier, and more prosperous with a Clean Energy Standard guaranteeing that America meets 80 percent of its energy needs from advanced low carbon energy, as the President has proposed, if coupled with a strong target of 35 percent renewable energy and efficiency by 2035, as the Center for American Progress has suggested. This is a policy prescription to stabilize and reduce consumer energy bills, even as we create U.S. jobs, enhance our competitive position, cut energy imports, and reduce pollution. That is a smart investment in the future.

Note

1. In 1965, Gordon Moore predicted that the number of computer transistors on a chip will double with no increase in cost every two years.

> "It stands to reason that a RES [renewable energy standard] would raise electricity prices. After all, if electricity created by wind and other renewables were cost competitive, consumers would use more of it without a federal law to force consumption."

Renewable Energies Will Increase Energy Prices

David W. Kreutzer et al.

David W. Kreutzer is a research fellow in energy economics and climate change in the Center for Data Analysis at the Heritage Foundation, a conservative public policy and research institute. His co-authors are also affiliated with the Heritage Foundation. In the following viewpoint, Kreutzer and his colleagues argue that Congress should not impose a renewable energy standard on the United States. In their opinion, mandating increased dependence on renewable energies is tantamount to raising the costs of energy for consumers. As these authors contend, though renewable sources such as wind and solar power are free to acquire, they are not free to generate and transmit. Using wind power as an example, Kreutzer and colleagues point out that there is a cost to build wind turbines

David W. Kreutzer, Karen A. Campbell, William W. Beach, Ben Lieberman, and Nicolas D. Loris, "A Renewable Electricity Standard: What It Will Really Cost Americans," *Heritage Foundation Center for Data Analysis Report #10-03*, May 5, 2010. Copyright © 2010 The Heritage Foundation. Reproduced by permission.

and to lay the lines that will connect them to points of use. More significantly they state that the wind is intermittent and cannot promise continual generation, leading to switchover costs associated with ramping up and powering down alternate power sources to fill in the gap when the wind is not blowing. All these hidden expenses, the authors maintain, will raise consumer electricity bills beyond what most people can afford.

As you read, consider the following questions:

1. By what percent do the authors expect electricity prices for households will increase if the proposed RES is enacted?
2. As stated by the authors, what is the Energy Information Administration's levelized cost per megawatt hour for conventional coal power? What is the levelized cost for onshore wind power?
3. As Kreutzer and colleagues measure, what will be the added price per megawatt hour for wind power after taking into account the costs of transmission and gas-turbine fill-gap expenses?

Congress is once again [Spring 2010] considering major energy legislation, focused largely on promotion of energy sources that produce few or no greenhouse gases. This current concentration on promoting so-called renewable energy sources assumes that congressional action now will lead to such significant growth in renewable energy sources that the use of carbon-based energy will subside, thus reducing the expansion of atmospheric carbon dioxide and other global warming gases.

Congress's effort to expand renewable energy sources starts from a relatively meager production base. Nearly half of America's electricity is generated from coal, with natural gas and nuclear energy adding about 20 percent each. Most of the rest is provided by renewable sources, primarily hydroelectric energy at 6 percent.

Non-hydro renewables like wind and solar energy and biomass total only 3 percent.

For many years, federal energy and environmental policy has nudged production of some electricity sources over others, either through "sticks," such as costly air quality regulations targeting coal, or through "carrots" like tax credits and subsidies for wind. Proposed global warming legislation would alter the electricity mix to an unprecedented degree by putting a price on emissions of greenhouse gases, chiefly carbon dioxide from fossil fuel combustion. Coal is the most carbon-intensive energy source, and any stringent cap-and-trade provisions would significantly curtail its use in favor of other sources in the decades ahead. Such legislative measures, however, are very costly, and the prospects for passage in 2010 are uncertain.

Congress is also considering achieving similar but less ambitious goals via a renewable electricity standard (RES). Twenty-nine states have versions of a RES, but Washington is considering a nationwide standard. Under this mandate, a growing percentage of electricity would have to be produced by approved renewable energy sources. Much of the RES would be met with increased energy generation from wind turbines.

The Real Cost of Renewables

It stands to reason that a RES would raise electricity prices. After all, if electricity created by wind and other renewables were cost competitive, consumers would use more of it without a federal law to force consumption. Recent experience with the mandate for renewable fuels like corn ethanol also suggests significant cost increases as well as technical shortcomings.

While proponents argue that wind is free, harnessing it into useful electricity certainly is not. However, the question of how much a RES will affect electric bills does not have a straightforward answer.

Perhaps easiest to calculate is the direct cost of purchasing, installing, and operating the increasing number of wind turbines needed to meet the RES. A bit murkier are questions about the costs of the necessary additional transmission lines to deliver the electricity from where it is generated—the most desirable sites for wind are often remote mountain ridges or sparsely populated plains—to the cities where it is needed. The economics of a RES is further complicated by the legal and administrative objections to establishing appropriate sites for wind farms and transmission lines, which already are quite common and would only grow with a RES.

It is particularly difficult to take into account the substantial costs created by the intermittent and unreliable nature of wind. Simply put, the wind does not always blow, and it is difficult to predict and impossible to control. Given the need for electricity 24 hours a day seven days a week and the reality that times of peak demand—hot summer days—are precisely when the wind is usually still, a mandate for increased wind-generated energy is also a mandate for increased non-wind backup systems for balancing wind fluctuations. In effect, increased wind power cannot simply be added to the existing grid without transforming the grid in ways that introduce both significant costs and operational inefficiencies.

These shortcomings will not be overcome through increases in scale. Connecting a large number of widely dispersed wind farms to the grid will not smooth the overall supply enough to make balancing unnecessary. Though variability can be reduced, a recent analysis states, "These results do not indicate that wind power can provide substantial baseload power simply through interconnecting wind plants."

There are federal studies of the costs of a RES that conclude that it would add no more than a few percent to electric rates, but these studies do not take the full cost of wind and other renewables into account. This Center for Data Analysis (CDA) Report provides such a comprehensive economic analysis.

CDA analysis projects that a RES as outlined below would:

- Raise electricity prices by 36 percent for households and 60 percent for industry;
- Cut national income (GDP [gross domestic product]) by $5.2 trillion between 2012 and 2035;
- Cut national income by $2,400 per year for a family of four;
- Reduce employment by more than 1,000,000 jobs; and
- Add more than $10,000 to a family of four's share of the national debt by 2035.

Comparing the Costs of Wind and Coal

The flow of wind is erratic and uncertain, which means that so is the power generated from wind. This unreliable nature is especially problematic when wind is used to generate utility-scale electricity for the power grid.

Keeping line quality, primarily voltage and frequency, within the necessarily close tolerances requires constant monitoring of demand and the constant monitoring and adjustment of supply. Even under the best of circumstances, these adjustments require a certain fraction of power to be delivered from generators that can be ramped up and down rapidly. For the most part, this easily ramped electricity comes from natural-gas fired turbines that are relatively expensive to operate compared to a baseload source such as coal, nuclear, or natural-gas combined-cycle power plants.

Though coal, nuclear, and gas combined-cycle power plants are much more sluggish in response to changing demand, their dependability is very high. Indeed, their output can be matched to sizeable, expected changes in demand when given sufficient lead time. Wind energy plants do not have this ability by themselves, so direct comparisons of wind costs per kilowatt hour to coal or gas costs are misleading.

Further, location choices for fossil and nuclear-fueled power plants have much greater latitude than those for wind turbines, which, like hydropower plants, must be located where the natural resource is best suited—not necessarily close to where the power is used. This feature adds additional transmission costs to wind energy.

With nuclear power not considered to be renewable, the least-cost renewable source for electricity is onshore wind. In an early-release version of its "Annual Energy Outlook 2010," the Energy Information Administration (EIA) lists the levelized costs of various sources of electricity projected for 2016 (in 2008 dollars).

The EIA levelized costs per megawatt hour are $78.10 for conventional coal power, $149.30 for onshore wind power, $191.10 for offshore wind power, $396.10 for photo-voltaic solar power, $256.60 for thermal solar power, and $139.50 for power generated by natural-gas conventional turbines.

Even though the $149.30 for the cheapest renewable power is already well above the cost of conventional power sources, it does not include any adjustment for reliability or additional transmission costs.

Wind cannot be turned on and off to match changes in demand. There are no feasible energy storage options for most wind farms. So, unlike power from conventional sources, wind power must be used when the wind is actually blowing.

Geography puts wind at another disadvantage. To keep the cost of wind power as low as possible, it is necessary to locate the wind farms in areas with the strongest and steadiest winds. As is the case with solar power, many of the best areas for wind power are located far from the major population centers. This requires construction of new, high-capacity transmission lines. A review of transmission costs suggests a median cost of $15 per megawatt hour.

Dependability Issues

The dependability problem is more complicated. Power-grid management requires constant and instantaneous balancing of supply and demand. Sophisticated analysis and long experi-

The High Cost of Renewable Energy Systems

Using wind and solar energy systems to provide 100 percent of electricity could double or triple household electric bills.

Average Electricity Bill for a Family of Four, by Energy Source

Energy System	Costs Monthly	Annually
Coal	$188.66	$2,263.90
On-shore wind	$339.58	$4,075.02
Off-shore wind	$403.65	$4,843.75
Solar thermal	$504.03	$6,048.34
Solar photovoltaic	$717.82	$8,613.85

TAKEN FROM: Heritage Foundation calculations, and US Energy Information Administration, "2016 Levelized Cost of New Generation Resources from the Annual Energy Outlook 2010," in David W. Kreutzer et al., "A Renewable Electricity Standard," Heritage Foundation Center for Data Analysis Report No. 10-03, May 5, 2010.

ence guide grid operators as they schedule the various sources of generation. Nevertheless, there will still be unanticipated changes in both supply and demand; further, there can be variations in demand that cannot easily be matched by the most efficient conventional sources (coal, nuclear power, and integrated combined-cycle gas) even if they are anticipated. The most common energy source for balancing these very short-run changes is natural gas turbines, which are less efficient than coal, nuclear power, or natural gas combined cycle.

Wind, like solar energy, is not a dispatchable power source; that is, it cannot be turned on at will. As a result, increasing dependence on wind adds variability and uncertainty to the power grid that must be offset by quick-ramping power sources like natural gas turbines to maintain a relatively constant flow of electricity.

This increased reliance on natural gas turbines comes from two sides of the balancing equation. When there is an unantici- pated decline in wind generation, or when the decline is antici- pated but is for too short a period to balance with coal, natural gas turbines fill the gap. On the other hand, when wind genera- tion is low compared to capacity, there is need for power sources that can be quickly ramped down. In this case, there would be additional need for natural gas generation so that unanticipated increases in wind power can be accommodated by rapidly cut- ting power from the natural gas turbines.

Gas turbines are not a renewable energy source, so swap- ping a megawatt hour of wind power for a megawatt hour of coal power also requires swapping power from natural gas turbines for additional coal. Since coal power is cheaper than power gen- erated by natural gas turbines, the difference must be added to the cost differential between wind and coal.

There is little research directly addressing the question of how much additional gas-turbine power will be needed. The the- oretical limits are zero (all fluctuations are perfectly anticipated and balanced with the cheapest coal power) and the inverse of the capacity factor, which would imply three megawatt hours of additional gas-turbine power for every megawatt hour of wind power. In theory, this could add as much as $179 per megawatt hour to the cost of wind power.

A study done for the National Renewable Energy Laboratory indicates that the spinning reserves must be increased about 0.2 megawatt capacity for each megawatt of wind power. "Spinning reserves" describes the power plants that must be warmed up and synchronized with the grid so that they can be brought on- line more quickly. They use fuel, but not as much as when they are called upon to supply power to the grid.

This measure is somewhat different from the necessary in- crease in actual gas-turbine electricity production, but it is very much related to the uncertainty and variability problem. Though 0.2 megawatt per hour may be a significant underestimate for the amount of additional gas-turbine power, it is the factor employed for this analysis. That is, for every megawatt hour of wind that is substituted for coal power, an additional 0.2 megawatt hour of gas-turbine power must be substituted for coal as well. Using this ratio adds $12 per megawatt hour instead of the theoretical maximum of $179 per megawatt hour to the cost of wind power.

After making these adjustments for transmission costs and additional gas-turbine generation, the cost of an additional megawatt of onshore wind power is $177 per hour. This is 126 percent above the cost of a megawatt of coal power per hour.

Put another way, the electric bill for a typical family of four would be $189 per month if it was powered entirely by coal, but it would rise to $340 per month if it was supplied entirely by onshore wind power.

Since onshore wind is the least expensive of the renewable electricity sources (ruling out conventional hydro and nuclear power), any plan that uses the more expensive renewable sources—such as offshore wind ($218 per megawatt hour); thermal solar power ($284 per megawatt hour); or photovoltaic solar power ($423 per megawatt hour)—would have even greater costs. As the mandated renewable-fraction of electric power rises, so does the average cost of electricity.

> "[Solar and wind power generators]
> gobble up land on a stunning scale that
> can make an oil refinery seem like a
> minor pothole on the migration route
> of wildlife."

Renewable Energy Sources Have Enormous Land Footprints

Bob Marshall

Bob Marshall is the conservation writer for Field & Stream, *an outdoor sports, recreation, and wildlife magazine. In the viewpoint that follows, Marshall reports that the rush to turn land into energy production sites for renewable energies such as wind and solar power should take heed of environmental impact. According to Marshall, these renewable generators—whether wind farms or solar arrays—require more land to produce the same energy derived from a coal plant. The large footprint of these renewables means that ecosystems may be harmed and fish and wildlife threatened. Thus, in Marshall's opinion, the desire to capitalize on one resource comes at the expense of curtailing another. Marshall encourages wildlife enthusiasts, fishers, and hunters to openly question the im-*

Bob Marshall, "Green Energy Land Rush," *Field & Stream*, vol. 114, December 2009–January 2010, pp. 38–40. Reproduced by permission.

pact of renewable energy structures before they begin to dominate wildlife areas.

As you read, consider the following questions:

1. What are some problems surrounding ethanol production that the author and other outdoor enthusiasts cite to recommend a cautious approach to the use of land for renewable energy production?
2. According to Marshall, on how many acres of land is the US Bureau of Land Management reviewing lease applications for renewable energy production?
3. According to a 2008 study by the US Department of Energy, cited in this viewpoint, how many gallons of water might be used up in the production of one megawatt-hour of solar-generated electricity?

As the nation begins addressing the problem of global warming by looking at renewable alternatives to fossil fuels, a new slogan is emerging from the conservation community, especially fish and wildlife advocates: *Remember ethanol!*

That's not a rallying cry. It's a call for caution.

Two years ago most sportsmen would have asked: What could possibly be bad about renewable power sources—ethanol, solar, wind, hydropower, wave, tidal, ocean thermal, and geothermal? What could be wrong with finding energy supplies that don't pour carbon into the air?

Today, leaders in fish and wildlife conservation have a quick answer: Remember ethanol. Made primarily from corn, ethanol was billed as a green fuel that would reduce our carbon footprint as well as our dependence on oil from countries that hate us. It was a win-win: good for the environment and good politics, too.

It was only after refineries were being built in corn country that problems surfaced. Corn-based ethanol, it turned out, actually created more carbon than it saved. It also gobbled up water supplies, polluted water, and increased nutrient loads in streams. Worst of all, as corn prices exploded to meet the new demand, landowners rushed to pull out of their Conservation Reserve Program [CRP] contracts so they could convert land to cropfields, which would have doomed wildlife habitat in many areas.

Since then steps have been taken to protect CRP, but the energy issue continues to pose challenges for fish and wildlife. Additionally, our persistent dependence on the diminishing supply of oil has been deemed a national security threat. So the nation is forging ahead with subsidies for green energy technologies, and while sportsmen agree that movement is necessary, they're right to be concerned about the cost of unintended consequences.

Those start with the impact on the landscape—and we're not talking aesthetics here.

The Demand for Land and Water

Solar and wind energy projects designed to produce power on scales large enough to light communities do not resemble the photovoltaic panels on your neighbor's roof, nor that windmill on the local farm. They gobble up land on a stunning scale that can make an oil refinery seem like a minor pothole on the migration route of wildlife.

Robert McDonald, a landscape ecologist for the Nature Conservancy, studied the land requirements to produce a terawatt-hour of energy—about the electricity generated by a small power plant. It came to 3.74 square miles for coal, 14.2 square miles for photovoltaic solar power, and 27.8 square miles for wind.

Last July [2009], the U.S. Department of the Interior moved to accelerate large-scale solar power plants on 670,000 acres of public lands in six Western states. The *New York Times* reported that the government-backed interest in solar has led to a "so-

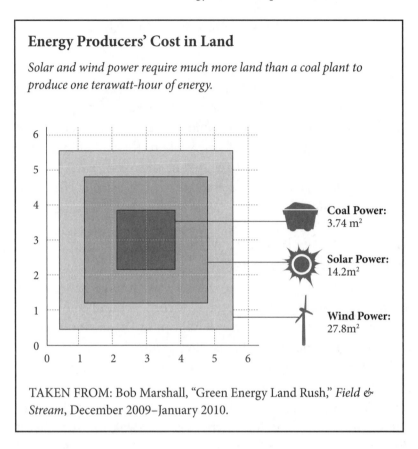

Energy Producers' Cost in Land

Solar and wind power require much more land than a coal plant to produce one terawatt-hour of energy.

Coal Power: 3.74 m²

Solar Power: 14.2m²

Wind Power: 27.8m²

TAKEN FROM: Bob Marshall, "Green Energy Land Rush," *Field & Stream*, December 2009–January 2010.

lar land rush" over the last two years, with the Bureau of Land Management now reviewing 158 lease applications on a total of 1.8 million acres. And this is only the beginning.

Unfortunately, solar power on an industrial scale doesn't go directly from the sun to batteries, like those flat panels on a suburban rooftop. Robert Glennon, author of *Unquenchable: America's Water Crisis and What to Do About It* and one of the nation's authorities on water use, noted in a *Washington Post* op-ed recently that "most large solar power projects use a system called concentrating solar power, or CSP, that heats a fluid that boils water to turn a turbine. CSP, just like any thermal power plant, produces waste heat as a byproduct. In most cases, cooling towers release the heat to the atmosphere through evaporation, a process that uses gobs of water."

According to a 2008 study by the U.S. Department of Energy, that water usage amounts to as much as 750 gallons per mega-watt-hour. One megawatt can power about 800 homes.

That rate of water usage becomes more critical because large solar farms will be located in areas where the sun shines most of the day—arid and desert regions of the West. Even a slight change in the water supply there can have disastrous effects on fish and wildlife.

Wind Turbines Interfere with National Environments

Wind energy is getting even more attention because it has a proven power-producing track record around the world. Windmills have been standing on hilltops in Europe for decades, and now are sprouting on landscapes across the U.S. But just as with solar, energy companies responding to new federal incentives (such as a 30 percent tax credit) know their profits rise with scale. Investors like the legendary oilman T. Boone Pickens are talking about covering huge expanses of the prairie states with thick forests of windmills; energy companies in wind-whipped areas of the Rocky Mountain West are already negotiating with ranchers to line ridgetops with windmills.

And while the Department of Energy tries to smooth over that footprint by saying that "it is important to note that the land be-tween the turbines—minus the 'footprint' area—is still usable for its original purpose," boosters of fish and wildlife would disagree.

"What impact would miles of windmills or solar panels have if they were placed in a migration corridor for antelope or mule deer?" asks Steve Belinda, who covers energy issues for the Theodore Roosevelt Conservation Partnership, a coalition of sportsmen's groups. "What happens to grouse or pheasants if the windmills or panels are located in a prime nesting or feed-ing area?

"I've seen these pictures the industry puts out of deer grazing near windmills, trying to claim no harm is done. Well, maybe in that case at that moment. But how many of those energy companies will want guys with guns or bows hunting around their investments?"

The amount of land required for wind turbines and solar panels is only part of the landscape equation. Many more miles will be consumed for power lines to carry the energy to the power grid. It's all part of the environmental cost of environment-friendly energy production.

Getting Involved to Protect Ecosystems

Belinda is careful to stress that sportsmen's groups are not opposed to development of renewable energy; in fact, they see it as necessary for the future of the entire planet, not just fish and wildlife. But they want to make sure solar, wind, wave, and the others do not become another exercise in ethanol.

To that end, sportsmen's groups are developing a strategy to have fish and wildlife values considered on the front end wherever alternative energy development is being discussed. They know they probably can't stop some projects, but they want to ensure that current ecosystems are protected or compensated.

"We want to know what fish, wildlife, and recreational values are in a proposed area before development, and what will be needed after development to sustain populations and traditional uses," Belinda says. "If you have 100 sage grouse nests in that area, you may be able to tell regulators we will need 70 left to sustain the resource at levels where it can be used."

Getting seats at the table during development is essential.

"We may be able to urge alternative sites for wind farms or transmission lines, based on the needs of wildlife and sportsmen," Belinda says. "This is all coming at us pretty fast, and from all sides. But it's an issue we can't ignore."

Just remember ethanol.

> *"An average square meter of land receives each year as much solar energy as a barrel of oil contains, and that solar energy is evenly distributed across the world within about twofold."*

Land Footprints of Renewable Energy Sources Are Exaggerated

Amory B. Lovins

Environmental scientist Amory B. Lovins is chairman and chief scientist of the Rocky Mountain Institute, a research organization dedicated to sustainable living. He is the author of such books as Small Is Profitable *and* Natural Capitalism. *In the following viewpoint, Lovins rebuts arguments that the land footprint of renewable energy production facilities—such as windmills and solar arrays—is larger than traditional fossil-fuel and nuclear energy production facilities. Lovins contends that wind farms are often placed in regions in which the intervening land between the windmills can be used for other purposes; he states that this is not the case for nuclear facilities that may have a smaller building footprint but normally prohibit the use of land around the buildings. Furthermore Lovins claims that photovoltaic solar panels are typi-*

Amory B. Lovins, "Renewable Energy's 'Footprint' Myth," *Electricity Journal*, vol. 24, July 2011, pp. 40–47. Reproduced with permission from Elsevier.

cally placed on building roofs, thus requiring no additional real estate for energy production. Finally Lovins points out that nuclear power plants require even more land to mill and refine the fissionable materials and to bury the hazardous waste products.

As you read, consider the following questions:

1. According to Lovins and the Brookhaven National Laboratory, how much land does a 1 GW plant use over a forty-year life cycle?
2. What percent of the land on a wind farm site can be used for purposes other than producing energy, in Lovins's opinion?
3. As Lovins states, what percent of photovoltaic accumulators are placed on building roofs, thus using no extra land?

L and footprint seems an odd criterion for choosing energy systems: the amounts of land at issue are not large, because global renewable energy flows are so vast that only a tiny fraction of them need be captured. For example, economically exploitable wind resources, after excluding land with competing uses, are over nine times total national electricity use in the U.S. and over twice in China; before land-use restrictions, the economic resource is over 6 times total national electricity use in Britain and 35 times worldwide—all at 80-meter hub height, where there's less energy than at the modern ≥100 m [meter]. Just the 300 GW [gigawatt] of windpower now stuck in the U.S. interconnection queue could displace two-fifths of U.S. coal power. Photovoltaics [PV], counting just one-fifth of their extractable power over land to allow for poor or unavailable sites, could deliver over 150 times the world's total 2005 electricity consumption. The sunlight falling on the Earth about every 70 minutes equals humankind's entire annual energy use. An average square meter of land receives each year as much solar energy as a barrel of oil contains, and that solar energy is evenly distributed across the world within about twofold. The U.S., "an intense user of energy, has about 4,000 times more solar energy than its annual electricity use. This same number is about 10,000 worldwide [so] . . . if only 1 percent of land area were used for PV, more than 10 times the global energy could be produced," [states a US Department of Energy and Electric Power Research Institute 1997 report].

Nonetheless, many nuclear advocates argue that renewable electricity has far too big a land "footprint" to be environmentally acceptable, while nuclear power is preferable because it uses orders of magnitude less land. If we assume that land-use *is* an important metric, a closer look reveals the opposite is true.

Comparing Footprints

For example, Stewart Brand's 2010 book *Whole Earth Discipline* cites novelist and author Gwyneth Cravens's claim that "A nuclear plant producing 1,000 megawatts [peak, or about 900 megawatts average] takes up a third of a square mile." But this direct plant footprint omits the owner-controlled exclusion zone ($\sim$1.9–3.1 mi^2 [square mile]). Including all site areas barred to other uses (except sometimes a public road or railway track), the U.S. Department of Energy's nuclear cost guide says the nominal site needs 7 mi^2, or 21 times Cravens' figure. She also omits the entire nuclear fuel cycle, whose first steps—mining, milling, and tailings disposal—disturb nearly 4 mi^2 to produce that 1 GW plant's uranium for 40 years using typical U.S. ores. Coal-mining to power the enrichment plant commits about another 22 mi^2-y of land disturbance for coal mining, transport, and combustion, or an average (assuming full restoration afterwards) of 0.55 mi^2 throughout the reactor's 40-year operating life. Finally, the plant's share of the Yucca Mountain spent-fuel repository (abandoned by DOE [US Department of Energy] but favored by Brand) plus its exclusion zone adds another 3 mi^2. Though this sum is incomplete, clearly Brand's nuclear land-use figures are too low by more than 40-fold—or, according to an older calculation done by a leading nuclear advocate, by more than 120-fold.

Exaggerating Renewables' Land Use

This is strongly confirmed by a new, thorough, and authoritative assessment I found after completing the foregoing bottom-up analysis. Scientists at the nuclear-centric Brookhaven National Laboratory and at Columbia University, using Argonne National Laboratory data and a standard lifecycle assessment tool, found that U.S. nuclear-system land use totals 119 m^2 [square meters] /GWh [gigawatt hour], or for our nominal 1 GW plant over 40 years, 14.5 mi^2—virtually identical to my estimate of at least 14.3 mi^2. . . .

Of this 119 m^2/GWh of land-use, Brand counts only 2.7 m^2/GWh—1/16th of the power-plant site—or 2.3 percent. Not that he's unaware of the concept of a fuel cycle, which he bemoans for coal. His land-use errors for renewables, however, are in the opposite direction. "A wind farm," he says, "would have to cover over 200 square miles to obtain the same result [as the 1 GW nuclear plant], and a solar array over 50 square miles." On page 86 he quotes Jesse Ausubel's claim of 298 and 58 square miles respectively. Yet these windpower figures are about 100–1,000 times too high, because they include the undisturbed land *between* the turbines—about 98–99+ percent of the site—which is typically used for cultivation, grazing, wildlife, or other uses (even solar collection) and is in no way occupied, transformed, or consumed by windpower. For example, the turbines that make 15 percent of Iowa's electricity rise amidst farmland, often cropped right up to the base of each tower, though wind royalties are often more profitable than crops. Saying that wind turbines "use" the land between them is like saying that the lampposts in a parking lot have the same area as the parking lot: in fact, about 99 percent of its area remains available to drive, park, and walk in.

The area actually *used* by 900 average MW [megawatt] of windpower output—unavailable for other uses—is only about 0.2–2 mi², not "over 200" or "298." Further, as noted by Stanford's top renewables expert, Prof. Mark Jacobson, the key variable is whether there are permanent roads. Most of the infrastructure area, he notes, is *temporary* dirt roads that soon revegetate. Except in rugged or heavily vegetated terrain that needs maintained roads, the long-term footprint for the tower and foundation of a modern 5 MW tubular-tower turbine is *only about 13–20 m²*. That's just about 0.005 mi² of actual windpower footprint to produce 900 average MW: not about 50–100 times but *22,000–34,000 times* smaller than the unused land that such turbines spread across. Depending on site and road details, therefore, Brand overstates windpower's land use by two to four orders of magnitude.

Solar Panels Require the Least Additional Land Use

His photovoltaic land-use figures are also at least 3.3–3.9 times too high (or ≥4.3 times *versus* an optimized system), apparently due to analytic errors. Moreover, some 90 percent of today's photovoltaics are mounted not on the ground but on rooftops and over parking lots, using *no* extra land—yet 90 percent are also tied to the grid. PVs on the world's urban roofs alone could produce many times the world's electricity consumption. [In 2006] the National Renewable Energy Laboratory found that:

> In the United States, cities and residences cover about 140 million acres of land. We could supply every kilowatt-hour of our nation's current electricity requirements simply by applying PV to 7% of this area—on roofs, on parking lots, along highway walls, on the sides of buildings, and in other dual-use scenarios. We wouldn't have to appropriate a single acre of new land to make PV our primary energy source! . . . [I]nstead of our sun's energy falling on shingles, concrete, and under-

Land Use Requirements for Nuclear, PV, and Wind Systems

mi²/900 av. MW	Stewart Brand's Claim	Evidence-Based Literature Findings
Nuclear	0.33	≥14.3 (Lovins); 14.5 (Brookhaven National Laboratory)
Windpower	>200 to 298	In flat open sites, ~0.2–2 (max. 5) actually used with permanent roads; without permanent roads, ~0.005
Photovoltaics	>50 to 58	≤15 with horizontal panels in av. U.S. sites; ≤13.5 if optimized; 0 if on structures

TAKEN FROM: Amory B. Lovins, "Renewable Energy's 'Footprint' Myth," *Electricity Journal*, July 2011.

used land, it would fall on PV—providing us with clean energy while leaving our landscape largely untouched.

and concludes: "Contrary to popular opinion, *a world relying on PV would offer a landscape almost indistinguishable from the landscape we know today.*" This would also bypass the fragile grid, greatly improving reliability and resilience.

Table 1 summarizes, then, the square miles of land area used to site and fuel a 1 GW nuclear plant at 90 percent capacity factor, *versus* PV and wind systems with the same annual output.

Thus *windpower is far less land-intensive than nuclear power; photovoltaics spread across land are comparable to nuclear if mounted on the ground in average U.S. sites, but much or most of that land (shown in the table) can be shared with livestock or wildlife, and PVs use no land if mounted on structures, as about 90 percent now are.* Brand's "footprint" is thus the opposite of what he claims.

Material Production Costs for Nuclear and Renewables

These comparisons don't yet count the land needed to produce the materials to build these electricity supply systems—because doing so wouldn't significantly change the results. Modern wind and PV systems are probably no more, and may be less, cement-, steel-, and other basic-materials-intensive than nuclear systems—consistent both with their economic competitiveness and with how quickly their output repays the energy invested to make them. For example, a modern wind turbine, including transmission, has a lifecycle embodied-energy payback of under seven months; PVs' energy payback ranges from months to a few years (chiefly for their aluminum and glass housings); and adding indirect (via materials) to direct land-use increases PV systems' land-use by only a few percent, just as it would for nuclear power according to the industry's assessments. Indeed, a gram of silicon in amorphous solar cells, because they're so thin and durable, produces more lifetime electricity than a gram of uranium does in a light-water reactor—so it's not only nuclear materials, as Brand supposes, that yield abundant energy from a small mass. Their risks and side effects, however, are different. A nuclear bomb can be made from a lemon-sized piece of fissile uranium or plutonium, but not from any amount of silicon. Only for that purpose is energy or power density a meaningful metric. For civilian energy production, it's merely an intriguing artifact. What matters is economics and practicality.

Periodical Bibliography

The following articles have been selected to supplement the diverse views presented in this chapter.

Liam Denning   "Risky Patriot Games for Renewable Energy," *Wall Street Journal*, December 28, 2010.

Mary Engel and Nolan Hester   "Everyone Wants Clean Energy—But Where Do We Put the Turbines?," *Wilderness*, 2009–2010.

Carolyn Fischer   "Renewable Portfolio Standards: When Do They Lower Energy Prices?," *Energy Journal*, 2010.

Mark Fischetti   "Growing Vertical," *Scientific American* Special Edition, September 2008.

Douglas Fox   "New Energy: Climate Change and Sustainability Shape a New Era," *Christian Science Monitor*, November 8, 2010.

Al Gore   "Climate of Denial," *Rolling Stone*, July 7, 2011.

Human Events   "Top 10 Proofs Obama Wants High Energy Prices," June 20, 2011.

Bjorn Lomborg   "Mr. Gore, Your Solution to Global Warming Is Wrong," *Esquire*, August 2009.

Kumi Naidoo   "The Safe Bet: Renewables," *Nation*, June 27, 2011.

Michael Parfit   "Future Power," *National Geographic*, August 2005.

Gus Speth   "Interview with Gus Speth: Communicating Environmental Risks in an Age of Disinformation," *Bulletin of the Atomic Scientists*, July 19, 2011.

Melinda E. Taylor   "How Green Is Green Power?," *Power*, May 2010.

CHAPTER 2

What Must Be Done to Transition from Nonrenewable to Renewable Energy?

Chapter Preface

The authors included in the following chapter examine how the United States and the world can best make the transition from an energy supply chiefly derived from fossil fuels to a new system that replaces those old stocks with renewable energies such as wind, solar, and biomass. While critics challenge the notion that a transition will be easy or even practical, those who advocate the change insist that the mission is urgent and that developing alternative energies will proceed quickly because of the need. In the United States, the federal government has set aside billions of dollars in loans to fast-track renewable technologies and installation projects. Though the administration of President Barack Obama has not set a national timeline for converting to renewables, several states have imposed their own schedules. California, for example, aims at having 35 percent of its energy portfolio composed of green energies by 2020. New York has the ambitious goal of generating 30 percent of its electricity from renewable resources by 2015. Many foreign governments have also projected similar achievements over the next two decades.

Stephen Lacy, a reporter with ClimateProgress.org, doubts such targets are feasible. Though he does not deny the power and motivation of timelines in this matter, Lacy claims that history would suggest that the transition will be slow. In an April 22, 2010, post on RenewableEnergyWorld.com, Lacy states, "Switching from one energy source to another takes a long time. And many energy experts would say that this latest transition from fossil resources to renewables is no different. Although it might feel like a new, urgent time, a broader historical look shows that it's very similar to all other previous energy transitions." Building off the theories of Professor Vaclav Smil of the University of Manitoba, Canada, Lacy maintains that past transitions from one form of energy to another—such as when coal took over from biomass as the engine that drove industrialization in the 1800s—took time to permeate global society. He believes that because the transition to renewables must take into effect the unprecedented growth of energy demand and the desire for energy producers to pay off their carbon-based infrastructures, there is reason to believe that the transition to renewables may take many decades. "The need for a mass penetration of cleaner, renewable sources of energy is clear," Lacy contends. "But while big goals like [former Vice President Al Gore's hope for] '100% renewable by 2020' sound good, they don't really give the enormity of the task much justice."

What may speed the change to renewables has as much to do with fiscal outlooks as it does with environmental concerns. For years naysayers have argued that the price of solar energy, for example, could not compete with coal or natural gas. More recently, though, studies in Germany—which has an aggressive wind and solar commitment of its own—suggest that the price gap may not be as great as technology improves and that other benefits will accrue as the transition continues. Ned Haluzan, writing on July 28, 2011, for Renewables-info.com, claims that reports from the Fraunhofer Institute for Systems and Innovation Research ISI in Karlsruhe indicate "that the transition to renewable energy will stimulate growth in the job market in the coming decade which should for EU [European Union] bring more than 2.8 million employments within the EU renewable energy industry." However, even with these incentives, Haluzan cautions, "Renewable energy technologies have only started developing which means we have to be patient with them and not expect some overnight miracles."

> *"Renewable-energy proponents eager to act now are furious when tripped up by fellow environmentalists. They've raced to engineer technology that allows them to compete with fossil fuels . . . only to be undercut by their closest allies."*

Large Scale Renewable Energy Projects Are Necessary

Tim Dickinson

In the viewpoint that follows, Tim Dickinson, a noted American political correspondent and writer for Rolling Stone, Wired, *and* Outside *magazines, describes how large-scale renewable energy projects are being confounded not by fossil-fuel lobbies but by environmental activists. As Dickinson contends, local environmentalists often object to the building of massive solar and wind projects because of their potential impact on wildlife and ecosystems. Dickinson asserts that these activists have valid arguments, but, according to him, they are missing the big picture—namely, that some environments will have to be sacrificed if renewable energy is to help stave off further climate change. Dickinson worries that these local environmentalists are holding up the only projects that can meet the country's enormous energy demands and replace the fossil-fuel resources that are adding to the problem of global warming.*

Tim Dickinson, "Electric Bugaboo," *Outside*, vol. 35, May 2010, pp. 46–124. Reproduced by permission.

As you read, consider the following questions:

1. What type of renewable energy does Dickinson say can produce more energy than photovoltaics?
2. What is "disruptive" technology, according to Silicon Valley lingo?
3. How many square miles of federal land has the Obama administration deemed solar energy study areas, according to Dickinson?

Loggers felling primeval sequoias, oil barons raising derricks like so many middle fingers on the horizon, Japanese dolphin hunters engaged in horrific bloodsport—environmentalists have rarely had any trouble identifying the *bad guy*.

But as America embarks on a clean-energy moon shot, scaling up massive solar and wind projects, the black-and-white ethics that have guided greens since the days of [*Silent Spring* author and activist] Rachel Carson appear suddenly . . . quaint. There's a new and widening fault line within the movement itself. On one side: environmentalists seeking to stave off a climate holocaust by fast-tracking renewable-power development. On the other: environmentalists determined to protect important habitat and sacred landscapes, no matter what. These conflicts, playing out in town halls, courtrooms, and the U.S. Senate, pit vast solar arrays against desert tortoises in California; towering wind turbines against sage grouse in the northern Rockies; and an offshore wind farm against Native American waters near Cape Cod. They've been billed in the media as a case of Green v. Green. Which is true. But this isn't some internecine spat among the Prius [hybrid car] set.

Differing Environmentalists' Perspectives

The fact is, alternative energy is no longer alternative. It's big business, backed by giants like Bechtel and Goldman Sachs. This is a *good* thing.

If the U.S. is going to break its dependence on coal and oil, we're going to need massive renewable-energy projects and all the capitalist spirit we can marshal. And, yes, we're going to have to do some building on sensitive landscapes. Leaders of most of the big environmental groups—the Sierra Club, the Natural Resources Defense Council [NRDC], and the National Wildlife Federation—get this. They know that unchecked pollution and rising global temperatures will decimate the wild world, so they're willing to sacrifice some of the public lands that they would have fought tooth and nail to protect a generation ago. Not that it's easy.

"This challenges people. Hell, it challenges me!" says Carl Zichella, director of the Sierra Club's renewable-energy program for the West. "But we can't not do it."

Yet many conservationists, especially on the local level, aren't buying in. Having spent their lives fighting developers, they refuse to let any into their backyards now, even if they're wearing green hard hats. Instead, they're resorting to the same obstructionist tactics honed over decades of fighting polluters. A manifesto from a group calling themselves People Only Wanting Energy Responsibility (POWER!) declared: "Big Solar, wind farms, hydroelectric plants, along with the necessary transmission lines are nothing less than Domestic Terrorism being perpetrated on . . . our Desert Southwest's premier wildlands."

According to Colorado-based energy analyst Randy Udall, "Renewable-energy developers are running headlong into half a century of very successful environmentalist opposition to large energy projects." Udall has a name for this kind of shortsighted obstructionism: *stopology.*

Massive Solar Projects

John Woolard is not a man environmentalists should be trying to stop. The 45-year-old CEO of BrightSource Energy, a solar-power company based in Oakland, California, grew up kayaking in Virginia and spent an epic post-college summer living out of his truck in California, working as a rafting guide. After a stint leading trips on Zimbabwe's croc-infested Zambezi, he entered grad school in the early nineties intending, he recalls, "to fight all the bad corporations."

That orientation began to shift during Woolard's studies at the Institute for Environmental Negotiation, a group at the University of Virginia that looks for market incentives to solve environmental problems. He became obsessed with energy efficiency while earning an M.B.A. at Berkeley, and his first startup, Silicon Energy, identified energy savings for industrial clients equivalent to two massive coal plants. Woolard cashed out in 2003 and became a venture capitalist, seeking opportunities to "decarbonize" America's electric works. "I was looking for something that could actually make a difference," he says.

His quest led him to BrightSource, a solar-thermal startup founded by Arnold Goldman, who pioneered solar in California in the seventies. Solar thermal can generate vastly more energy than photovoltaics, at a lower cost. BrightSource's version involves a 1.5-mile-wide circle in the desert, packed with concentric rings of seven-by-ten-foot mirrors, each mounted on a steel post. These "heliostats"—66,000 of them—track the sun like android sunflowers, concentrating light on a boiler tower some 45 stories tall, superheating steam to drive a turbine. (To ensure consistent output even on cloudy days, the steam can also be heated by natural gas from a 1,000-square-foot complex below the tower.) Line up three of these circles on an axis and you can produce 392 megawatts—enough to power Pasadena, with 400,000 fewer tons of CO_2 emissions than from a coal-fired plant.

In the lingo of Silicon Valley, this is *disruptive* technology, meaning that, kilowatt for kilowatt, it's cost-competitive with new natural-gas plants—even without factoring in the costs of pollution. Not surprisingly, BrightSource has attracted backing from Chevron, Google, and Morgan Stanley and is under contract with California's largest utilities to produce 2.6 gigawatts of power.

Of course, any installation covering five square miles of desert is also plain *disruptive*. But this is where having a CEO with a master's degree in environmental planning makes a world of difference. "From the beginning, we set down fundamental principles that we would seek the lowest environmental impact," Woolard tells me when we meet in his 21st-story boardroom, with a panoramic view of the San Francisco skyline.

BrightSource wants its plants far from critical wilderness and close to preexisting electrical-transmission and gas pipelines. Its design calls for heating and cooling water in a closed loop, using a 25th of the water of a traditional steam-driven solar plant. And unlike the previous generation of plants, BrightSource won't blade the desert to create a level surface for its panels.

For one of its initial sites, BrightSource targeted Broadwell Dry Lake, a dust bowl of federal land outside Barstow that was once proposed as a nuclear-waste dump. Out of view from two interstates, bisected by transmission lines and crisscrossed by dirt roads, next to a gas pipeline, and—most important—close to Los Angeles, it seemed an ideal spot.

Green Opposition

But try telling that to David Myers, director of the Wildlands Conservancy, a California nonprofit that's fought BrightSource as though it were ExxonMobil. "You couldn't pick a worse place to put solar," says Myers, who believes the project would displace migration routes of wildlife from surrounding wilderness. In the nineties, Wildlands raised $45 million to subsidize the government's acquisition of Broadwell, among 266,000 acres of desert formerly deeded to the Southern Pacific Railroad, with the understanding that it would be preserved.

How serious an impact would the plant really have? We'll never know. Last fall, Senator Dianne Feinstein—herself a fierce defender of the California desert and the main reason there's a Joshua Tree National Park—effectively blocked development at Broadwell when she included it in a proposed Mojave Trails

National Monument. The senator's move, made after lobbying by Wildlands and other groups, killed not only BrightSource's installation but a dozen other renewable projects across the Mojave.

File this one under They Just Don't Get It: The 941,000-acre monument would celebrate not only desert wilderness but also car culture, preserving what a Wildlands press release called "the most pristine, undeveloped remaining stretch of historic Route 66." Renewable-energy proponents eager to act now are furious when tripped up by fellow environmentalists. They've raced to engineer technology that allows them to compete with fossil fuels—the tipping point greens have been waiting for—only to be undercut by their closest allies. "We finally come up with a solution," says a top climate advocate who spoke on condition of anonymity, "and now it's our own side that's killing us!"

The infighting is both splintering traditional alliances and producing strange bedfellows. The Sierra Club is eager to see BrightSource break ground at another site, Ivanpah, a plot of degraded former grazing land in the Mojave, down the road from a golf resort and just across the state line from a pair of Nevada casinos and a natural-gas plant. But last fall [2009], the Club's own Desert Committee sought to block Ivanpah, because it would force the relocation of a handful of endangered desert tortoises and cover up several square miles of what committee chair Terry Frewin calls "viable habitat"—a fuzzy designation that can be applied to all sorts of land. Frewin says he applauds the national Sierra Club's drive to eliminate the use of coal in America but doesn't want the desert "to be sacrificed for that goal to be met."

Meanwhile, in the northern Rockies, where the struggling sage grouse could easily have been turned into the next spotted owl, the Sierra Club and NRDC are partnering with wind developers to help them mitigate habitat loss. "People are willing to work with us because we're approaching these issues from the context of solving problems," says Carl Zichella. On the other side, Wyoming's Northern Laramie Range Alliance, a group fending off "outside interests . . . trying to industrialize our pristine mountain country," has been linked to oil-drilling businesses.

I understand where the conservationists are coming from: It makes no difference to a sage grouse if its habitat is destroyed by an oil derrick or a wind turbine. But even if you don't fault them for failing to see the big picture—that climate change is a greater threat than renewable-energy development—it's hard to excuse those who reflexively oppose big projects simply because they're big.

As Frewin admits, "If anything, it's the size of these things that shake most of us up." In the mind's eye of a hardcore conservationist, the new age of clean energy is all about rooftop solar panels and windmill hats. The reality is that we do need those kinds of small contributions, just like we need all the energy efficiency we can muster, but they'll hardly be enough. "The bitter truth is that we're going to need to do large-scale renewable energy," says Zichella, "and that's something people have been very reluctant to accept."

But why? Consider the thousands of square miles flattened in the quest for Appalachian coal or under lease to oil and gas developers. To succeed, renewable-energy advocates have to fight big with big. "The notion that if we just cover rooftops, we can leave the deserts alone, that we don't need new wind farms, and don't need to build new transmission lines—that doesn't pass the mathematical sniff test," says Udall. "What I say to these people is: Buy a calculator. Run the numbers. We're going to have to scale up renewable energy in a way we can hardly imagine."

Difficulty Moving Forward

If there's one point of agreement, it's that there are no easy answers. "It's fascinating," says Woolard. "The environmental community is at this soul-searching moment where everyone is trying to figure out, What the hell do we do?"

Fortunately, the solution isn't an endless horizon of solar plants and wind farms. America's energy needs could be met, for example, by the solar power generated from less than 2 percent of the U.S. land area. There's enough exploitable wind in this country to power the nation nine times over.

If projects could be sited according to unified scientific standards that protect vital habitat and uncommon "viewscapes," the renewable revolution could proceed without all the Sturm und Drang [German phrase meaning turmoil]. Problem is, there are no such standards. So every project gets bogged down by NIMBYism ["Not In My BackYard"] and a tangle of overlapping bureaucracies. "At the end of the day," says Woolard, "there's not a single project of any size or scale moving forward without environmental opposition."

State and federal governments helped make the mess by offering rich incentives for renewable development without providing the rules of the road. The feds are now slowly catching up. The Interior Department has streamlined interagency reviews for renewable-energy proposals, and the [Barack] Obama administration has established 1,054 square miles of Solar Energy Study Areas, including land in the Mojave, intending to pre-clear appropriate areas. "We can do this right, in less time, without cutting corners in environmental law if we just get better organized," says Zichella. "That's what they've done."

And some projects are moving forward. In February [2010], BrightSource downsized Ivanpah by nearly 50 megawatts to mitigate the loss of tortoise habitat. A week later, the Department of Energy blessed the project with nearly $1.4 billion in provisional loan guarantees. The bad news? The biggest battles are still to come. So far, renewable-energy projects have been feeding power into an existing network of transmission lines that's quickly maxing out. Placing new lines, which don't have the feel-good vibes of wind turbines or solar panels, will be a dogfight. Scaling up to just 20 percent wind power will require building nearly 20,000 miles of new transmission lines, subject to the resistance of every municipality through which they pass.

"We're trying to get things built with the least amount of controversy," says Zichella, "but the one thing I've learned in three years of trying: Everything is harder than it seems."

Small Scale Renewable Energy Projects Will Democratize Energy

John Farrell

John Farrell is the senior researcher for the Institute for Local Self-Reliance, an organization that provides research to communities wishing to increase their sustainability and become more self-sufficient. In the following viewpoint, Farrell advocates for expanding the "distributed generation" networks of renewable energy providers. In his opinion, individuals and communities should generate their own power through solar panels and wind turbines, and this power should be integrated into the existing power grid. To Farrell this will revamp the top-down model of energy production that forces citizens to rely on industrial power plants and will, therefore, democratize power generation. In addition Farrell argues that because renewable generators can be widely distributed,

John Farrell, *Democratizing the Electricity System: A Vision for the 21st Century Grid*, Institute for Local Self-Reliance, June 2011. Reproduced by permission.

the new model will create more efficient delivery and help reduce overloads and outages.

As you read, consider the following questions:

1. As Farrell states, what percent of Germany's overall energy production comes from renewable resources?
2. According to the author, how will distributed renewable energy affect backup generation needed during peak or emergency hours?
3. In Farrell's view, what can the Federal Energy Regulatory Commission do to break down barriers against distributed power generation?

Wind and sun are available everywhere, so renewable energy can be economically harnessed at small scales across the country, state and community. This nature of renewable energy, coupled with an exponential increase of renewable energy generation here and abroad promises to transform the structure and scale of the nation's grid system. But the greater transformation is the democratization of the electric grid, abandoning a 20th century grid dominated by large, centralized utilities for a 21st century grid, a democratized network of independently-owned and widely dispersed renewable energy generators, with the economic benefits of electricity generation as widely dispersed as the ownership.

Local Power, Independently Owned

This paradigm of energy production—called "distributed generation" because it is geographically dispersed and connects to the existing (distribution) electric grid infrastructure—is changing the nature of energy generation. It's the same way in which personal computers replaced mainframes, or how Wikipedia and the internet have supplanted the library encyclopedia.

Germany has installed over 10,000 MW [megawatts] of distributed solar photovoltaics (PV)—mostly on rooftops—in the past two years and renewable energy now constitutes 17 percent of overall electricity generation. Half of their wind power and three-quarters of German solar is locally owned.

California intends to generate 12,000 megawatts from renewable distributed power plants by 2020. Utilities are testing and developing new energy storage technologies just as manufacturers are prepared to put 100,000 fully electric vehicles on U.S. roads by 2012. Sixteen states have added a solar or distributed generation mandate to their renewable electricity requirements. The potential for local ownership and economic benefits from energy generation—energy self-reliance—has never been greater.

The rapid growth of distributed renewable energy has led utility planners and state and local governments to examine what the new rules of electricity generation and distribution will be in an age where households and businesses will be both producers and consumers of electricity. The result is a historic opportunity to democratize energy, develop energy efficiency, [create] energy self-reliance and renew local communities.

Integrating with the Existing Grid

Until recently, utilities believed that even small amounts of variable renewable energy like solar and wind would generate problems on the local electric grid. But currently in Kona, Hawaii, a 700 kilowatt (kW) solar array provides 35% of the capacity of the local distribution feeder. In Las Vegas, 10 MW of commercial solar PV on a distribution line provides 50% of capacity (and up to 100% during periods of low load). In each case, the utility has reported no significant issues managing the integration of local distributed solar power.

The growth of democratic, distributed renewable energy will also mitigate the need for new backup generation to smooth the variations in wind and solar power production. Geographic dispersion will significantly reduce backup requirements, and existing fossil fuel power plants (particularly natural gas) will have sufficient capacity to smooth out the remaining variations in wind and solar generation for many years.

In the long term, the increasingly renewable energy electricity grid will also use more energy storage. New technological developments and an increasing recognition of the many system benefits of storage (e.g., frequency regulation, voltage support, etc.) has led the Federal Energy Regulatory Commission (FERC) to issue new rules that give storage and generation equal standing. This opens the door for large energy storage systems from batteries to pumping systems to compete with fossil fuel backup power to smooth out wind and solar power production.

The new distributed grid paradigm is already being tested by utilities. Xcel Energy installed and has been testing a 1-MW (7.2 MWh [megawatt hour]) sodium-sulfide battery integrated with a 11.5-MW wind energy project in Luverne, MN. The Long Island Power Authority is considering a proposal to meet growing demand with a 400 MW battery storage facility rather than new power generation.

Value to the Grid and the Economy

A cornerstone of the democratization of the grid with distributed renewable energy is its economic competitiveness. New wind, hydro, and geothermal power can increasingly compete head-to-head with new fossil fuel power plants with the use of federal tax incentives. Solar power is competitive in a few select regions with high electricity prices and a strong solar resource, but its rapidly declining costs (50% in 5 years) suggest a pending explosion of distributed solar power.

This transition is aided by re-evaluations of the value of distributed energy by regulators and utilities. Municipal utilities in Colorado, Florida, and Texas have found valuable benefits beyond its electricity output. . . .

Furthermore, distributed generation reduces efficiency losses from long-distance transmission of electricity and can help reduce the incidence of blackouts (just 500 MW of distributed solar could have prevented the massive Northeast blackout of 2003, saving $6 billion).

The modest economies of scale in wind and solar power also create a positive feedback loop of cost effectiveness and economic value. Wind power is most cost effective in arrays of 5–20 MW, a handful of utility-scale turbines. The economies of scale of solar PV are largely captured at the modest size of 10 kW, with modest additional savings for community-scale (up to 1 MW) projects.

The small scale cost-effectiveness of distributed wind and solar enables the democratization of energy production and local ownership. For states and cities looking to maximize the local value of renewable energy, the 1.5 to 3.4 times greater economic returns of local ownership compared to absentee ownership are compelling.

Breaking Down Barriers

While technology advances and costs drop, the major obstacle confronting distributed generation is a century of rules and institutional structures predicated on the outdated assumption that power plants will continually grow in size and electricity will continue to be transmitted over ever-longer distances. From federal energy incentives to rules issued by the Federal Energy Regulatory Commission (FERC) to state interconnection rules, there is a systemic bias toward centralized power and one-way grid systems.

Expanding and adopting new policies can help level the playing field.

Federal. The Federal Energy Regulatory Commission can abandon its policy of providing lavish and unnecessary incentives to new high-voltage transmission at the expense of democratic, distributed generation. The federal government can also aid the transformation to a 21st century grid by extending the cash option in lieu of tax credits that dramatically broadens the potential participation in renewable energy generation.

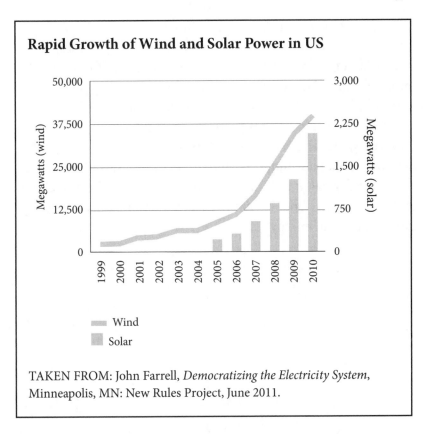

Rapid Growth of Wind and Solar Power in US

TAKEN FROM: John Farrell, *Democratizing the Electricity System*, Minneapolis, MN: New Rules Project, June 2011.

State. CLEAN [Clean Local Energy Accessible Now] Contracts (i.e., feed-in tariffs) make electricity generation "plug and play," democratizing the grid and allowing energy consumers to become producers. Data sharing rules enforced by state public utility commissions require utilities to publish information about their distribution network to let distributed generators locate the best opportunities for developing new projects. Interconnection reform at the federal and state level can drastically simplify the process of connecting distributed generation to the electricity grid.

Local. Community choice aggregation and municipalization can give communities the power and authority to establish energy self-reliance. Lacking these major moves, communities can increase democratic, local energy development by passing solar access laws giving everyone a right to capture sunshine on their property for solar electricity and by changing building codes to encourage or require more on-site power generation.

The U.S. electric grid is poised for a transformation. Without new rules, the renewable energy future and its economic benefits will be developed under an outdated paradigm and owned by the same few large utilities. With new rules, we can unlock the potential of distributed generation and the potential of people to power the clean energy future.

"A fully sustainable renewable power
supply is the only way we can secure
energy for all and avoid environmental
catastrophe."

Renewable Energy Sources Can Satisfy Energy Demands

World Wildlife Fund, Ecofys, and Office for Metropolitan Architecture

The following viewpoint is an extract from a report undertaken by the World Wildlife Fund (WWF), Ecofys (a consulting firm for sustainable energy projects), and the Office for Metropolitan Architecture. The viewpoint summarizes the findings of an Ecofys study that predicted the world can switch from fossil fuels to a fully renewable energy future by 2050. According to the study, most energy will be electricity-based, and that energy will be supplied chiefly by solar power. Wind power, geothermal heat, and water power will also serve to create electricity and heat homes. Finally the Ecofys scenario argues that biofuels will be needed to power some transport systems and industrial processes that require liquid fuels. According to the WWF and Ecofys, the renewables-driven future will save money, stall climate change, and create a sustainable energy system.

The Energy Report: 100% Renewable Energy by 2050, World Wildlife Fund, Ecofys, and Office for Metropolitan Architecture, May 2011. Reproduced by permission of WWF.

As you read, consider the following questions:

1. According to the WWF, by what percent does the International Energy Agency predict oil and gas reserves will fall by 2030?
2. What percent of the world's energy needs does Ecofys claim can be satisfied by renewables in 2050?
3. Why does Ecofys's scenario only provide for a small increase in hydropower by 2050?

The way we produce and use energy today is not sustainable. Our main fossil fuel sources—oil, coal and gas—are finite natural resources, and we are depleting them at a rapid rate. Furthermore they are the main contributors to climate change, and the race to the last 'cheap' fossil resources evokes disasters for the natural environment as seen recently in the case of the [2010] BP oil spill in the Gulf of Mexico. In the developing world, regional and local desertification is caused by depletion of fuelwood and other biomass sources that are often used very inefficiently, causing substantive indoor pollution and millions of deaths annually. A fully sustainable renewable power supply is the only way we can secure energy for all and avoid environmental catastrophe.

Risks and Harms of Fossil Fuels

While most of us take energy for granted as a basic right, a fifth of the world's population still has no access to reliable electricity—drastically reducing their chances of getting an education and earning a living. As energy prices increase, the world's poor will continue to be excluded.

At the same time, more than 2.7 billion people are dependent on traditional bioenergy (mainly from wood, crop residues and animal dung) as their main source of cooking and heating fuel. This is often harvested unsustainably, causing soil erosion and increasing the risk of flooding, as well as threatening biodiversity and adding to greenhouse gas emissions. Traditional stoves are also a significant health problem: the World Health Organization (WHO) estimates that 2.5 million women and young children die prematurely each year from inhaling their fumes. With many developing societies becoming increasingly urban, air quality in cities will decline further.

Finite and increasingly expensive fossil fuels are not the answer for developing countries. But renewable energy sources offer the potential to transform the quality of life and improve the economic prospects of billions.

Vanishing Oil and Gas

Supplies of cheap, conventional oil and gas are declining while our energy demands continue to increase. It is clear that our reliance on fossil fuels cannot continue indefinitely. With the world's population projected to increase to over nine billion over the next 40 years, "business-as-usual" is not an option.

According to the International Energy Agency (IEA), production from known oil and gas reserves will fall by around 40–60 per cent by 2030. Yet the developed world's thirst for energy is unabated, while demand is rocketing in emerging economies, such as China, India and Brazil. If everyone in the world used oil at the same rate as the average Saudi, Singaporean or U.S. resident, the world's proven oil reserves would be used up in less than 10 years. Competition for fossil fuel resources is a source of international tension, and potentially conflict.

Energy companies are increasingly looking to fill the gap with unconventional sources of oil and gas, such as shale gas, oil from deep water platforms like BP's Deepwater Horizon, or the Canadian tar sands. But these come at an unprecedented cost—and not just in economic terms. Many reserves are located in some of the world's most pristine places—such as tropical rainforests and the Arctic—that are vital for biodiversity and the ecosystem services that we all depend on, from freshwater to a healthy atmosphere. Extracting them is difficult and dangerous, and costly to businesses, communities and economies when things go wrong.

Processing and using unconventional fossil sources produces large quantities of greenhouse gasses and chemical pollution, and puts unsustainable demands on our freshwater resources, with severe impacts on biodiversity and ecosystem services. . . .

Switching to Renewables

The global energy crisis is a daunting challenge. Yet we do not have to look far for the solutions. Energy derived from the sun, the wind, the Earth's heat, water and the sea has the potential to meet the world's electricity needs many times over, even allowing for fluctuations in supply and demand. We can greatly reduce the amount of energy we use through simple measures like insulating buildings, recycling materials and installing efficient biomass stoves. Biomass from waste, crops and forest resources has potential to provide a renewable source of energy—although this raises significant social and environmental issues. . . .

Around the world, people are taking steps in the right direction. In 2009, China added 37 GW [gigawatts] of renewable energy, bringing its total renewable capacity to 226 GW—equivalent to four times the capacity required to satisfy the total peak electrical power consumption of Great Britain or over twice the total electric capacity of Africa! In Europe and the U.S., more than half of all new power capacity installed in 2009 came from renewable sources. In the developing world, more than 30 million households have their own biogas generators for cooking and lighting. Over 160 million use "improved" biomass stoves, which are more efficient and produce less greenhouse gas and other pollutants. Solar water heating is used by 70 million households around the world. Wind power capacity has grown by 70 per cent, and solar power (PV) by a massive 190 per cent in the last two years (2008 and 2009). During the same period, total investment into all renewables has increased

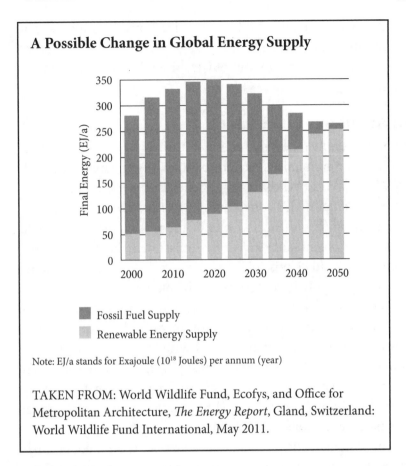

A Possible Change in Global Energy Supply

Fossil Fuel Supply
Renewable Energy Supply

Note: EJ/a stands for Exajoule (10^{18} Joules) per annum (year)

TAKEN FROM: World Wildlife Fund, Ecofys, and Office for Metropolitan Architecture, *The Energy Report*, Gland, Switzerland: World Wildlife Fund International, May 2011.

from about $US 100 billion in 2007 to more than $US 150 billion in 2009.

But the pace of change is far too slow. Non-hydro renewables still only comprise a mere 3 per cent of all electricity consumed. Huge quantities of fossil fuels continue to be extracted and used, and global carbon emissions are still rising. Government subsidies and private investments in fossil fuels and nuclear power ventures still vastly outweigh those into renewable energy and energy efficiency, even though the latter would give a far greater long-term return. While thousands of houses throughout the world, especially in Germany and

Scandinavia, have been built to "passive house" standards that require almost no energy for heating and cooling, many more construction projects follow old-fashioned, energy-inefficient designs.

An Ambitious Undertaking

Moving to a fully renewable energy future by 2050 is a radical departure from humanity's current course. It is an ambitious goal. But WWF [World Wildlife Fund] believes that it is a goal we can and must achieve. This conviction led us to establish a collaborative partnership with Ecofys, one of the world's leading climate and energy consultancies. We commissioned Ecofys to assess whether it would be possible to secure a fully renewable, sustainable energy supply for everyone on the planet by 2050.

The Ecofys scenario . . . is the most ambitious analysis of its kind to date. It demonstrates that it is technically feasible to supply everyone on the planet in 2050 with the energy they need, with 95 per cent of this energy coming from renewable sources. This would reduce greenhouse gas emissions from the energy sector by about 80 per cent while taking account of residual land-based emissions from bioenergy production.

The task ahead is, of course, a huge one, raising major challenges. However, the scenario Ecofys has mapped out is practically possible. It is based only on the technologies the world already has at its disposal, and is realistic about the rate at which these can be brought up to scale. Although significant investment will be required, the economic outlay is reasonable, with net costs never rising above 2 per cent of global GDP [gross domestic product]. The Ecofys scenario accounts for projected increases in population, long-distance travel and increased economic wealth—it does not demand radical changes to the way we live.

The scenario . . . is not the only solution, nor is it intended to be a prescriptive plan. Indeed, it raises a number of major challenges and difficult questions—particularly for a conservation organization like WWF. . . . To realize our vision of a 100 per cent renewable and sustainable energy supply, we need to further advance the Ecofys scenario; and we propose some of the social and technological changes that could help us do this.

In presenting the Ecofys scenario, WWF aims to show that a fully renewable energy future is not an unattainable utopia. It is technically and economically possible, and there are concrete steps we can take—starting right now—to achieve it.

The Ecofys Scenario

In 2050, energy demand is 15 per cent lower than in 2005. Although population, industrial output, passenger travel and freight transport continue to rise as predicted, ambitious energy-saving measures allow us to do more with less. Industry uses more recycled and energy-efficient materials, buildings are constructed or upgraded to need minimal energy for heating and cooling, and there is a shift to more efficient forms of transport.

As far as possible, we use electrical energy rather than solid and liquid fuels. Wind, solar, biomass and hydropower are the main sources of electricity, with solar and geothermal sources, as well as heat pumps providing a large share of heat for buildings and industry. Because supplies of wind and solar power vary, "smart" electricity grids have been developed to store and deliver energy more efficiently.

Bioenergy (liquid biofuels and solid biomass) is used as a last resort where other renewable energy sources are not viable—primarily in providing fuels for aeroplanes, ships and trucks, and in industrial processes that require very high temperatures. We can meet part of this demand from waste products, but it would still be necessary to grow sustainable biofuel crops and take more wood from well-managed forests to meet demand. Careful land-use planning and better international cooperation and governance are essential to ensure we do this without threatening food and water supplies or biodiversity, or increasing atmospheric carbon.

By 2050, we save nearly € [euro] 4 trillion per year through energy efficiency and reduced fuel costs compared to a "business-as-usual" scenario. But big increases in capital expenditure are needed first—to install renewable energy-generating capacity on a massive scale, modernize electricity grids, transform goods and public transport and improve the energy efficiency of our existing buildings. Our investments begin to pay off around 2040, when the savings start to outweigh the costs. If oil prices rise faster than predicted, and if we factor in the costs of climate change and the impact of fossil fuels on public health, the pay-off occurs much earlier.

At the moment, more than 80 per cent of our global energy comes from fossil fuels (oil, gas and coal). The remainder comes from nuclear and renewable energy sources, mainly hydropower, and traditional biomass fuels such as charcoal, which are often used inefficiently and unsustainably. Under the Ecofys scenario, fossil fuels, nuclear power and traditional biomass are almost entirely phased-out by 2050, to be replaced with a more varied mixture of renewable energy sources.

The Ecofys scenario takes into account each resource's overall potential, current growth rates, selected sustainability criteria, and other constraints and opportunities such as variability of wind and solar sources. Technological breakthroughs, market forces and geographic location will all influence the ways in which renewable energies are developed and deployed, so the final energy breakdown could well look very different—while still based on 100 per cent sustainable renewables.

Solar Will Supply Half of Electrical Energy

The sun provides an effectively unlimited supply of energy that we can use to generate electricity and heat. At the moment, solar energy technology contributes only 0.02 per cent of our total energy supply, but this proportion is growing fast. In the Ecofys scenario, solar energy supplies around half of our total electricity, half of our building heating and 15 per cent of our industrial heat and fuel by 2050, requiring an average annual growth rate much lower than the one currently sustained year on year.

Solar energy provides light, heat and electricity. Photovoltaic (PV) cells, which convert sunlight directly into electricity, can be integrated into devices (solar-powered calculators have been around since the 1970s) or buildings, or installed on exposed areas such as roofs. Concentrating solar power (CSP) uses mirrors or lenses to focus the sun's rays onto a small area where the heat can be collected—for example to heat water, which can be used to generate electricity via a steam turbine or for direct heat. The same principle can be used on a small scale to cook food or boil water. Solar thermal collectors absorb heat from the sun and provide hot water. Combined with improved insulation and window architecture, direct sunshine can also be used to heat buildings.

For developing countries, many of which are in region that receive the most sunlight, solar power is an especially important resource. Solar energy can generate power in rural areas, on islands, and other remote places "off-grid".

One obvious drawback of solar power is that the supply varies. Photovoltaic cells don't function after dark—although most electricity is consumed in daylight hours when sunshine also peaks—and are less effective on cloudy days. But energy storage is improving: CSP systems that can store energy in the form of heat—which can then be used to generate electricity—for up to 15 hours, are now at the design stage. This issue of variability can also be addressed by combining solar electricity with other renewable electricity sources.

Wind Power

Wind power currently supplies around 2 per cent of global electricity demand, with capacity more than doubling in the last four years. In Denmark, wind already accounts for one-fifth of the country's electricity production. Wind could meet a quarter of the world's electricity needs by 2050 if current growth rates continue—requiring an additional 1,000,000 onshore and 100,000 offshore turbines. Electricity from offshore wind is less variable, and turbines can be bigger.

Although wind farms have a very visible effect on the landscape, their environmental impact is minimal if they are planned sensitively. When turbines are sited on farmland, almost all of the land can still be used for agriculture, such as grazing or crops. Unlike fossil fuel and nuclear power plants, wind farms don't need any water for cooling. Both on- and offshore wind developments need to be sensitively planned to minimise the impact on marine life and birds, and more research is needed in this area. Floating turbines, which would have less impact on the seabed and could be sited in deeper water, are being trialled.

Geothermal to Heat Buildings

The ancient Romans used the heat from beneath the Earth's crust to heat buildings and water, but only relatively recently have we begun to rediscover its potential. Under the Ecofys scenario, more than a third of building heat comes from geothermal sources by 2050. This is not restricted to volcanically active areas: direct geothermal heat can provide central heating for buildings in almost all parts of the world.

When temperatures are high enough, geothermal energy can be used to generate electricity and local heating, including high-temperature heat for industrial processes. Unlike wind or solar power, which vary with the weather, geothermal energy provides a constant supply of electricity. Iceland already gets a quarter of its electricity and almost all of its heating from its molten "basement". In the Philippines, geothermal plants generate almost a fifth of total electricity.

Geothermal electric capacity is growing at around 5 per cent each year; the Ecofys analysis suggests we could reasonably hope to at least double this growth rate to provide about 4 per cent of our total electricity in 2050. Geothermal would also provide 5 per cent of our industrial heat needs. Exploiting geothermal resources will undoubtedly affect the surrounding environment and the people who live there. Geothermal steam or hot water used for generating electricity contains toxic compounds, but "closed loop" systems can prevent these from escaping. If sites are well chosen and systems are in place to control emissions, they have little negative environmental impact. In fact, because geothermal plants need healthy water catchment areas, they may actually strengthen efforts to conserve surrounding ecosystems.

Tidal Power and Hydropower

The motion of the ocean, through both waves and tides, provides a potentially vast and reliable source of energy—but there are significant challenges in converting it into electricity. Several pilot projects are underway to harness wave energy and to design sustainable tidal systems, but this is a relatively new technology. Recognising this constraint, the Ecofys scenario assumes that ocean power accounts for only 1 per cent of global electricity supply by 2050. However, it is likely to provide a significantly larger percentage in some particularly suitable areas, like America's Pacific Northwest and the British Isles.

Wave and tidal power installations could affect the local marine environment, coastal communities, as well as maritime industries such as shipping and fishing. It is critical that appropriate sites are selected and technologies developed that minimize any negative impacts.

Hydropower is currently the world's largest renewable power source, providing nearly one-fifth of all electricity worldwide. Large-scale hydropower plants store water in a reservoir behind a dam, and then regulate the flow according to electricity demand. Hydropower can provide a relatively reliable source of power on demand, helping to balance variable sources like wind and solar PV.

However, hydropower can have severe environmental and social impacts. By changing water flow downstream, dams threaten freshwater ecosystems and the livelihoods of millions of people who depend on fisheries, wetlands, and regular deposits of sediment for agriculture. They fragment habitats and cut off fish access to traditional spawning grounds. Creating reservoirs means flooding large areas of land: 40–80 million people worldwide have been displaced as a result of hydroelectric schemes.

The Ecofys scenario reflects these concerns with a relatively small increase in hydropower. Hydropower would provide 12 per cent of our electricity in 2050 compared with 15 per cent today. New hydropower schemes would need to meet stringent environmental sustainability and human rights criteria, and minimize any negative impacts on river flows and freshwater habitats.

Biofuels for Transportation and Industry

Energy from biomass—materials derived from living or recently living organisms, such as plant materials or animal waste—is potentially the most challenging part of the Ecofys scenario. Bioenergy comes from a large variety of sources and is used in many different ways. Wood and charcoal have traditionally provided the main source of fuel for cooking and heating for hundreds of millions of people in the developing world. More recently, biofuels have begun to replace some petrol and diesel in vehicles.

In principle, biomass is a renewable resource—it is possible to grow new plants to replace the ones we use. Greenhouse gas emissions are lower than from fossil fuels, provided there is enough regrowth to absorb the carbon dioxide released, and good management practices are applied. Bioenergy also has potential to provide sustainable livelihoods for millions of people, particularly in Africa, Asia and Latin America. However, if produced unsustainably its environmental and social impacts can be devastating. We need comprehensive policies and mandatory certification to ensure bioenergy is produced to the highest standards.

Although the Ecofys scenario favours other renewable resources wherever possible, there are some applications where bioenergy is the only suitable replacement for fossil fuels. Aviation, shipping and long-haul trucking require liquid fuels with a high energy density; they cannot, with current technology and fuelling infrastructure, be electrified or powered by hydrogen. Some industrial processes, such as steel manufacturing, require fuels not only for their energy content, but as feedstocks with specific material properties. By 2050, 60 per cent of industrial fuels and heat will come from biomass. 13 percent of building heat will come from biomass and some biomass will still be needed in the electricity mix (about 13 per cent), for balancing purposes with other renewable energy technologies.

We can derive a significant proportion of the bioenergy needs in the Ecofys scenario from products that would otherwise go to waste. These include some plant residues from agriculture and food processing; sawdust and residues from forestry and wood processing; manure; and municipal waste. Using these resources up to a sustainable level has other environmental benefits, such as cutting methane and nitrogen emissions and water pollution from animal slurry, and reducing the need for landfill. In developing countries, more than 30 million households have their own biogas digesters for cooking and lighting. Some residues and waste products are already used, for example as soil conditioners; the Ecofys scenario accounts for these.

The second major source of biomass comes from forests. According to the Ecofys scenario, we will need more than 4.5 billion cubic metres of wood products for energy purposes by 2050 coming from harvesting and processing residues, wood waste and "complementary fellings"—the difference between the amount of wood we use and the maximum amount that we could sustainably harvest in forests that are already used commercially. This is preferable to taking wood from virgin forests and disturbing important habitats, although more intensive forestry is bound to affect biodiversity. In addition, some of the biomass traditionally used for heating and cooking in the developing world, which will largely be replaced by renewable energy sources such as solar energy, can also be used for more efficient bioenergy uses. All the same, meeting demand sustainably will be a huge challenge.

Bioenergy crops provide a possible source of liquid fuel—either vegetable oils from plants such as rapeseed, or in the form of ethanol derived from crops high in sugar, starch or cellulose. The Ecofys scenario suggests we will need around 250 million hectares of bioenergy crops—equal to about one-sixth of total global cropland—to meet projected demand. This has the potential to cause deforestation, food and water shortages, and other social and environmental impacts, so must be considered with utmost care.

With an expected 2 billion more mouths to feed by 2050, it is vital that increased biofuel cultivation does not use land and water that is needed to grow food for people or to sustain biodiversity. This is no easy challenge. While Ecofys has applied a series of safeguards in its analysis, land and water implications of bioenergy feedstock production will need further research, especially at the landscape level.

A possible long-term alternative source of high-density fuel included in this scenario is algae. Algae can be grown in vats of saltwater or wastewater on land not suitable for agriculture. Large-scale cultivation of algae for biofuel is currently in development. In the Ecofys scenario, algae begins to appear as a viable energy source around 2030, and only a fraction of its potential is included by 2050.

The apparent need for large amount of land for bioenergy is the aspect of the Ecofys scenario that produces the hardest challenges and raises the hardest questions.

"It would be difficult to find a more
taken for granted, unquestioned
assumption than that it will be possible
to substitute renewable energy sources
for fossil fuels."

Renewable Energy Sources Cannot Satisfy Energy Demands

Ted Trainer

Ted Trainer is a lecturer in the School of Social Work at the University of New South Wales in Australia. He has focused his studies on global issues including energy sustainability. He is the author of The Conserver Society: Alternatives for Sustainability *and other works. In the following viewpoint, Trainer argues that renewable energy resources are not capable of providing the power needed to replace fossil-fuel power generation. Whether noting the intermittent quality of wind power or the enormous land requirements of biomass, Trainer insists these resources, while useful, cannot provide even enough power to support present day, consumer-capitalist living standards. Trainer suggests the only answer is to dismantle the consumer-capitalist agenda of unmitigated*

Ted Trainer, "Renewable Energy: No Solution for Consumer Society," *International Journal of Inclusive Democracy*, vol. 3, January 2007. Reproduced by permission of the publisher and the author.

growth and create smaller community-focused, sustainable living patterns.

As you read, consider the following questions:
1. Why does Trainer believe that if humanity builds a lot of wind generators, it may have to build just as many coal plants as well?
2. According to the author, what is the winter performance capability of solar thermal power plants when compared to summer performance?
3. Why does Trainer remark that it is a problem if the projected biomass needs of 2060 will require 24 billion hectares of plantations?

Suddenly the energy and greenhouse problems have hit the headlines and everyone knows that significant steps have to be taken. What steps? Well, obviously just move to technologies that will get rid of the problems . . . without threatening the economy of course.

It would be difficult to find a more taken for granted, unquestioned assumption than that it will be possible to substitute renewable energy sources for fossil fuels, while consumer-capitalist society continues on its merry pursuit of limitless affluence and growth. There is a strong case that this assumption is seriously mistaken.

The limits to renewable energy have been almost totally ignored as a topic of study, even (especially) within the renewable energy field. There are powerful ideological forces at work here. No one wants to even think about the possibility that these sources might not be able to underwrite ever-rising affluent living standards and limitless economic growth.

It is necessary to divide a discussion of renewable energy potential into two parts, one to do with electricity and the other to do with liquid fuels. Liquid fuels set the biggest problem.

When the Wind Won't Blow

Many sources could contribute some renewable electricity, but the big three are wind, photovoltaic solar and solar thermal.

An examination of wind maps indicates that the annual quantity of wind energy that is available could well be considerably greater than demand, but the important question is what fraction of this can be harvested in view of the *variability* problem; that is, sometimes there is little or no wind. In the past it was usually assumed that for this reason wind might be able to contribute up to 25% of demand. However, the Germans with far more wind mills than any other country, and the Danish with the world's highest ratio of wind output to electricity consumption, have run into problems "integrating" wind into the grid while wind is supplying only about 5% of demand. (Denmark's output is equivalent to c. [circa] 18% of demand but most of this is not used locally and is exported.)

A mill at a good site might run over time at 33% of its maximum or "peak" capacity, but this should not be taken as a performance likely from a whole wind system. [In a 2005 article for Incoteco, a Danish company, Hugh] Sharman reports that even in Denmark in 2003 the average output of the wind system was about 17% of its peak capacity and was down to around 5% for several months at a time. The E.On Netz [Wind Report 2005] for Germany, the country with more wind mills than any other, also says that in 2003 system capacity was 16%, and around 5% for months. They stress that 2003 was a good wind year.

Another significant problem is that because the wind sometimes does not blow at all, in a system in which wind provided a large fraction of demand there might have to be almost as much back-up capacity from other sources as there is wind generating capacity. E.On Netz has emphasised this problem with respect to the German experience. So if we built a lot of wind farms we might have to build almost as many coal, gas or nuclear power stations to turn to from time to time. This means that renewable sources tend to be *alternative* rather than *additive*. We might have to build two or even four separate systems (wind, PV [photovoltaic], solar thermal and coal/nuclear) each capable of meeting much or all of the demand, with the equivalent of one to three sitting idle all the time. This would obviously be very expensive.

In addition, electricity distribution grids would have to be reinforced and extended, especially to cope with the new task of enabling large amounts of power to be sent from wherever the winds were high at that time. Centralised coal or nuclear generators do not have this problem. These costs must be added to get the full cost of renewable systems.

[Robert] Davey and [Peter] Coppin carried out a valuable study [in 2003] of what the situation would be if an integrated wind system aggregated output from mills across 1,500 km [kilometers] of south east Australia. Coppin points out that this region has better wind resource than Europe in general. Linking mills in all parts of the region would reduce variability of electricity supply considerably, but it would remain large. Calms would affect the whole area for days at a time. My interpretation of their [data] is that the aggregated system would be generating at under 26% of capacity about 30% of the time, and for 20% of the time it would be under 20% of capacity. Clearly a very large wind system would have to be backed up by some other large and highly reliable supply system, and that system would be called on to do a lot of generating (. . . and would exceed safe greenhouse emission limits).

These problems of variability and integration could be overcome if electricity could be stored in large quantities. This can't be done and satisfactory solutions are not foreseen. The best option is to use electricity to pump water up into dams, then generate with this later. This works well, but the capacity is very limited. World hydro generating capacity is about 7–10% of electricity demand, so there would often be times when it could not come anywhere near topping up supply.

The Uncertainty of Solar Power

The big problem with PV is that it too is an intermittent source, and its possible contribution to a wholly renewable energy system is therefore quite limited without the capacity for very large scale storage. No matter how cheap it became, it can power nothing for some 16 hours a day, or over a run of cloudy days. It is fine (though costly) when it can feed surpluses from house roofs etc., into a grid running on coal, while drawing power from that grid at night. But this only works when a lot of coal or nuclear power plants are running all the time to act as a giant "battery" into which PV can send surpluses.

After wind, Europe's best option for renewable electricity will probably be solar thermal plants located in the Sahara region. These will impose significant transmission losses but their big advantage is their capacity to store energy as heat to generate and transmit electricity when it is needed. However, the magnitude of the potential is uncertain, and especially doubtful in winter. Solar thermal trough systems do not work very well in lower solar incidence. Even in the best locations output in winter is about 20% of summer output. The winter incidence of solar energy in the Sahara is not that impressive, perhaps 6 kWh/m/d [kilowatt-hours per meter per day] towards Libya and Egypt and a long way south of the Mediterranean.

Solar thermal dishes perform better than troughs in winter, but they cost more and their big disadvantage is that because each tracks the sun it is difficult to take heat via flexible couplings to a central generator or store. They are being developed with Stirling engine generators at each focal point, meaning that heat energy can't be stored to generate electricity when it is needed. Central receiver or tower systems can store, but like troughs they have reduced winter performance.

It is likely that solar thermal systems will be located only in the hottest regions, will have to supply major demand centres by long transmission lines, and will not be able to make a large contribution in winter.

Could the gaps left when there is little sun or wind be filled by use of coal without risking the greenhouse problem? Unfortunately the gaps are far too big. The IPCC [Intergovernmental Panel on Climate Change] emission scenarios indicate that to keep the carbon concentration in the atmosphere to a safe level, world per capita fossil fuel use should cut world carbon emissions to no more than 2 GT/y [gigatons per year]. For the expected 9 billion people this means average per capita carbon use would have to be about .11 tonnes p.a. [per annum (year)]. This amount would generate about .03 kW [kilowatts] . . . *which is about 3% of the rich world per capita electricity consumption rate.*

Renewables could provide a considerable fraction of electricity demand, probably in excess of 25% in some countries, but a) much of the generating capacity would have to be duplicated in the form of fossil or nuclear plant for use when there is little sun or wind, b) the amount of coal use still required would far exceed safe greenhouse gas emission limits.

Hydrogen Inefficiency

There are weighty reasons why we are not likely to have a hydrogen economy. If you make hydrogen from electricity you lose 30% of the energy that was in the electricity. If you then compress, pump, store and re-use the hydrogen, the losses at each of these steps will result in something like only 25% of the energy generated being available for use, e.g., to drive the wheels of a fuel-cell powered car.

Not Enough Land to Fabricate Biofuels

The limits to the hope of meeting liquid fuel demand via renewable energy sources are much clearer than those for meeting electrical demand. A very large scale supply would have to be via ethanol produced from woody biomass. The current view among the main researchers and agencies is that in the future it will be possible to produce about 7 GJ [gigajoules] of ethanol (net of all production energy costs) from each tonne of biomass.

A Supplement, Not a Replacement

Wind power . . . is every bit as consistent as is the wind when you fly your kite. Some days it works, some days it doesn't. Solar power, today, is every bit as efficient as the day you decide to get a tan and it rains. That's not to say we shouldn't continue to enhance the collection capabilities in these areas—just a reminder that they aren't like batteries you can dig out of the drawer and know they will work every day, rain or shine, daytime or nighttime.

We need all the wind, solar, geothermal, biomass and hydroelectric supplementation that we can afford. But let's think of it rationally; today and for the foreseeable future, these sources will supplement the giant batteries nature has created [i.e., fossil fuel's stored energy]; they will not provide a cost-effective alternative.

Joseph L. Shaefer, "The Truth About Fossil Fuels and Renewable Energy (Part II)," Seeking Alpha, August 9, 2009. http://seekingalpha.com.

People in rich countries such as Australia use about 128 GJ of liquids (oil plus gas) per year, so to provide this via ethanol would require 16.3 tonnes of biomass each year.

It is probable that for very large scale biomass production the yield will be 7 t/ha/y [tons per hectare per year]. This would mean each person would need 2.6 hectares of land growing biomass to provide for their liquid and gas consumption (in the form of ethanol net, not primary energy amount.) To provide the 9+ billion people we will probably have on earth by 2060 we would therefore need *24 billion hectares of biomass plantations.*

This is a slight problem here . . . because *the world's total land area is only 13 billion* hectares, and the total forest, cropland and pasture adds to only about 8 billion hectares, just about all heavily overused already. So vary the above assumptions as you wish (e.g., assume 15 t/ha/y for willows grown in Europe) and there is no possibility of explaining how all people could ever have something like the present rich world liquid fuel consumption from biomass.

Renewables Cannot Sustain Future Growth

All of the above references have been to the difficulty or impossibility of meeting *present* energy demand from renewables. That is not the focal problem for the evaluation of the energy viability of consumer-capitalist society. The crucial question is can renewables meet *the future* demand for energy in a society that is fiercely and blindly committed to limitless increases in "living standards" and economic output. The absurdity of this commitment is easily shown.

If 9 billion people were to rise to the "living standards" we in rich countries will have in 2070 given 3% p.a. economic growth, then total world economic output would be *60 times as great as it is now!* . . .

Such multiples mean that the problems cannot be solved without enormous reductions in the volumes of industrial/commercial producing and consuming going on, perhaps to 10% of present levels. The numbers are so big that no plausible assumptions regarding technical advance, energy conservation, etc. could show that the problems can be solved without moving to a zero-growth economy on a fraction of present GDP [gross domestic product]. . . .

The End of Consumer-Capitalism

The only way out of this alarming and rapidly deteriorating situation is to move to some kind of Simpler Way. . . . This must involve non-affluent (but quite sufficient) material living standards, mostly small, highly self-sufficient local economies. Economic systems under social control and not driven by market forces or the profit motive and highly cooperative and participatory systems. Obviously, such radical systemic changes could not be made without profound change in values and world view, away from some of the most fundamental elements in Western culture, especially to do with competitive, acquisitive individualism.

There are good reasons for thinking that we have neither the wit nor the will to face up to changes of this order, especially given that they are not on the agenda of official or public discussion. A major factor that has kept them off the agenda has been the strength of the assumption all wish to believe, that renewable energy sources can substitute for fossil fuels and therefore can sustain consumer-capitalist society.

"A hybrid [nuclear-renewables] system would take advantage of the complementary strengths of nuclear, wind, and solar power, along with biofuels, to become more economically viable and efficient."

Renewable Energy Sources Work Best if Supplemented with Nuclear Power

Charles Forsberg

In the following viewpoint, Charles Forsberg advocates combining nuclear and renewable energy production systems to wean the world off fossil fuels. Arguing that nuclear power already has a proven record of delivering baseload energy, Forsberg believes the future of nuclear energy lies in its ability both to supplement renewable energies and in the production of biofuels and hydrogen resources. That is, as Forsberg describes, nuclear power plants could provide backup energy when renewables are not functioning at peak performance and it could produce the heat needed to manufacture hydrogen as well as ethanol and other biofuels. By working in tandem with renewable energies, nuclear power can help ensure a low-carbon future, Forsberg maintains. An award-

Charles Forsberg, "The Real Path to Green Energy: Hybrid Nuclear-Renewable Power," *Bulletin of the Atomic Scientists*, vol. 65, November 2009, pp. 65–71. Reproduced by permission of *Bulletin of the Atomic Scientists: The Magazine of Global Security News and Analysis*.

winning nuclear engineer, Charles Forsberg is the executive direc-
tor of the Nuclear Fuel Cycle Project at the Massachusetts Institute
of Technology.

As you read, consider the following questions:

1. According to Forsberg, what percent of the fossil fuel
   energy used in the making of ethanol could be replaced by
   low-pressure steam from nuclear power plants?
2. As Forsberg explains, what energy source does the United
   States currently rely upon to provide backup electricity
   during peak use times?
3. What is high-temperature electrolysis, according to the
   author, and what could be the role of nuclear power in
   this process?

Since the beginning of the industrial revolution, the world has
developed an energy monoculture based on fossil fuels. And
for good reason: Fossil fuels are easily transported; easily stored
in coal piles, oil tanks, or underground; and easily scalable, from
small home furnaces to massive factories.

Yet the emissions generated from burning fossil fuels are im-
periling the planet. As such, the Group of Eight [industrialized
nations] has pledged to reduce greenhouse gas emissions 80 percent by 2050 to combat the growing threat of climate change.
Meanwhile, the developed world desperately wants to end its dependency on increasingly unstable oil resources that primarily
come from a highly unstable region of the world—the Middle
East. Oil, however, accounts for 35 percent of total world energy
consumption and 39 percent of U.S. energy consumption. So
weaning the developed world, and especially Americans, from
it will not be easy.

Nuclear power has been proposed as a solution. And, again,
for good reason: Nuclear power generates electricity without
releasing carbon dioxide and offers a stable source of base-load

power, or power night and day without interruption. But beyond directly producing base-load electricity, nuclear power also may prove to be surprisingly useful when paired with renewable energy sources such as biofuels, wind, and solar. In such a hybrid nuclear-renewable energy system, heat and hydrogen from nuclear reactors could provide the necessary carbon-emission-free energy to operate biomass-to-liquid fuel plants and provide backup electricity for intermittent wind and solar energy. In short, a hybrid system would take advantage of the complementary strengths of nuclear, wind, and solar power, along with biofuels, to become more economically viable and efficient.

The Benefits of Biofuels

Gasoline and diesel are the fuels of choice for the transportation sector because of their high energy densities, relative nontoxicity, and ease of storage. Existing technologies, such as the hybrid Toyota Prius and other high fuel efficiency vehicles, and near-term technologies, such as plug-in hybrid vehicles, may eventually reduce oil demand by one-half, but the transport sector will still need a transportable fuel. Hence the interest in biofuels such as ethanol and biodiesel.

The problem is that producing liquid fuels from fossil fuels or biomass is itself an energy-intensive process—U.S. oil refineries constitute roughly 7 percent of the country's total energy demand. The fuel cycle for liquid fuels includes obtaining the feedstock, or raw materials; converting that feedstock to liquid fuels; transporting the liquid fuels to the user; and burning the liquid fuel in a car, truck, or airplane. Each of these steps consumes energy and releases carbon dioxide.

Liquid fuels can be made from any feedstock containing carbon, but the less similar the feedstock is to gasoline or diesel fuel, the more energy it takes to convert it. This applies to crude oil, natural gas, heavy oil, shale oil, coal, and biomass to differing degrees. Using coal as a feedstock, for example, is so inefficient that the liquefaction process consumes more energy than is available in the resulting fuel. Converting biomass into liquid fuels also is energy intensive. It differs from fossil fuels, however, in one key way: In theory, burning the resulting ethanol or diesel does not increase the total amount of carbon dioxide in the atmosphere. (Instead, it simply returns carbon dioxide to the air that had been removed by whatever crops are used as a feedstock.) With the caveat, of course, that non-fossil energy sources are used to produce it.

Using Nuclear Power to Create Biofuels

Today, most fuel ethanol is made from corn. So much energy is used to grow, transport, and convert that corn into ethanol that the production process consumes 70–80 percent of the final energy available in the fuel (and most of that energy comes from burning fossil fuels). But about one-half of this fossil fuel energy input could be replaced by supplying low-pressure steam from nuclear power plants to ethanol plants—an economically feasible way to reduce the greenhouse gas emissions from ethanol production. Already, this has been done commercially in Canada. And in Switzerland, Russia, and a few other countries, nuclear power plants sell low-pressure steam to nearby industrial customers—a strategy that should (and likely will) be adopted in the United States for biofuels production.

Ethanol is by no means the only available liquid fuel production method for biomass. The energy content of liquid fuels per ton of biomass can be further maximized by converting the organic feedstocks to gasoline or diesel fuel rather than ethanol. The current way to do so is the Fischer-Tropsch Process—the same process used to convert coal into liquid fuel. (It dates back to the 1930s.) Studies, such as one by Idaho National Laboratory, have described how nuclear energy could be used to convert all of the carbon atoms in coal into liquid fuel without creating carbon dioxide emissions from the coal liquefaction process. In such a system, nuclear reactors would be used to produce hydrogen from water,

---

Nuclear Power Can Quickly Decrease Carbon Emissions

I would love it if we powered our entire economy from renewables but I see no political will to achieve this aim. We would need to invest billions now in renewable technologies. Without nuclear, reducing carbon emissions at high speed is impossible. We might end up keeping old coal power stations open for the next 30 years.

Chris Goodall and Jose Etcheverry, "Is Nuclear Power Necessary for a Carbon-Free Future?," New Internationalist, *June 2011.*

---

which would be combined with carbon monoxide from coal in the presence of a catalyst (e.g., iron) to produce synthetic liquid fuels. The same approach can be used for converting biomass into gasoline and diesel fuel, where the biomass is the feedstock while nuclear energy provides the heat and hydrogen to the biorefinery.

Biofuels by themselves could meet perhaps one-third of our liquid transportation fuel needs when biomass is used as both the feedstock and the energy source for a biorefinery. The combination of nuclear energy and biomass, however, could produce enough gasoline and diesel fuel to replace oil in the U.S. transportation system. Furthermore, assessments indicate that countries around the world have similar access to biomass as does the United States. Thus, the ability of biofuels to replace oil for global transportation needs depends upon the availability of external energy sources to power biorefineries. While some countries have more biomass than others, wide-scale biofuels production theoretically could disrupt energy monopolies that exist today based on nothing more than geology and geography.

Using Nuclear Power as a Backup to Renewable Energy Sources

A major issue in the large-scale adoption of renewable energy sources (e.g., wind and solar) for electricity production is the need for backup electricity. In addition to short-term variations in output (if the sun isn't shining or the wind isn't blowing), renewables have seasonal production patterns that don't match U.S. electricity demand. Wind production peaks in the spring—a time of low electricity demand. Likewise, peak solar electricity production is from April through August—a time of both some of the lowest and highest months of electricity demand.

Currently, the primary fuel to generate such backup electricity in the United States is natural gas. Its use as a backup power source, only fired up when demand spikes, makes sense economically—most of the cost is associated with the purchase of fuel and plant operation, not the initial plant construction. In contrast, for capital-intensive nuclear, renewable, and fossil fuel-burning power plants equipped with carbon-sequestration technology, most of the cost of electricity is associated with paying for the plant's construction. So if such plants operate only one-half of the time as backup power sources, electricity costs will almost double because the capital costs remain fixed while electricity production is cut in half. In other words, operating capital-intensive, electric-generating technologies at anything but full capacity results in high electricity costs. That would seem to make them useless in any hybrid energy system. Yet there are solutions that allow nuclear power and renewable sources to work together to maximize efficiency and economic viability.

Hydrogen's Role in Hybrid Nuclear-Renewable Systems

One set of options involves the production and use of hydrogen. Hydrogen can be produced from electricity when excess electricity is available. This hydrogen then can be used later to produce liquid fuels from biomass and to cover any electricity shortfalls. The important characteristic of hydrogen in the context of the electrical grid is that it can be stored inexpensively for days, weeks, or months in large underground facilities using technology originally developed to store natural gas. In the United States, commercial technology currently exists to store hydrogen on a scale sufficiently large enough to cover seasonal variations in electricity demand.

There are major thermodynamic incentives to produce hydrogen with electricity in tandem with nuclear reactors as opposed to using electricity alone. In traditional electrolysis, electricity is used to break water's chemical bonds and release hydrogen and oxygen. Today, high-temperature electrolysis is being developed where heat is used to convert water to steam; then it is electrolyzed to produce hydrogen with much lower inputs of electricity. If high-temperature electrolysis and similar technologies are commercialized (high-temperature electrolysis is currently in a pilot phase), energy sources that produce heat and electricity will have significantly lower hydrogen production costs than energy sources that solely produce electricity. Thus, nuclear reactors, which produce high-pressure, high-temperature steam at about one-third the cost of electricity, and solar thermal power plants, where mirrors concentrate sunlight on a central point to heat up a fluid and produce steam, would have economic advantages in hydrogen production relative to "cooler" energy technologies such as wind farms and solar cells.

High-temperature electrolysis may create other incentives for hybrid nuclear-renewable energy systems as well—for example, take wind farms, where relatively small differences in wind velocity can have large impacts on electricity production costs. In the United States, most of the high-quality wind resources are on the Great Plains, with the Dakotas having the strongest and most sustained winds. Yet long-distance transport of electricity or hydrogen for liquid fuels production is expensive because the intermittent characteristics of wind means that pipelines operate at partial capacity for most of the year and power lines suffer long-distance transmission losses. In a hybrid system, however, when significant electricity output is coming from wind farms, the steam from nuclear plants would be diverted to the high-temperature electrolysis system with wind providing electricity for high-temperature electrolysis and to the grid. The nuclear and wind systems would each do what they do most economically to maximize efficient high-temperature electrolysis hydrogen production. If electricity is needed when windmills are still, the nuclear reactor and hydrogen from storage would be used to produce electricity. The economic feasibility of the system would be based on geographically isolated, low-cost renewable energy resources (such as remote wind farms), the economic gains of the high-temperature electrolysis process relative to traditional electrolysis, and the more efficient use of energy transmission facilities by maximizing transmission even when the wind farm is not operating.

A hybrid nuclear-renewable system that uses hydrogen at times of low wind or sun could incorporate other technologies to further maximize efficiency. Solid-oxide, high-temperature fuel cells are being developed by Siemens and other companies for electricity production as stand-alone units and are being integrated into combined-cycle gas turbines where the fuel cell functions as a "burner" that produces electricity. For peak-power applications, this technology has an advantage because a fuel cell operates as a high-temperature electrolysis unit producing hydrogen when operated in reverse. By using the same piece of equipment for both electricity and hydrogen production, the system's capital costs are minimized. This combination would allow the nuclear power station at times of excess renewable electricity production to be a consumer of electricity (nuclear steam plus grid electricity for hydrogen production and storage) and a producer of peak electricity (nuclear and fuel cells) at times of high electricity demand. It is a non-fossil method allowing for rapid responses to demand fluctuations.

Replacing Fossil Fuels

If biofuels are to replace oil, biofuel production will require massive quantities of heat and hydrogen. Today, steam from existing nuclear power plants could help biofuel production reduce its reliance on fossil fuels. In the long-term, as biofuels and hydrogen production technologies are developed, hybrid nuclear-renewable energy systems can become the prominent energy source to maximize biofuels production per ton of biomass.

Currently, hydrogen is used to produce liquid fuels from oil, tar sands, and coal. In the future, its primary use likely will be to maximize liquid fuels production from biomass. How hydrogen is produced will have major impacts on the electricity grid (not to mention future greenhouse gas emissions). If hydrogen is produced using electricity from nuclear and renewable sources and heat from nuclear reactors, its production can be easily varied. It also allows for the full utilization of capital intensive nuclear and renewables.

We are in a transition from a fossil-fuel dominated economy to a more diverse energy system. Such a future, where hybrid nuclear-renewable energy systems exist, will allow the different characteristics of each energy source to work best and allow for the ultimate replacement of fossil fuels.

> "We must make significant cuts in the carbon emissions today—and natural gas offers the fastest way to do that."

Renewable Energy Sources Work Best if Supplemented with Natural Gas

Richard Ward

In the following viewpoint, Richard Ward, the director of energy initiatives at the Aspen Science Center and a senior energy advisor to the United Nations Foundation's Energy Future Coalition, claims that renewable energies in the United States are not yet developed enough to provide the power to replace coal and oil. However, in Ward's opinion, natural gas could be used as a supplement to fill energy needs while solar, wind, and other renewables are improving their technologies. According to Ward, natural gas is more carbon efficient than coal and emits less carbon dioxide when burned. Thus, if natural gas was used in tandem with burgeoning renewable resources, the United States could produce less greenhouse gas emissions while moving toward a more diverse energy future, Ward claims.

Richard Ward, "Ally Renewables with Natural Gas," *Earth Island Journal*, vol. 26, Spring 2011, pp. 49–50. Reproduced by permission.

As you read, consider the following questions:

1. According to Ward, how many tons of carbon dioxide does coal emit in the production of electricity per year in the United States?
2. Why does Ward contend that natural gas could easily be ramped up to meet electricity generation needs in the United States if the country cut back on coal burning?
3. According to the Clean Air Task Force, cited in this viewpoint, about how many premature deaths were caused in 2010 by fine particle pollution, mercury, and other harmful gases of the sort emitted by coal-fired power plants?

The scientific consensus is stark: Earth systems are dangerously close to tipping points which, once crossed, could ignite negative feedback loops and catastrophic climate change beyond human capacity to remedy. Because burning hydrocarbons is the cause, many environmentalists advocate a complete ban on carbon fuel sources in favor of renewables. This is compelling until we consider the numbers. The US uses about 100 quadrillion BTUs [British Thermal Units] of energy a year and emits 6 billion tons of the world's 30 billion tons of CO_2 [carbon dioxide]. We use nearly 40 quads [quadrillion (10^{15}) BTUs] of oil for transportation and about 40 quads of energy for electric power. By contrast, our production from wind and solar is only 0.5 quads. To replace the 67 quads of oil, coal, and natural gas with wind and solar would take decades. In this time, the emissions from coal and oil would drive the planet over the brink.

Switching to Gas to Cut CO_2 Emissions

Even if we were to able ramp up solar and wind power by 20 times our current capacity over the next 20 years, the total contribution would only be 10 percent of the energy we need. We do not have time to be purists. The renewables revolution must occur. But we must make significant cuts in the carbon emissions today—and natural gas offers the fastest way to do that.

Each year, coal emits 2 billion tons of CO_2 for electric power generation in the United States. Because natural gas is 50 to 70 percent more carbon efficient than coal for the same energy output, switching our coal generation to natural gas will radically reduce the nation's emissions by up to 500 million tons of CO_2 per year in the near-term (1–2 years) and by more than a billion tons per year in the medium-term (10 years). There are no other options that provide these volumes of reductions this fast. Rapidly transitioning our energy infrastructure away from coal and oil toward renewables backed up by clean burning natural gas makes good sense. Renewables emit no greenhouse gases, and when the sun is not shining and the wind is not blowing, burning natural gas creates far less health and environmental damage than coal and oil. As we expand our renewables portfolio, the natural gas electricity generation could be ratcheted back.

The reason that natural gas generation can be ramped up so quickly in the US is that the infrastructure for electrical generation is sitting idle most of the time. For most of the year, the natural gas-fed electric power plants are used less than 40 percent of the time. The Congressional Research Office estimates that by simply dispatching gas ahead of coal, the US could reduce 400 million tons of CO_2 per year with existing infrastructure.

Unjust Rumors About the Risks of Natural Gas

Just because transitioning from coal to renewables and natural gas is smart doesn't mean it will be easy. The coal lobby will not go away quietly. They sponsor climate skeptics, support efforts to shut down natural gas development, and flood the air space with disingenuous information. Fear is their best tool. The latest example is that leaking pipes will make a shift to natural gas more dangerous and emit more methane than staying with coal. Environmentalists must not be fooled. It is good that the EPA

[Environmental Protection Agency] has raised leaking flanges and compressors as a concern, not to discredit natural gas, but to improve regulations to ensure that the gas stays in the pipes until it is burned.

Coal-fired power plants remain among the top emitters of fine particle pollution, mercury, SO_2 [sulfur dioxide] and NO_x [nitric oxide and nitrogen dioxide] in the country. According to the Clean Air Task Force, this pollution caused over 13,000 premature deaths in 2010, almost 10,000 hospitalizations, and more than 20,000 heart attacks. Shifting to renewables and natural gas is the patriotic thing to do because significantly more Americans die every year from coal emissions than have died in the World Trade Center attack and the eight years of Iraq and Afghan wars combined (nearly 11,000 fatalities).

In the transportation sector, electric cars charged by a grid that is powered by renewables and natural gas would deliver tremendous CO_2 emissions reductions. For larger vehicles, natural gas can substitute directly for oil. Take as just one opportunity our long-haul 18-wheeler fleet which cannot be run on batteries. If we converted 40 percent of 18-wheel trucks to natural gas, we would displace about 20 percent of our diesel consumption and reduce CO_2 emissions by approximately 40 million tons per year.

Working Together Is Vital

Making a transition from oil to renewables and natural gas would have other benefits. In an average month, the US imports more than 300 million barrels of oil. In 2011, we will send approximately a third of a trillion dollars out of the country to pay for our gasoline and diesel. Switching to electric cars and to natural gas powered trucks would reduce our dependence on foreign oil, improve national security, reduce our trade deficit, strengthen our economy, and radically reduce our greenhouse gas emissions.

Environmental groups are rightly concerned about the impact that "unconventional" natural gas drilling has on ground-

Renewable Natural Gas Can Also Help North America Transition from Fossil Fuels to Renewables

Nowhere is the relationship between natural gas and renewable energy more connected than with pipeline quality natural gas produced from renewable resources such as biogas. The development of biogas upgrading equipment that can convert biogas from landfills and anaerobic digesters into a direct substitute for conventional natural gas has opened up a vast network of natural gas pipelines in North America as a new distribution method for renewable energy. . . . These pipelines ultimately lead to millions of clean and efficient end-use appliances in residential, commercial and industrial applications.

Peter Taglia, "Making the Case for Renewable Natural Gas," BioCycle, *June 2011.*

water, surface water, communities, and biodiversity. Currently, shale gas exploration and production is governed by a complex set of federal, state, and local laws. This fragmented regulatory landscape poses a challenge to ensuring responsible production practices and address public concerns about the environment. We must launch a multilateral effort that encourages pro-active participation and collaboration by NGOs [nongovernmental organizations], industry, elected officials, and regulators to do it right. A critical goal must be to demonstrate that government, NGOs and industry can work together.

We must resolve these environmental and public health concerns as quickly as possible so that natural gas can be used without harm. The technical solutions are well known; no inventions are necessary. We just need the will to come together and work it out. We have missed so many chances in the past to shift our energy system. This could be our last chance; we cannot miss this opportunity.

Periodical Bibliography

The following articles have been selected to supplement the diverse views presented in this chapter.

Mike Abram	"Climate Change Demands Large-Scale Investment," *Farmers Weekly*, September 17, 2010.
Alan Borst	"Bring It on Home: Local Ownership of Renewable Energy Helps 'Keep It on the Farm,'" *Rural Cooperatives*, September–October 2006.
Martin Cohen	"Profits of Doom," *Times Higher Education*, July 29, 2010.
Scott Gibson	"Green Energy Breakthroughs," *Mother Earth News*, December 2009–January 2010.
Ethan E. Goffman	"Smart and Smarter," *E: The Environmental Magazine*, June 30, 2010.
Allison MacFarlane	"Nuclear Power—A Panacea for Future Energy Needs?," *Environment*, March–April 2010.
Jessica Marshall	"Who Needs Oil?," *New Scientist*, July 7, 2007.
Lyndsay Moseley	"We Have the Technology," *Sojourners Magazine*, July 2011.
Bret Stephens	"Al Gore's Doomsday Clock," *Wall Street Journal*, July 22, 2008.
Peter Taglia	"Making the Case for Renewable Natural Gas," *BioCycle*, June 2011.
USA Today Magazine	"Systematic Transfer Will Take Decades," April 2010.
Matthew L. Wald	"US, Seeking to Reshape Electric Grid, Adopts a Power Line Rule," *New York Times*, July 22, 2011.

OPPOSING
VIEWPOINTS®
SERIES

What Renewable Energy Sources Are Viable Parts of the World's Energy Future?

Chapter Preface

While solar, wind, geothermal, hydropower, and biomass are often touted as the electricity pathways toward a future free from rapidly depleting and environmentally unfriendly fossil fuels, the focus on electrical generation is only part of the proposed solution to carbon independence. Another critical aspect of a renewable energy future has always been the conversion of the world's gas-guzzling and polluting vehicular fleets away from oil and diesel reliance toward low-or-zero-emissions, alternative fuel automobiles. To achieve this, countries have been experimenting for decades with electric cars, vehicles powered by ethanol or other green fuels, and even hybrid automobiles that are run on electric-battery power but can be switched to gasoline power when needed.

According to a 2008 discussion paper from Australia titled "Renewable Transport: How Renewable Energy and Electric Vehicles Using Vehicle to Grid Technology Can Make Carbon Free Urban Development," the most promising investment for that country—or any country—would be in electric vehicles. The authors, Andrew Went, Peter Newman, and Wal James, insist that "Electricity offers several key advantages over other alternative fuel sources. . . . It is already ubiquitously accessible, requires no significant technological breakthrough, does not compete with land that can be used to grow food and can reduce mechanical complexity in the vehicle. Furthermore, urban air quality is greatly improved as electric propulsion emits no emissions from the vehicle's tailpipe and, if the electricity is supplied from renewable sources, no overall CO_2 emissions at all." Part of their plan is to create a vehicle-to-grid (V2G) system that will allow these electric autos to draw power from a renewables-powered energy grid when needed and feed power from vehicle batteries back into the grid when they sit idle. The V2G concept is not only inherent to the Australian proposal; the model has gained popularity in the United States and other countries as well. With more than one million electric vehicles sold in the United States alone, the number of 10 kilowatt storage batteries on board could make significant grid contributions while keeping vehicle fleets emissions free.

Some US scientists and policy makers may be pushing for electric vehicles because the advocacy for alternative biofuels has met with mixed results in the States. Ethanol production has come under fire because it requires farmers to plant corn crops specifically for ethanol manufacture, taking land away from food crops. Ethanol derived from the inedible cellulose refuse of food crops seems a better alternative, but the government appears hesitant to commit to production because of the expense. Writing for Reuters on July 25, 2011, Tom Doggett reports, "Battered by recession, funding remains scarce for $100-million-plus plants needed for commercial-scale production so cellulosic can compete against cheaper ethanol-based corn." Despite the George W. Bush administration setting a goal of 16 billion gallons of cellulosic ethanol by 2022, only recently has the country broken ground on the building of cellulose processing plants. Experts predict the United States will not produce a drop of commercial-grade cellulosic ethanol in 2011, signaling a lack of progress toward the government's target.

Although cellulosic ethanol production in the United States may be stalled and the V2G projects still in the conceptual stage worldwide, it is clear that alternative vehicular fuels comprise a significant segment of proposed renewable energy plans. In the following chapter, advocates and critics of specific fuel options debate what role these energy resources can play in the global future.

"With appropriate carrots and sticks,
biofuels could play a big role in the
energy portfolio of the future."

The Biofuels
Future

Rachel Ehrenberg

Rachel Ehrenberg reports in the viewpoint that follows how biofuels are slated as a replacement for oil and gasoline. According to Ehrenberg, corn-produced ethanol pointed the way toward a new engine fuel for automotive transport. However, as Ehrenberg states, the production of corn ethanol had some environmental and energy-consumption drawbacks that made observers wary of biofuels. New methods of manufacturing biofuels, though, from waste products, switchgrass, and other cellulose plants have scientists predicting that biofuels can be both economically competitive and environmentally safer than ethanol, Ehrenberg writes. She also explains that new crop management techniques and new processing technologies are helping ensure that biofuels become a major part of the world's energy future. Rachel Ehrenberg is a writer for various news sources including Science News, *in which she covers interdisciplinary science and chemistry.*

Rachel Ehrenberg, "The Biofuel Future," *Science News*, vol. 176, pp. 24–29. Reproduced by permission.

As you read, consider the following questions:

1. According to an online review published in *Environmental Science and Technology*, cited in the viewpoint, waste-based ethanol emits how much less greenhouse gas emissions than corn-based ethanol?
2. What two plant characteristics does Ehrenberg claim are "generally desirable" for all biofuel crops?
3. What is consolidated bioprocessing, as Ehrenberg defines it?

Scientists seek ways to make green energy pay off.

Biofuels are liquid energy Version 2.0. Unlike their fossil fuel counterparts—the cadaverous remains of plants that died hundreds of millions of years ago—biofuels come from vegetation grown in the here and now. So they should offer a carbon-neutral energy source: Plants that become biofuels ideally consume more carbon dioxide during photosynthesis than they emit when processed and burned for power. Biofuels make fossil fuels seem so last century, so quaintly carboniferous.

And these new liquid fuels promise more than just carbon correctness. They offer a renewable home-grown energy source, reducing the need for foreign oil. They present ways to heal an agricultural landscape hobbled by intensive fertilizer use. Biofuels could even help clean waterways, reduce air pollution, enhance wildlife habitats and increase biodiversity.

Yet in many respects, biofuels are in their beta version. For any of a number of promising feedstocks—the raw materials from which biofuels are made—there are logistics to be worked out such as how to best shred the original material and ship the finished product. There is also lab work—for example, refining the processes for busting apart plant cell walls to release the useful sugars inside. And there is math. A lot of math.

The only way that biofuels will add up is if they produce more energy than it takes to make them. Yet, depending on the crops and the logistics of production, some analyses suggest that it may take more energy to make these fuels than they will provide. And if growing biofuels creates the same environmental problems that plague much of large-scale agriculture, then air and water quality might not really improve. Prized ecosystems such as rain forests, wetlands and savannas could be destroyed to grow crops. Biofuels done badly, scientists say, could go very, very wrong.

"Business as usual writ larger is not an environmentally welcome outcome," states a biofuels policy paper authored by more than 20 scientists and published in *Science* last October.

Many scientists have expressed concern that political support for the biofuels industry has outpaced rigorous analyses of the fuels' potential impacts. Others see this notion as manure. Research needed to resolve that disagreement is now underway, as scientists in industry, national labs and universities across the country are assessing every aspect of these fuels, from field to tailpipe. Researchers are growing crops, evaluating yields and comparing harvesting techniques. Computer models are providing stats on each crop's effect on environmental factors such as soil nutrients and erosion. The plant cell wall is under attack from several angles. And chemists and microbiologists are cajoling an expanding menagerie of microorganisms into producing higher fuel yields.

Ideally, high biofuel yields come with minimal environmental baggage and maximum efficiency at every step. The raw materials for these fuels run the gamut from corn to municipal waste to algae, and each has its own benefits and headaches. To make fuels, researchers must first process the raw material to create fermentable sugars or a crude oil-like liquid. Further refinement yields fuels such as ethanol, butanol, jet fuel or biodiesel.

In some cases, such as algae-based biodiesel, the technologies are far from mature. Squeezing ethanol from crops such as corn, on the other hand, uses a technology as old as whiskey. An infrastructure already exists for growing and moving grain, and distillation and fermentation techniques work at large scales.

But grain-based fuels raise several environmental issues, such as emissions of the potent greenhouse gas nitrous oxide from heavy fertilizer use. So, many scientists see corn ethanol as a bridging technology for use until the next-generation feedstocks fulfill biofuels' real promise. Nonfood plants rich in cellulose or even residual waste diverted from landfills may define the biofuel future.

Several studies attest to the benefits of fuels made from such feedstocks, although the degree of benefit varies depending on what factors are included in the analysis. Overall, dedicated energy crops such as switchgrass and waste residues from sources like commercial logging fare better than corn-based ethanol, concludes a recent modeling analysis and literature review citing more than 100 papers. Published online May 27 in *Environmental Science & Technology*, the analysis reports that municipal waste-based ethanol production emits an estimated 60 to 80 percent less greenhouse gas than corn-based ethanol production. Dedicated energy crops, especially when grown on marginal land, also fare better than corn in terms of greenhouse gas emissions, and require less water and generate less air pollution, report researchers from the National Renewable Energy Laboratory in Golden, Colo., and E Risk Sciences in Boulder, Colo.

Research also suggests that these new fuels will be priced competitively with gasoline from petroleum. A new assessment coauthored by Lee Lynd, head scientist and cofounder of the Boston-based ethanol start-up Mascoma Corp., found that the production costs of cellulose-based ethanol, when made on a commercial scale, could be competitive with gasoline at oil prices of $30 or more per barrel.

Both of these recent big-picture studies, while optimistic, call for continued research to improve existing production processes and better define each fuel's associated trade-offs.

Such research is in progress at the Idaho National Laboratory in Idaho Falls, where scientists David Muth Jr. and Thomas Ulrich take part in a coordinated, national effort to watch grass grow.

Biomass Benefits over Corn

Greenhouse gas emissions drop, and air and water quality improve, when switchgrass and forest residues from logging replace corn as a raw material for fuel, suggests a recent life cycle analysis. The chart below shows the improvement relative to corn for these two next-generation biofuel hopefuls.

		Potential percent reduction	
What	**Type**	**Forest residue**	**Switchgrass**
Greenhouse gases	Carbon dioxide	93%	90%
Air pollutants	Lead	87%	88%
	Ozone	99%	89%
Water use	Groundwater	100%	100%
Water pollutants	Nitrates	100%	100%

TAKEN FROM: Williams et al., *Environmental Science and Technology 2009*, cited in Rachel Ehrenberg, "The Biofuel Future," *Science News*, August 1, 2009.

In partnership with scientists at Oak Ridge National Laboratory in Tennessee and at several universities, Muth and Ulrich are keeping track of more than 50 field trials of various feedstocks across the country. The researchers are growing switchgrass and *Miscanthus*, an 11-foot-tall perennial grass. Energy cane, an über-biomass relative of sugar cane, is also under study.

The research suggests that there is not one silver bullet source for biofuels. While there are some generally desirable plant characteristics—such as needing few nutrients and flourishing on degraded land—the future biofuels landscape will likely be a patchwork of different sources that work best in different regions.

"What's emerging pretty quickly is how site-specific both the production systems and problems are," says Muth.

Energy cane, for example, has "huge yields, but it is a water sink," he says. So it may be best for water-rich Gulf Coast states. *Miscanthus*, which has been tested in Europe for several years, produces very high yields and has the genes to withstand cold climates.

Part of biofuels' allure lies in the variety of ingredients from which the fuels may be spun. The Idaho National Lab is also investigating strains of algae that pump out oils as a raw material for biodiesel. At other sites agricultural and municipal waste, such as straw stalks, corn cobs and tree cuttings, are under investigation. Some researchers are focused on crops dedicated to energy, such as prairie grasses, and fast-growing softwoods, such as willow, poplar and eucalyptus. A pilot-scale system for growing the diminutive pond plant duckweed on wastewater is underway at North Carolina State University.

In Idaho, Muth is also using several computer models to calculate the effect that growing and removing the feedstocks has on factors such as soil's nutrients, carbon and water content. This information, along with yields and quality of plant material, is all being entered into a database to help predict which plants will grow best where.

Biomass Breakdown

Bioenergy is not just about growing crops up, though. It's even more about tearing them down. Biomass must be harvested from the field or forest, perhaps stored, and then shipped to a refinery for processing. Harvesting equipment, travel distances and processing methods must all be considered to determine whether biofuels make economic and energy sense.

"What is becoming a bigger and bigger issue to people is the logistics of it all—that's becoming a barrier to the whole thing," says J. Richard Hess, the technology manager of the Idaho National Lab program.

An essential part of biofuel logistics is the preprocessing of plants—cutting, baling and hauling the bales somewhere for storage before transporting them to a refinery. Those preprocessing steps pose problems with a material that isn't very dense or evenly shaped. "It's like moving air or feathers," Hess says.

Ideally, preprocessing would provide an end product that is uniform and easy to handle, like grain—the biomass equivalent of crude oil. "We're not aiming for a certain size, but a certain density that's easy to ship, is flowable," says INL's Christopher Wright.

Wright and Neal Yancey, also of INL, are trying to achieve the optimal density by finding the right balance of shredding and compacting, ultimately producing something like the alfalfa pellets fed to pet rabbits, or perhaps Matchbox car-sized blocks. This crude can then be shipped to a refinery to be heated into an oil-like liquid or broken down by enzymes into the desired fuel.

Breaking biomass down into fuel is no small task. The dominant method is known as biochemical conversion: processes that use heat, chemicals or enzymes to turn the biomass into sugars that can be fermented by microbes such as yeast into ethanol. This ethanol is the same whether its origins are corn or other biomass. But it is currently a lot easier to get the fermentable sugars out of a starchy corn kernel than from something like wood chips or a weedy grass.

Plant cell walls are about 75 percent complex sugars, but getting at these sugars is a bit like trying to get the mortar and minerals out of a castle's rampart. Cell walls, one of the defining features of plants as a life-form, were made to resist degradation. Even termites and cows need special microbes in their guts to get the job done.

That's because those sugars are embedded in a complex architectural structure called lignocellulose—cellulose (long, unbranched chains of glucose) embedded in a matrix of more sugars (hemicellulose) embedded in the tough, glue-like lignin. (Biofuels researchers refer to the "recalcitrance" of the cell wall, as if it were an obstinate child.) Not only did cell walls evolve for strength, they also are a primary defense against microbial attack, and critters that are up to the task aren't common.

"Lignin is a highly problematic polymer from the point of view of processing, but an exemplary evolutionary achievement," researchers at the University of York in England commented in May 2008 in *New Phytologist*.

To prep for the cell wall attack, plant matter is usually pretreated: the shredded, chopped or pelletized biomass is typically mixed with dilute acids or ammonia. At a biofuels symposium held in May in San Francisco, scientists presented work describing pretreatment with proton beam irradiation, steam explosion and microwave reactors. Ionic liquids—basically liquid salts— are also under investigation.

"Cellulose doesn't liquefy in minutes to hours—it's hours to days," says Jim McMillan of the national lab in Golden. This step is the main bottleneck in cellulosic fuel production, Lynd and several other researchers conclude in a February 2008 commentary in *Nature Biotechnology*.

Lignin is typically removed after pretreatment and then burned in the refinery's boiler, replacing some fossil fuel use. The remaining plant matter is then broken into simple sugars, typically by a cocktail of microbial enzymes known as cellulases. Other microbes are then called in to ferment the sugars into ethanol.

Breaking down cellulose with enzymes is usually a separate step from fermentation—and a very costly one. But recent attempts to combine the conversion of cellulose to sugars with the conversion of sugars to fuel—called consolidated bioprocessing—have been successful. A strain of the soil-dwelling bacterium *Clostridium phytofermentans* will happily munch biomass such as wood pulp waste and will ferment it into ethanol. That discovery, by microbiologist Susan Leschine of the University of Massachusetts Amherst, led to the development of Qteros, a cellulosic-ethanol start-up in Marlborough, Mass. And in May, Mascoma researchers reported the engineering of a yeast and the bacterium *Clostridium thermocellum* to produce cellulases and ethanol in a single step.

At the San Francisco conference, posters reported on investigations of even more enzymes from various sources: bacteria that live in the deep sea, penicillin, diseased sea squirts, the bread mold *Neurospora*, a yeast that grows on wood-boring beetles and soil microbes from a Puerto Rican rainforest. Scientists are also fighting recalcitrance from the inside out by breeding lines of low-lignin plants.

Of course, getting a lot of ethanol in a benchtop flask is one thing. Scaling up to a silo-sized bioreactor is another. Industrial models exist—such as wringing pulp from trees for the paper industry or mass-producing cornstarch. "But we haven't done it with cellulose yet," says McMillan.

More than a dozen pilot plants for producing cellulosic ethanol are under construction and a handful are operating, with 2011 seen as the year for cellulosic technologies to walk the walk. The group at Idaho National Lab hopes to be able to demonstrate a system from field to refinery by autumn of 2010.

Environmental Cost

Yet concerns remain that the environmental side of the biofuels equation is still not worked out. Some argue that the numbers are too fuzzy to proceed with confidence that environmental burdens and benefits have been fully considered.

"There are people who say we don't have enough knowledge to move forward—to some extent that is true," says Michigan State University's Philip Robertson, coauthor of the *Science* policy paper. "But we do know a lot about sustainability—enough to implement logical science-based standards." This includes things like the strategic use of cover crops, fertilizer and tilling.

There is also the consideration of land-use changes—if forests are cleared for biofuels production, far more carbon will be released than is saved by the nonpetroleum fuels, several studies suggest. Such findings have led to scrutiny that has stung many in the industry who argue that biofuels are being held to a much higher standard than fossil fuels. If the petroleum isn't "charged" for the greenhouse gas emissions of the U.S. military keeping supply lanes open in the Persian Gulf, why should emissions from cleared forests be included in the biofuels ledger? asks Bruce Dale of Michigan State University in a recent editorial in the journal *Biofuels, Bioproducts & Biorefining*.

Congress is now considering legislation that may determine whether indirect land use can or cannot be a mark on the ruler used by the U.S. Environmental Protection Agency to measure biofuels' impacts. Eventually, many researchers hope, a more detailed picture will emerge of the benefits and costs across all stages of the life cycles of fossil and next-generation fuels.

"Some really interesting services are going to emerge from these crops," says Muth, of the Idaho National Lab. Some biofuel plants help sequester carbon in the soil, for example. A 2002 analysis reported that by the second or third planting year, switchgrass plots experience far less soil erosion than annual crops such as corn. Species that do well near wetlands can act as filters, preventing nitrates and phosphates from getting into the water, Muth says. "If there is a value on carbon sequestration . . . a value on clean water, there may be economic benefits for a lot of these crops."

Robertson adds, "If certain practices were being promoted with incentives, it would ensure that we have a biofuels industry that is sustainable with a net benefit, not a cost. We don't have that yet—I say 'yet' hopefully."

With appropriate carrots and sticks, biofuels could play a big role in the energy portfolio of the future. There may even be a day when, *Back to the Future* style, garbage can be thrown into a personal-sized bioreactor that yields fuel. (Trash biomass in the form of sugar beet pulp, tomato pomace, cashew apple, grape pomace, sweet gum and coffee pulp are all being investigated.) Several lines of research are investigating biofuel "coproducts," high-value molecules that can be extracted during processing, such as proteins for animal feed or aromatics for perfumes and drugs. These products will also bring the net costs of these fuels down, one of several variables that can help the biofuels math add up to success as a fossil fuel substitute.

"It's difficult to compare the costs of not changing with the costs of changing," Lynd said at the May meeting in San Francisco. "Asking is this or that realistic is well-intentioned, but all solutions involve changes—we don't have an option. Business as usual? Well, we think of it as a baseline, but it is a fantasy— even if you don't care about carbon—just as a supply issue. Fossil fuels will all be gone. They'll all be gone."

> "While some carefully managed fuel crops could have a useful role to play, a profit-driven attempt to ramp up biofuels to a level where they replace a large chunk of our fossil fuels is a one-way road to failure."

Biofuels Are Not a Viable Renewable Energy

Danny Chivers

In the following viewpoint, Danny Chivers debunks notions that biofuels can replace large portions of global energy needs currently fed by fossil fuels. Chivers explains that biofuel crops would need an inordinate amount of land to flourish, intruding on food crops and thus threatening the food security of the planet. In addition, biofuels may be more carbon-intensive than expected, Chivers states, making them less useful in redressing climate change. Regardless, Chivers believes biofuels may function best on a local level and should not be proposed as a cure-all for the unsustainable global demand for oil and gas. A climate change activist and researcher, Danny Chivers is the author of The No-Nonsense Guide to Climate Change.

Danny Chivers, "Fields of Burning Gold: Where Now for Biofuels?," *New Internationalist*, July 2011, pp. 25–29. Reproduced by permission.

As you read, consider the following questions:

1. How many hectares of cropland does Chivers say would have to be turned over to biofuel production in order to power the world's vehicles?
2. As Chivers writes, how many countries now have mandates that pledge to mix biofuels into their transport fuel supplies?
3. What percent of renewable electricity production in the United States comes from the burning of wood and other organic material, according to the author?

It seems like quite a nice idea, if you don't think about it too hard. Why not grow some fresh new energy rather than relying on finite fossil fuels that are cooking the climate? Why not swap some of those dirty coal mines and oil wells for fields of fuel crops, powered by the sun, delivering clean, renewable energy year after year?

Sadly, as soon as you *do* start thinking about it, you realize that things aren't so simple. We'd need to turn around 600 million hectares of cropland—accounting for almost half of current global food production—over to biofuels just to power the world's vehicle fleet. Despite this, over the past 20 years, the dream of a plant-powered world has grown from a green-tinted vision to a globe-spanning industry. Millions of hectares of African land have been set aside for energy crops like jatropha and oil palm. Forty per cent of the US corn crop now feeds cars rather than people. More than a third of the fuel in Brazilian cars started life as sugar cane. Neste Oil has just completed the world's largest biofuel refinery in Singapore, with a processing capacity of 800,000 tonnes per year. A whole host of problems have followed the push to exploit biofuels, from land grabs and deforestation to food price rises and increased carbon emissions.

Biofuels Reality vs. the Hype

But are these problems inevitable? Could energy crops have a useful role to play in helping to wean us off fossil fuels, if we could just manage them properly, or grow them in the right places and in the right way?

In [its] recent report *Zero Carbon Britain 2030*, the Centre for Alternative Technology in Wales suggests that a limited amount of domestically grown biofuels made from wood and grasses could be useful for powering the sectors of society for which no alternatives to liquid fuels are currently available: aviation, shipping, some heavy goods vehicles and some farm machinery. [The Centre] notes that this would only work if overall energy use in all these sectors fell dramatically through a shift to more sustainable forms of transport; if the crops were organically grown and carefully managed; and if the necessary land was freed up by a shift from livestock farming to vegetables and grains.

This cautious vision of a carefully controlled bundle of biofuels is a far cry from the profit-driven rush for biogold that's happening in the real world.

The Rush for Profits

Making fuel from crops is nothing new—the original Model T Ford was built to run on ethanol. However, the recent biofuel boom has its roots in the 1990s, when growing public awareness of climate change and oil scarcity spurred interest in alternative fuels.

Because plants suck carbon out of the air as they grow and then release it when they burn, it was first assumed that the greenhouse gas emissions from a fuel crop would pretty much balance themselves out. However, this doesn't take account of all the chemical and energy inputs to the crop, the effects of deforestation and lost soil carbon. Once these things are included, the carbon savings from biofuels are small at best, and in many cases they are worse for the climate than fossil fuels. As these figures were revealed by new research, along with the effect of biofuels on livelihoods and food supplies, environmentalists who had previously cautiously welcomed these fuels quickly withdrew support—but by this time, big energy and agricultural companies had spotted the potential of biofuels as a profitable new income stream.

Jim Thomas from the technology watchdog ETC Group explains: 'If you look at BP and Shell, they've dropped their support for other so-called renewables and are focusing on biofuels. Exxon only ever went for biofuels. It's because it's something they're already used to dealing with—a liquid fuel they can put in cars—and they have the existing infrastructure to handle and refine it.' He places liquid biofuels in the same category as oil from tar sands or deepwater drilling—an opportunity for the energy companies to keep squeezing out more profits as sources of conventional crude dry up.

At the same time, powerful agricultural interests—from US corn growers to Brazilian sugar cane magnates—saw the opportunity for a whole new fuel-based market for their products. The seeds of the biofuel boom had been sown.

Government Support Ignores Downside of Biofuels

Pressure from the industrial lobby plus other local factors (such as calls for energy security and 'rural development' in the US, and greenhouse gas reduction targets in the EU [European Union]) spurred governments around the world into launching pro-biofuel policies. Forty-nine countries (including the 27 members of the EU) now have a mandated 'blending' target—a pledge to mix a certain percentage of biofuel into their transport fuel supply, typically between 5 and 20 per cent. Some, like the US and Brazil, have progressed a long way towards these targets; others, like Australia, are still in the early stages.

By guaranteeing ever-increasing demand for biofuels, these policies have flung open the farm gates to large-scale energy crop development. Meanwhile, more and more evidence is piling up about the negative impacts of these crops. For example, switching a piece of food-growing farmland over to biofuels means that someone elsewhere will need to grow some extra food to compensate—and they may well be felling a forest or carving up peatland to do it, leading to sizeable 'indirect' carbon emissions.

Meanwhile, the use of biofuels is thought to have played a significant role in the current disastrous spike in global food prices. The US drive for corn ethanol—supported by the government through a 10 per cent blending mandate, a subsidy and an import tariff—is seen as a major culprit. According to Marie Brill, Senior Policy Analyst at ActionAid USA, 'It's definitely not the only factor, but it plays a big role. We're currently producing over 13 billion gallons of corn ethanol per year. Combined with recent weather shocks, this has left our stocks of corn at a dangerously low level, and pushed prices up to record highs. As the world's biggest corn exporter, US corn prices have a direct impact on global prices.'

Brill also points out that the US itself is not insulated from these price shocks—by chasing the will-o-the-wisp of energy security (which corn ethanol could never come close to achieving), the country could—ironically—be putting its own food security at risk.

The EU's target of making 10 per cent of its vehicle transport 'renewable' by 2020 was supposed to drive the development of all kinds of new sustainable technology. Instead, it's become a *de facto* biofuels target, as industries have seen this as the easiest route to follow. The EU is now rolling out a set of accompanying 'sustainability standards' to try to limit the negative impacts of the biofuels it imports; however, these standards do not cover social issues, water scarcity, agrochemical use, impacts on food prices or indirect land use change, and seem impossible to enforce on the ground. The same problems seem to hold for similar 'sustainable' biofuel standards around the world.

Biofuels aren't just powering cars. Half of renewable electricity generation in the US comes from wood and other organic material, and a major expansion of tree-burning power stations is being planned. Similar schemes are afoot in Britain, including a proposal for the world's biggest wood-fuelled power station at Tilbury. This is likely to have knock-on effects on forests, people's

Growing Fuel Versus Growing Food

Using food crops to produce ethanol raises major nutritional and ethical concerns. Nearly 60% of humans in the world are currently malnourished, so the need for grains and other basic foods is critical. Growing crops for fuel squanders land, water, and energy resources vital for the production of food for people. Using food and feed crops for ethanol production has brought increases in the prices of US beef, chicken, pork, eggs, breads, cereals, and milk of 10% to 20%. In addition, Jacques Diouf, Director General of the UN Food and Agriculture Organization, reports that using food grains to produce biofuels already is causing food shortages for the poor of the world. Growing crops for biofuel not only ignores the need to reduce natural resource consumption, but exacerbates the problem of malnourishment worldwide by turning food grain into biofuel.

David Pimentel et al., "Food Versus Biofuels: Environmental and Economic Costs," Human Ecology: An Interdisciplinary Journal, *February 2009.*

health, soil quality, and the climate—even if a new tree is planted for every tree that's burned, it can take decades for the new tree to absorb as much carbon as was lost from the old one. There are no firm standards to prevent wood fuel being imported from ex-rainforest plantations in South America or Africa.

Biofuels Work Better for Small-Scale Projects

So far, all of the liquid biofuels produced on a large scale have been so-called 'first generation' ethanol and biodiesel crops—

mainly corn, sugar cane, soya, rapeseed, sugar beet and cereals. Following heavy criticism, the industries are keen to develop 'next generation' crops. In Australia, for example, growing concerns about the use of fresh water and arable land for biofuel production rather than food have led to calls to produce biofuels from wood and waste instead, particularly for aviation. Corporate pairings from an environmentalist's nightmare—Exxon and Synthetic Genomics, Shell and Amyris Biotechnologies, Total and Cargill—have come together to compete in a race to develop more efficient ways to process farm waste, grasses and algae into fuel. While they may not compete directly with food crops in the same way as first generation fuels, these 'next gen' energy sources all face similar problems and limits. None are yet in full-scale development, and aren't expected to be until at least 2020.

Some of these technologies may indeed turn out to be useful—but only on a relatively small scale. Solid and liquid fuels from trees, grasses and some agricultural wastes could have a specialized role in local energy use. Methane from food waste and recycled cooking oil both have a limited but helpful role to play. Jatropha is traditionally grown on parts of some African farms as a wind break, and to provide a small amount of oil for lanterns, soaps and medicinal purposes. Brazilian farmers from the Movement of Small Peasants (MPA), have set up a co-operative (Cooperativa Mista de Produção, Industrialização e Comercialização de Biocombustíveis) to challenge the Brazilian monoculture model: they each grow a small amount of sugar cane along with their other crops and then share the use of a communal micro-mill. This produces ethanol to power their farm machinery, as well as *cachaça* spirit and other sugar products for sale.

However, there is a limited amount of productive land in the world, and it usually makes more sense to use it to feed people rather than cars or power stations. In many cases, we need to use that land (or ocean) only lightly or not at all, in order to maintain the species and ecosystems that share the planet with us. There are usually better ways to get (or save) energy than growing it—as Fatou Mbaye points out, in Africa it is far more efficient to harness solar power directly for cooking or electricity generation than to use it to grow jatropha. Marie Brill notes that the US grand plan to replace 10 per cent of the country's vehicle fuel with corn ethanol would save the same amount of imported oil as properly pumping up the nation's tyres.

Rather than putting in place all the tricky infrastructure and policies that we need for a high-quality zero-carbon future—good public transport powered by wind and solar energy, low-input regional food networks, energy-efficient homes, land reform and trade justice in the South, economies not based on consumerism and endless growth in the North—governments and business are pretending that we can carry on as usual by pouring the planet's bioproductivity into our petrol tanks and power stations. While some carefully managed fuel crops could have a useful role to play, a profit-driven attempt to ramp up biofuels to a level where they replace a large chunk of our fossil fuels is a one-way road to failure, with plenty of casualties along the way.

Bursting the Biobubble

It doesn't have to be this way. Resistance to the biofuel boom is spreading. Campaigning by Kenyan civil society has so far prevented biofuel development in the Dakatcha area. Local groups are springing up to oppose wood- and palm-oil-burning power stations in Northern nations. The EU is under increasing pressure to remove biofuels from its renewables target. A highly unusual alliance is coming together in the US to challenge corn ethanol subsidies, with such strange bedfellows as Move On, FreedomWorks, Americans for Limited Government, ActionAid, the National Chicken Council and Oxfam all heading into battle together.

The next batch of biofuels isn't yet out of the blocks, and we have an opportunity to redefine the debate before they get here. The Rio +20 Sustainable Development Summit in Brazil in 2012 will be a crucial moment—biofuels are currently a large part of the agenda. We still have time to debunk the myth of 'sustainable' large-scale fuel crops, and shift the Rio agenda towards genuine energy solutions. We can all live good lives within planetary limits—but we need to remember that one of those limits is productive land. As Mark Twain famously said: they're not making it any more.

> *"At the same time oil is becoming more difficult to find, expensive to drill, and harmful to the environment, corn ethanol is improving as an even more sustainable, efficient, and cleaner alternative to fossil fuel."*

Ethanol Provides a Sustainable Alternative to Gasoline

American Coalition for Ethanol

In the following viewpoint, the American Coalition for Ethanol (ACE) explains that ethanol is a practical and safe alternative to gasoline. As the coalition argues, ethanol has no harmful greenhouse gas emissions, and new technologies are ensuring that the amount of energy needed to make ethanol from corn is only half of that produced by the final product. Finally ACE disputes claims that the use of land for ethanol production is reducing land available for food crops and thus prompting deforestation to make up for that lost land. As the coalition points out, while ethanol production has risen over the past decades, global deforestation has declined. The American Coalition for Ethanol is a nonprofit advocacy group formed in 1988 to bring together business interests, agricultural industries, and others concerned with the growing production of ethanol as a viable fuel source.

"Ethanol Is Safer and Cleaner than Gasoline," American Coalition for Ethanol, March 31, 2011. Reproduced by permission.

As you read, consider the following questions:

1. According to ACE, the amount of ethanol used in 2010 was equivalent to the removal of the emissions from how many vehicles from US roads?

2. By what percent have ethanol producers reduced overall energy use (in the making of ethanol) since 2001, as ACE explains?

3. As ACE states, how many gallons of biofuel does the Energy Independence and Security Act of 2007 require for use by 2022?

E thanol is the cleanest and safest fuel on the market today. According to the U.S. Department of Energy's Argonne National Laboratory, the 13 billion gallons of corn ethanol produced in 2010 reduced greenhouse gas (GHG) emissions from motor vehicles by nearly 22 million tons. In other words, use of ethanol in 2010 was equivalent to removing the emissions of 3.5 million automobiles from U.S. roads.

Increased use of higher blends of ethanol could also substantially reduce the emissions of cancer-causing aromatics and other harmful toxics. Aromatics are produced during the refining of crude oil into gasoline and when these aromatics, such as benzene, toluene, and xylene, are combusted by motor vehicles, they result in a major source of toxic pollution. Ethanol combustion does not produce these deadly carcinogenic aromatics, which are also the primary toxic components of cigarette smoke, due to their chemical composition.

Ethanol Poses No Health Risks

With enactment of the 1990 Clean Air Act Amendments, Congress required the U.S. Environmental Protection Agency (EPA) to take steps to protect human health by significantly reducing carcinogenic aromatics used by petroleum refiners to increase octane levels in motor gasoline. However, thus far EPA has not honored Congressional intent. In the fifteen years since the law took full effect, EPA has imposed restrictions on benzene, but the agency has failed to curb the use of toluene and xylene aromatics by refiners. *ACE believes it is critical that EPA immediately enforce existing Clean Air Act restrictions on all of these cancer-causing aromatics.*

Ethanol is a source of clean octane that does not pose a threat to human and environmental health. Furthermore, ethanol can help automakers comply with the new federal vehicle fuel economy standards because automakers will likely need to downsize motors and apply new technologies to increase engine compression ratios, and these technologies place a premium on octane.

Ethanol Is an Efficient and Sustainable Alternative

At the same time oil is becoming more difficult to find, expensive to drill, and harmful to the environment, corn ethanol is improving as an even more sustainable, efficient, and cleaner alternative to fossil fuel.

- In 2009 corn farmers averaged nearly 165 bushels per acre to produce the largest corn crop in U.S. history at 13.2 billion bushels. This bin-busting production record was accomplished on 7 million fewer acres than were required to produce the 2nd largest corn crop in 2007.

- Since 2001, ethanol producers have reduced overall energy use 26 percent and reduced water use 21 percent, according to the Department of Energy's Argonne National Laboratory.

- Ethanol's net energy balance is positive and continues to improve. Recent USDA [US Department of Agriculture] research shows that ethanol produces nearly two times more energy in the form of ethanol delivered to customers than it uses for corn, processing and transportation. The ratio is about 2.3 BTU [British Thermal Units] of ethanol for 1 BTU of energy inputs.

Ethanol Is Not Responsible for Deforestation

The Energy Independence and Security Act of 2007 (EISA) modified and expanded the Renewable Fuels Standard (RFS2) to require the use of 36 billion gallons of biofuel by 2022. In order for biofuels to qualify under RFS2, EPA must determine that biofuels meet minimum thresholds for reducing lifecycle GHGs. EPA considered both direct effects and indirect effects, such as so-called indirect international land use changes (ILUC) when estimating the carbon intensity of biofuels.

The theory of ILUC predicts that using corn for ethanol in the U.S. results in land use changes across the globe, specifically deforestation of the Amazon, to compensate for "lost" corn or soybean meal for feed use. Computer models assume that the carbon released from the predicted deforestation is attributed to ethanol's carbon footprint.

New computer models relying upon updated data indicate corn ethanol's lifecycle carbon footprint is likely much smaller than previously predicted by ethanol opponents. According to models released by Purdue University in April of 2010, even assuming an ILUC penalty against corn ethanol, it emitted less than 14 grams of CO_2 [carbon dioxide] per mega joule (g/MJ) compared to an original estimation of more than 100 g/MJ. Furthermore, according to satellite imagery from Brazil's National Institute for Space Research, as U.S. ethanol production has increased, deforestation rates in the Amazon have fallen.

*"When we assume the ethanol
production process is fully renewable, it
would take all the corn in the country
to displace about 3.5 percent of our
gasoline consumption."*

Ethanol Does Not Provide
a Sustainable Alternative
to Gasoline

James Eaves and Stephen Eaves

*In the following viewpoint, James Eaves and Stephen Eaves ar-
gue that investing in ethanol as a replacement fuel for gasoline in
the United States is imprudent. According to the authors, ethanol production would consume too much of America's corn crops,
leaving little for food production. They also point out that variable crop yields and corn production's susceptibility to weather
shocks would destabilize prices and adversely affect the overall
supply of fuel. For these reasons, the authors contend that ethanol
is not a sustainable alternative to gasoline. James Eaves is a professor of finance at Laval University in Quebec, Canada. Stephen
Eaves is the vice-president of Eaves Devices, an energy storage
systems firm.*

James Eaves and Stephen Eaves, "Neither Renewable Nor Reliable," *Regulation*, Fall 2007,
pp. 24–27. Reproduced by permission.

As you read, consider the following questions:

1. What two alternative energy sources do Eaves and Eaves think would be better alternatives to ethanol production if the purpose of conversion is to rely more on domestic fuel sources?
2. How much net energy do the authors claim is left in a liter of ethanol once it reaches automobile gas tanks?
3. How many millions of tons of corn would be needed to replace only 15 percent of US gasoline consumption, as the authors determine?

Until recently, the process of producing ethanol was widely believed to use more energy than it created. But farming and ethanol conversion practices have improved, and ethanol proponents now argue that it is a sustainable and more secure alternative to gasoline. For instance, a particularly optimistic study conducted by the U.S. Department of Agriculture [USDA]—one widely cited by ethanol proponents—estimates that for every unit of energy used to produce ethanol from corn, 1.34 units are created.

Many politicians have embraced the notion that ethanol is a renewable, sustainable energy source. President [George W.] Bush, after signing the Energy Policy Act of 2005 that included a generous increase in the subsidies to ethanol producers, said, "The bill includes a flexible, cost-effective renewable fuel standard that will double the amount of ethanol and biodiesel in our fuel supply over the next seven years." More recently, a bipartisan group of Midwestern senators introduced a bill entitled "The BioFuels Security Act" that, as part of a new "renewable fuels standard," calls for the production of 227 billion liters of ethanol and biodiesel by the year 2030.

Clearly, the promise of a renewable automobile fuel is a major driving force behind support for ethanol. Nonetheless, there has been little or no discussion of how much gasoline could be displaced if ethanol were produced in a sustainable fashion.

Furthermore, though reliability is obviously a central component of an energy security policy, policymakers and researchers have paid little attention to the likelihood of an ethanol supply disruption relative to that of petroleum.

Determining Ethanol's Energy Value

If the objective of promoting ethanol is to rely more on domestic energy sources, then perhaps it would be more efficient to use natural gas and liquefied coal to power cars. Vehicles compatible with those energy sources have been operating on U.S. roadways for years, and reliance on those fuels would not disrupt the food supply. If, however, the objective of U.S. ethanol policy is to power cars with a sustainable, domestically produced fuel—the objective publicly promoted by the U.S. government—then the modeling approach used to analyze the policy should assume ethanol is produced in a sustainable fashion.

A simple way to do this is to create a balanced energy model where a portion of the ethanol output is fed back into the production and distribution process to make up for the energy used to farm, distill, and transport the ethanol. It is important to note that this approach is not meant to be literal; for example, ethanol would not typically be burned locally at distillation plants to power the process. Nonetheless, this approach simplifies the traditional analysis that mixes renewable and fossil fuel sources, which makes judging the relative merit of ethanol as a renewable energy source ambiguous. Therefore, in our analysis below, we convert energy contribution from fossil fuel sources to equivalent amounts of ethanol, and subtract the ethanol from the gross production values.

Virtually all ethanol produced in the United States comes from corn. Farmers grow the corn that converts solar energy into chemical energy. Then, the harvested corn is transported to a distillation plant where it is converted into ethanol. Finally, the ethanol is trucked to fueling stations.

Table 1 shows the USDA's estimate of the energy required at each stage of this process to produce one liter of ethanol. In

Ethanol's Net Energy

USDA estimate of the net energy gained from producing one liter of corn ethanol

	MJ/L
Energy in one liter of ethanol	23.6
USDA credit	3.8
Grow corn	(6.0)
Transport corn to distillation plant	(0.6)
Operate distillation plant	(14.4)
Transport ethanol to fueling stations	(0.4)
Net energy	**6.0**

TAKEN FROM: James Eaves and Stephen Eaves, "Neither Renewable Nor Reliable," *Regulation*, Fall 2007.

particular, approximately 6.0 megajoules per liter (MJ/L) are required at the corn-growing stage, 0.6 MJ/L are required to transport the corn to the ethanol plant, 14.4 MJ/L are required to operate the ethanol plant, and 0.4 MJ/L are required to truck the ethanol to fueling stations. A liter of ethanol contains approximately 23.6 MJ of energy.

The USDA study adds an "energy credit" of about 3.8 MJ to account for energy contained in co-products. The logic behind the energy credit is that co-products (mostly feed for cattle) have economic value and would require energy to produce if they were not produced during the ethanol process. (In establishing this credit, the USDA ignores the fact that if enough ethanol were produced to actually displace significant amounts of gasoline, the supply of co-product would exceed the demand and thus energy would be required to dispose of the excess co-product.) The inclusion of this energy credit brings the gross energy output of ethanol to near 27.4 MJ/L.

After subtracting the 21.4 MJ required to power this process, the net energy remaining for automobile fuel is approximately 6 MJ/L, which, in essence, means that 25.6 percent of each liter of ethanol created represents a net energy gain.

Not Enough Corn to Fulfill Ethanol's Promise

Using the net energy yield reported in Table 1, we can calculate how much corn would be required to displace 15 percent of U.S. gasoline consumption. The estimate requires some assumptions regarding how much corn the United States can produce. We assume that the number of metric tons of corn harvested per hectare is 9,400, equal to the 2006 average (which was a record-setting yield). Further, we assume the number of hectares harvested is approximately 30.4 million, which equals the 2005 harvest (the second-largest on record). Those assumptions imply a total harvest of 28.45 million metric tons. Finally, consistent with the USDA study, we assume that a metric ton of corn produces 4,000 liters of ethanol.

Based on the Bureau of Transportation Statistics, 15 percent of our annual gasoline consumption is over 98.6 billion liters. Since, according to the Department of Energy, flex-fuel vehicles typically get about 20–30 percent fewer miles per liter when fueled with the ethanol-gasoline blend E85, this means that a minimum of 123.3 billion liters of ethanol would be required to replace 15 percent of U.S. gasoline consumption.

According to the USDA study, the net energy (including the offsetting energy credit for cattle feed) used to farm, distill, and transport one liter of ethanol is near 17.6 MJ. A liter of ethanol provides a heating value of about 23.6 MJ, so we will need to withhold 0.744 liters of ethanol to cover the production energy for every full liter produced. That leaves a net gain of 0.256 liters for sale to the customer.

The USDA study assumes the ethanol plant can yield 10.14 liters of ethanol for every bushel of corn. This converts to a yield of 2.5 kg/L [kilograms per liter] where one bushel of corn weighs 25 kg. Since only 25.6 percent of each liter of ethanol represents the energy gain, the United States will need to produce 9.77 kg of corn for every liter sold to the customer. Or inverting this, we will net 0.103 liters of ethanol for every kilogram of corn harvested. Consequently, 1,203 million tons of corn, or over 423 percent of the all-time high harvest, would be needed in order for ethanol to displace 15 percent of U.S. gasoline consumption. If we devoted 100 percent of all corn grown in the United States to producing ethanol, we could displace only about 3.5 percent of current gasoline consumption. . . .

Ethanol's Costs Increase with Weather Disruptions

Relying on ethanol exposes the economy to an entirely new risk—an undesirable link between ethanol supply disruptions and ethanol demand shocks created by their joint dependency on weather. In the case of gasoline, there is no obvious link. For example, during a particularly hot and dry summer the demand and price for gasoline increases as we drive longer distances to escape the heat, spend more time on congested roads, and use our air conditioning more often. But the hot weather does not increase the cost of producing gasoline, so increases in the price of gas have an unambiguously positive impact on the supply of gas. . . .

The market supply curve, which depends on the marginal cost of producing gasoline, does not shift because the marginal cost is not affected by the heat wave. . . . But, because corn yields are especially sensitive to rainfall shortages during July and high temperatures during August, the heat wave also shifts the supply curve back as lower corn yields, or increased input costs, increase the marginal cost of producing ethanol.

The result of the correlation between demand shocks and supply shortages is to weaken the supply response relative to that of gasoline. . . .

Corn Crops Are Better Used for Food

When we assume the ethanol production process is fully renewable, it would take all the corn in the country to displace about 3.5 percent of our gasoline consumption—only slightly more than we could displace by making sure drivers' tires are inflated properly. There are also ethical considerations. In particular, the United States is responsible for over 40 percent of the world's corn supply and 70 percent of total global exports. Even small diversions of corn supplies to ethanol could have dramatic implications for the world's poor, especially considering that researchers believe that food production will need to triple by the year 2050 to accommodate expected demand. Furthermore, ethanol would not necessarily be a more reliable source of fuel. By displacing gasoline with ethanol, we are displacing geo-political risk with yield risk, and historical corn yields have been about twice as volatile as oil imports. Finally, because high temperatures can simultaneously increase fuel demand and the cost of growing corn, the supply response of ethanol producers to temperature-induced demand shocks would likely be weaker than that of gasoline producers.

> "Because electric cars consume no gasoline at all, they are a great option for drivers concerned with energy security and our nation's oil dependence."

Electric Vehicles Are Worthwhile Alternatives to Fossil-Fuel Vehicles

James Kliesch

James Kliesch is a senior engineer at the Union of Concerned Scientists, a nonprofit science advocacy organization. He claims in the viewpoint that follows that electric vehicles are cleaner and more efficient than those powered by fossil fuels. Kliesch asserts that electric vehicles have better overall fuel costs and emit zero vehicle emissions. He maintains that while "upstream" emissions from electrical power plants are still a concern, the change to renewable energy sources could lessen the impact of carbon emissions from the energy needed to power electric vehicles.

As you read, consider the following questions:

1. What does Kliesch state is the current driving range of an electric vehicle from one fuel charge?

James Kliesch, "Why Electric Cars Are Cleaner," *Mother Earth News*, vol. 244, February–March 2011, pp. 58–64. Reproduced by permission.

2. Accounting for "upstream" emissions, how many pounds of carbon dioxide are emitted from gasoline-powered vehicles for every gallon of gas used, according to Kliesch's measurements?

3. In Kliesch's analysis, what is the average cost per mile to fuel an electric car in 2011?

A s of 2011, the electric car is no longer a hypothetical car of the future. Thanks to unveilings from major automakers, corporate investment, dedicated government backing and steady improvements to the technology itself, electric cars are ready to claim a spot as a car of the present. It's been quite a ride. After first appearing in the early 1900s and then flirting with a return in the 1990s, electric cars (sometimes called EVs, for electric vehicles) fell back to niche status. But recent history has seen nearly the entire auto industry recharge about electric cars. Some notable buzz:

- General Motors is back in the game with production of the Chevy Volt, a plug-in hybrid capable of traveling 25 to 50 miles on electricity alone. The Volt has already won several notable awards, including the *Motor Trend* 2011 Car of the Year and the 2011 Green Car of the Year from *Green Car Journal.*

- Toyota is working on a small electric car, the FT-EV II, and has bought a significant stake in electric car specialist Tesla Motors, maker of the electric Roadster sports car. Tesla and Toyota are developing an electric version of Toyota's RAV4, a small SUV.

- Nissan sold out the preorder waiting list for its all-electric Leaf sedan in 2010, and the car is expected to go on sale nationwide for about $25,000 (after tax credits) by the end of 2011.

- Honda plans to sell its Fit EV, which will have a 70-mile driving range, in 2012.

- Mitsubishi plans to bring its electric compact car, the i-MiEV, to U.S. showrooms by the end of 2011.
- Fisker Automotive, maker of the luxury Karma sedan, received a $529 million federal loan to help develop its plug-in hybrid vehicles.

This resurgence is a testament to recent advances in electric car technology. While pure electric cars will continue to face challenges—such as expensive batteries, a limited driving range compared with conventional cars (although the 70 to 100 miles per charge offered by most electric cars is sufficient for many drivers), somewhat lengthy charging times, and a limited number of public recharging stations—they bring numerous benefits to the table.

Benefits of Electric Vehicles

Because electric cars consume no gasoline at all, they are a great option for drivers concerned with energy security and our nation's oil dependence. They offer the convenience of being able to "refuel" a vehicle at home, and they're more efficient and less expensive to operate compared with gas-only cars. They also reduce noise pollution in most driving circumstances. Finally, of course, they're perhaps best known for being zero-emission vehicles, and their lack of tailpipe emissions is a great step toward an improved environment.

Hold it right there, say some critics. Aren't electric cars simply moving emissions from the vehicle's tailpipe to a power plant smokestack? (This is the "long tailpipe" critique.) Aren't there still greenhouse gas emissions and other pollutants associated with creating the electricity these vehicles use? And if that's the case, are electric cars *really* all they're cracked up to be?

"These are valid questions deserving of a thorough assessment," says Bill Moore, editor in chief of EV World, a transportation technology and news website. While lamenting misinformation that perpetuates in the blogosphere and elsewhere, Moore values criticism that encourages progress. "We don't want [electric cars] to become a burden on society, so we need to hear those criticisms, we need to weigh them, and we need to move forward to improve the technology," he says.

Electric car emissions depend on multiple factors—particularly how your electricity is generated, which, for most, depends on where you live. Smog-forming pollution at the power plant from the use of an electric car can have higher emissions rates than typical gas-only or hybrid cars (such as the Toyota Prius), a fact owed largely to the effectiveness of catalytic converters in today's gas cars. It's important to note, though, that from a health standpoint, one major advantage of "moving" pollution from the tailpipe to the power plant is that it gets pollutants farther away from pedestrians and other drivers, lowering the pollutants' adverse health impacts on the concentrated population.

However, some pollutants, such as those related to climate change, affect the environment regardless of where they are released. In terms of climate change emissions, electric cars are generally much cleaner than conventional gas vehicles. In areas of the country that have the cleanest power generation (more wind, solar and hydropower), electric cars emit far less greenhouse gases, not only compared with conventional vehicles, but also compared with efficient hybrid-electric vehicles. In areas of the country with the dirtiest power generation (coal), an efficient hybrid may be your best environmental bet, though if you're gentle on the pedal, an electric car may yield comparable results. On a national average basis, an efficient electric car emits about half the amount of carbon dioxide as a conventional car, and roughly the same amount as an efficient hybrid. To fully understand these comparisons, we first need to understand the how, what and where of vehicle emissions.

Comparing Vehicle Emissions

The vast majority of cars and trucks on today's roads operate on internal combustion engines, which convert energy stored in a liquid fuel (usually gasoline) into mechanical motion by rapidly igniting an air-fuel mixture in the engine's cylinders. This combustion process emits engine exhaust that contains a number of pollutants, including (but not limited to) carbon monoxide, hydrocarbons, nitrogen oxides and particulate matter. But automotive engineers have found ways to reduce these pollutants, both by adding emissions-control devices (such as catalytic converters) to the exhaust plumbing, and by precisely rendering the cylinders' combustion process though computer control. The upshot is that, especially over the past decade, conventional vehicles have gotten much cleaner in terms of smog-forming pollution.

The bad news is that another pollutant created by combusting fuel—carbon dioxide, or CO_2—cannot be minimized through the use of emissions-control devices. Simply put, the more fuel your vehicle burns, the more CO_2 it emits. This is particularly troublesome because CO_2 is the primary human-caused greenhouse gas, contributing heavily to global warming. While a comparison of conventional vehicles and electric cars could be conducted for each of the major pollutants, the critical environmental issue today is the impact our vehicles have on global warming, which is why our calculations focus on CO_2 emissions.

A vehicle's emissions can be categorized into three types: in-use, upstream and vehicle-manufacturing emissions. In-use emissions—those produced when someone is actually driving the vehicle—constitute the majority of a typical car's lifetime emissions. Upstream emissions are those that result from producing and transporting the fuel a car uses to its point of use (in the case of gasoline, that means extracting crude oil, refining it and transporting it to gas stations). The third category is manufacturing-related emissions, which, according to the latest research, only account for about 10 to 20 percent of a vehicle's lifetime greenhouse gas output. (Given the modest impact of manufacturing emissions, calculations made in this [viewpoint] include only in-use and upstream emissions.)

Remarkably, burning 1 gallon of gasoline pushes more than 19 pounds of CO_2 out of your vehicle's tailpipe. One gallon of gasoline weighs only about 6 pounds, but the combustion process pulls in oxygen atoms from the surrounding air when creating carbon dioxide. But that's not all. In addition to those 19 pounds of CO_2 nearly another 5 pounds of CO_2 are produced "upstream" during the creation and transportation of that gallon of gas from the wellhead to the refinery to the corner station, all before being put in the car's tank. All told, our cars are responsible for emitting nearly 25 pounds of CO_2 for every gallon of gas they burn.

Unlike vehicles with internal combustion engines, electric cars have zero in-use emissions. They do, however, have upstream emissions: those resulting from producing the vehicle's fuel—in this case, the vehicle's electricity.

Electricity Production and Carbon Dioxide Emissions

When it comes to electricity, the resource used to generate it plays a major role in determining how environmentally friendly its electrons are. The cleanest type of electricity is that generated from *renewable energy sources*, such as solar, wind and hydropower. Such sources create electricity without producing greenhouse gases or smog-forming pollutants at a power plant. Electric cars powered by electricity created from renewable sources are, for all intents and purposes, true zero-emission vehicles.

Electricity generated by *natural gas plants* falls in the middle of the pack. It's cleaner than coal power, but not nearly as climate-friendly as power generated from renewable sources.

The worst electricity, from both a global warming and a smog-forming emissions standpoint, comes from *coal-fired power plants*. They emit the highest levels of carbon dioxide and, depending on the quality of the emissions-control devices on the plants, can emit high levels of smog-forming and toxic emissions as well, including particulate matter (soot).

Nuclear plants, while not a threat from a global warming or smog-forming pollution standpoint, pose the dangerous threats of nuclear disasters and nuclear proliferation. Safe, long-term storage of nuclear waste is also a serious concern. Because of these issues, nuclear energy isn't considered by many (including myself) to be an eco-friendly option at this time.

Today [Winter 2011], coal-fired power plants generate the majority of electricity in the United States (48 percent), followed by natural gas (22 percent), nuclear (19 percent) and renewables (9 percent). The efficiency of the power plant also affects the eco-friendliness of the electricity it generates. Some plants, such as combined heat and power facilities, make better use of waste energy, which reduces the amount of fuel necessary (and thus pollution emitted) to produce a given amount of energy. The cleanliness of power plant emissions is also tied to what pollution-control technology the plant utilizes. Plants can use scrubbers, for example, to control sulfur emissions. Short of still-invalidated carbon capture and storage processes, however, there is no method for controlling CO_2 emissions from power plants.

Different U.S. regions utilize vastly different electricity sources. The Northeast, Northwest and Pacific Coast generate electricity using large amounts of renewable hydroelectric power, while the Midwest uses a significant amount of coal.

What does all of this mean for the typical electricity consumer? In short, it means the cleanliness of your electricity determines how eco-friendly it would be to operate an electric car. For example, if you live in California, which has some of the cleanest electricity in the nation, an electric car driven 12,000 miles (a typical year's worth of driving) would emit about 1.6 tons of CO_2. By contrast, a hybrid such as the Toyota Prius would emit about 2.9 tons, and a 25-mpg gas car would emit about 5.9 tons per year. If you live in the Midwest, where coal is king, your electric car's annual emissions would be about 4.1 tons of CO_2 — more than that of an efficient hybrid, but still far less than that from a gas-only vehicle.

Electric Car Carbon Dioxide Emissions by Region

These numbers represent the estimated pounds of CO_2 emitted per year for a typical electric car driven in each region. An electric car in even the "worst" region yields cleaner emissions than a typical conventional gas car, whose CO_2 emissions do not vary by region. The calculations assume 12,000 miles driven annually (a typical year's worth of driving), and the emissions figure for gas-only cars assumes a fuel efficiency of 25 miles per gallon.

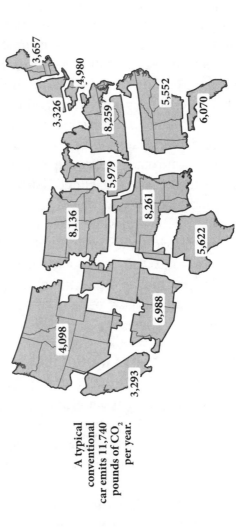

3,657

4,980

3,326

8,259

5,552

6,070

5,979

8,261

8,136

5,622

4,098

6,988

3,293

A typical conventional car emits 11,740 pounds of CO_2 per year.

TAKEN FROM: US Energy Information Administration and US Environmental Protection Agency, cited in James Kliesch, "Why Electric Cars Are Cleaner," *Mother Earth News*, vol. 244, February–March 2011.

So, how do the numbers shake out for the rest of the country? The U.S. Department of Energy tracks power plant emissions in more than a dozen different regions and subregions across the nation. This regional emissions information is a good starting point for estimating the environmental impact of electric cars in different regions of the country. Making subsequent calculations to account for regional transmission and distribution losses, vehicle charging equipment losses, and estimated impacts of energy extraction, transportation and processing, it's possible to estimate average electric car emissions around the country.

Another factor to consider is that, while power plants have multiple-decade lifetimes, emissions from the grid are not static. In time, electric cars have the potential to get even cleaner if concerted efforts are made to clean up our energy portfolio with cleaner fossil fuels (natural gas) and, far better yet, even more renewable energy. Each year, the U.S. Department of Energy projects how grid emissions are likely to change in the future. It predicts an electric car driven in California in 2035 will have 39 percent less annual CO_2 emissions than an electric car driven today. While constructive on a general level, this information should be viewed cautiously because of the many assumptions that go into such predictions. . . .

Cutting Fuel Costs by Going Electric

About 3 cents per mile driven is all it costs to "fuel" a typical electric car today, assuming an electricity rate of 10 cents per kilowatt-hour (kWh). By contrast, at a pump price of $2.75 per gallon, a 25-mpg conventional car costs more than *three times* that amount. Why? A big reason is the inherent efficiency of electric motors.

According to the Department of Energy and the Environmental Protection Agency, about 75 percent of the chemical energy stored in an electric car's battery can be translated to mechanical energy that rotates the wheels of the vehicle. By contrast, only about 20 percent of the energy stored in a conventional vehicle's tank of gas actually moves the vehicle down the road. The rest is simply lost—primarily to heat created during the combustion process, but also to other factors, such as friction and air-pumping losses in the engine.

The efficiency advantage of electric motors means excellent on-road "fuel" economy. Today's electric cars are rated at about 3 miles per kWh of electricity consumed. On a gasoline-equivalent basis, that's roughly 100 mpg, and a number of drivers report even better results when driving with efficiency in mind. All told, while expensive batteries add to the upfront cost of an electric vehicle, lower fuel and maintenance expenses allow electric car drivers to recoup much of those costs over the life of the vehicle.

"Numerous studies have found that electric and plug-in hybrid vehicles are simply not ready for prime time."

Electric Vehicles Are Not Worthwhile Alternatives to Fossil-Fuel Vehicles

Robert Bryce

A former veteran writer for the Austin Chronicle, *Robert Bryce is a journalist who focuses on energy issues and politics. In the following viewpoint, he maintains that electric cars have been the promise of US automakers since the dawn of the automotive age. Still, Bryce contends, no company has delivered a viable electric vehicle that can match or outperform combustion-engine vehicles. This has not deterred the federal government from subsidizing electric vehicles with taxpayer money, Bryce claims, wasting time and funding on vehicles that will never be as efficient as their gasoline-powered counterparts.*

As you read, consider the following questions:

1. According to Deloitte Consulting, a firm cited by the author, what percent of Americans will be amenable to electric vehicles by 2020?

Robert Bryce, "Unplugged! Why Electric Cars Are the Next Big Thing . . . and They Always Will Be," *Energy Tribune,* August 5, 2010. Reproduced by permission.

2. Even with the battery engine's efficiency advantage, gasoline will still have how much more energy density than
   the best car battery, as Bryce states?
3. According to Bryce, how much funding did fifty different
   US automakers and battery makers receive in 2010 as part
   of federal subsidies?

Imagine this scenario: Politicians at the state and federal levels
begin handing out billions of dollars in subsidies so that over
the next decade America's wealthiest people—those with household incomes of $200,000 or more—will be encouraged to buy
more vacation homes. Oh, and those homes should be concentrated in the areas around Los Angeles and San Diego.

The outrage at such an eventuality would be obvious and
immediate. The Democratic Party and the party's union-based
supporters would, no doubt, be particularly vociferous in their
objections. They would waste no time in pointing out that such
subsidies are ignoring the needs of working-class voters, particularly at a time when the US economy continues to be in recession, unemployment rates are near 10%, and chronic joblessness
could continue for years to come. Or given the California-
centric bias of the subsidies, imagine the reaction from a conservative Congressman hailing from Alabama, Mississippi, or
Arkansas.

Now toss aside that scenario and consider the real-life subsidies being lavished on the electric car, a vehicle which, if it
ever gains traction in the market place—and there's no indication that it will, given the sector's century-long history of failure
tailgating failure—will largely serve as driveway jewelry for the
wealthy.

A Toy of the Wealthy

In March [2010], *Der Spiegel* [a German newspaper] estimated that over the next five years, the US will provide about

$27 billion in subsidies for electric car development and production. Meanwhile, France will spend $2.7 billion and Germany $720 million.

There's no outrage at those massive subsidies even though the Americans who are most likely to buy electric cars are—according to a July study done by Deloitte Consulting—those with household incomes "in excess of $200,000" and "who already own one or more vehicles." Furthermore, Deloitte expects those buyers to be "concentrated around southern California where weather and infrastructure allow for ease of EV [electric vehicle] ownership."

Deloitte concluded that the US now has about 1.3 million consumers who "fit the demographic and psychographic profiles" of expected EV buyers. It went on saying that mass adoption of the EV "will be gradual" and that by 2020, perhaps 3% of the US car market could be amenable to EVs. The firm goes on saying that the keys to "mass adoption are 1) a reduction in price; and 2) a driving experience in which the EV is equivalent to the internal combustion engine."

Think about those numbers. Out of 300 million Americans, perhaps 1.3 million are likely to buy an electric vehicle, and yet, all we hear lately is that electric cars are the way of the future. Indeed, over the past few weeks, we've been carpet-bombed with happy talk about the electric car.

In late July [2010], the *New York Times* published a long profile of Elon Musk, the entrepreneur behind Tesla Motors, the startup that has produced about 1,000 electric sports cars. A few days after that, the news was dominated by the announcement of the sticker price ($41,000) of the new Chevrolet Volt. About that same time, Senate Majority Leader Harry Reid introduced a scaled-back energy bill that promises some $400 million in new subsidies for the electric-car business. The key photo op for the electric car came on July 30, when President Barack Obama visited a GM plant that will assemble the Volt. Obama reportedly pronounced the car as "pretty smooth."

But amid all of the hype, the essential question is obvious: Why is the government throwing so much money at a technology that shows so little promise?

A History of Failed Promises

Ever since we moved from horse-drawn power to automobiles, the electric-car industry has been promising that it was just on the cusp of viability. Today is no different. We are being told that this time things are different, that the technologies are better, the batteries are better, and that consumers are ready to adopt electrics like never before. Perhaps that's true. But consider this declaration: The electric car "has long been recognized as the ideal solution" because it "is cleaner and quieter" and "much more economical."

That story was published by the *New York Times* on November 12, 1911.

Or given that the new Chevy Volt costs as much as a new Mercedes-Benz C350, consider this assessment by a believing reporter: "Prices on electric cars will continue to drop until they are within reach of the average family."

That line appeared in the *Washington Post* on Halloween 1915.

And since the Volt is being built by GM, this news item says that the giant carmaker has found "a breakthrough in batteries" that "now makes electric cars commercially practical." The new zinc-nickel oxide batteries will provide the "100-mile range that General Motors executives believe is necessary to successfully sell electric vehicles to the public."

That story was published in the *Washington Post* on September 26, 1979.

Now fast-forward to July 2008, when Thomas Friedman of the *New York Times* declared that Shai Agassi—the founder of an electric-car company called Better Place—was "the Jewish Henry Ford." Friedman went on to claim that Agassi was launching "an energy revolution" that would end the world's "oil addiction."

Sticker Shock for Family Budgets

To store the electricity drawn from a power outlet, EVs [electric vehicles] require huge batteries that cost $10,000 to $15,000 apiece. This can drive the overall vehicle cost to nearly twice the levels of a comparable gas-powered car. For exotics like the $109,000 Tesla Roadster, sticker shock isn't really a problem. But for mass-market family cars, it is.

The Leaf, for instance, starts at about $33,000, compared with prices of less than $20,000 for a gas-powered hatch like the Mazda 3 or Volkswagen Golf.

Rick Newman, "5 Reasons Electric Cars Will Disappoint," U.S. News & World Report *Money blog, October 28, 2010. http://money .usnews.com.*

Never mind that when Friedman wrote his story Agassi's fleet of electric cars consisted of exactly one prototype.

The media's coverage of the electric-car sector demonstrates more than 100 years of gullibility. The gee-whiz factor of electric cars with their big batteries, small motors, and whisper-quiet locomotion appears to be so dazzling that reporters willingly give up their skepticism like star-struck groupies surrendering their panties.

That same lack of skepticism may explain why the Senate wants to throw hundreds of millions of additional dollars at electric cars without braking to consider the problems of physics and consumer demand. And those two factors are undoubtedly the biggest problems for the future of the electric-vehicle market. On a gravimetric basis, gasoline has 80 times the energy density of the best lithium-ion batteries. Of course, electric-car supporters will immediately retort that electric motors are about four times more efficient than internal combustion engines. Fine. Even with that four-fold advantage in efficiency, gasoline still has 20 times the energy density of batteries. And that is an essential advantage when it comes to automobiles, where weight, storage space, and of course, range, are critical considerations.

Lack of Consumer Confidence

Numerous studies have found that electric and plug-in hybrid vehicles are simply not ready for prime time. Perhaps the most damning report was published by the Department of Energy's [DOE] Office of Vehicle Technologies in January 2009. The report concludes that despite the enormous investments being made in plug-in hybrid-electric vehicles and lithium-ion batteries, four key barriers stand in the way of their commercialization: cost, performance, abuse tolerance, and life. The key problem, according the DOE analysts, was—predictably—the battery system. The report concludes that lithium-based batteries, which it calls "the most promising chemistry," are three to five times too expensive, are lacking in energy density, and are "not intrinsically tolerant to abusive conditions."

As for consumer choice, a May [2010] survey by Harris Interactive found that 75 percent of potential new car buyers said they were "not at all likely" to buy an electric vehicle and 70 percent said they were "not at all likely" to buy a plug-in hybrid electric vehicle.

Those findings are remarkable given that the new Senate energy bill is designed to facilitate the growth of both electric and plug-in electric hybrids. The same Harris Interactive survey found that consumers were far more likely to purchase vehicles that use diesel or compressed natural gas. They were also more amenable to conventional hybrids, like the Toyota Prius. But remember, the Prius, perhaps the most iconic "green" automobile in the world, did not steal, and has not stolen, the overall vehicle market. It took Toyota about a decade to sell 1 million copies of the Prius. That sounds like a lot of cars until you remember that the U.S. automotive fleet has about 250 million vehicles and the global fleet about 1 billion vehicles.

Automakers understand that consumers are wary of all-electric and plug-in hybrid-electric vehicles. Bill Reinert, the manager of Toyota's advanced technology group (he was also one of the lead designers of the Prius), told me last month that the market for electrics and plug-in hybrids remains a "niche of a niche." Reinert says potential buyers for those vehicles are a small subset of those who are inclined to buy a Prius. Reinert said that hybrid vehicles now account for about 3 percent of total car sales in the U.S.

Other auto industry officials see it the same way. Last September, Johan de Nysschen, president of Audi of America, was particularly blunt when asked about the prospects for the Chevrolet Volt. His memorable quote: "There are not enough idiots who will buy it." Of course, since then, Audi has announced that it, too, would begin building an all-electric vehicle, which leads to another obvious question: Why are so many companies rushing to build electric cars? The answer: fat government subsidies.

Lavish Subsidies Continue

Last September, Fisker Automotive, a startup that plans to start selling a plug-in hybrid (sticker price $87,900) this year, received a $529 million loan from the U.S. government. (One of Fisker's main financial backers is the venture-capital firm Kleiner Perkins Caufield & Byers.) Meanwhile, Nissan got a $1.6 billion federal loan and Tesla Motors got a $465 million loan for their electric-car projects. Two Phoenix-based companies, Electric Transportation Engineering Corp., and ECOtality, were given $99.8 million in federal stimulus money to help roll out an electric-vehicle pilot program in several U.S. cities. Johnson Controls, one of America's biggest battery makers, got a federal grant for $299.2 million to help it build batteries for electric and hybrid cars. General Motors got $105.9 million to help it produce battery packs for the Chevy Volt. In all, about 50 different entities were given federal grants (all provided by the stimulus package passed by Congress) that totaled some $2.4 billion as part of an "electric drive vehicle battery and component manufacturing initiative."

The Obama administration and Congress have given voters many justifications for these lavish subsidies, including stimulus, job creation, technology incubation, reduced oil consumption, etc. But by throwing billions of dollars at the electric-car sector, Congress is picking a technology winner and it is doing so in one of the world's most fiercely competitive markets. For that reason alone, taxpayers have plenty of reason to be concerned.

For the past two decades, Congress has been picking a technology winner in the automotive fuels sector by providing lavish subsidies for the corn ethanol scam. And yet despite decades of subsidies and mandates, the corn ethanol industry still cannot survive without subsidies. In fact, those very same subsidies have led to a situation where the ethanol industry has too much capacity and the only solution for that problem: even greater subsidies from taxpayers.

There is no doubt that electric cars are sexy. But no matter how much money the government throws at the electric-car business, it will remain a tiny fraction of the overall car market for years, or more likely, decades, to come. Why? For all the reasons stated above. Add the myriad problems posed by our inadequate electric grid and the long charging times needed to refuel electric vehicles and the challenges become yet more obvious. Sure, electric cars will improve dramatically in the years ahead. But so will conventionally fueled vehicles like the Honda Fit, which costs about one-third as much as the new Volt.

Indeed, when looking at the long history of the electric-car industry—and in particular the myriad problems posed by finicky batteries—one conclusion seems painfully obvious: All-electric cars are the Next Big Thing. And they always will be.

Periodical Bibliography

The following articles have been selected to supplement the diverse views presented in this chapter.

Katherin Bourzac	"Scaling Up Solar Power," *Technology Review*, March–April 2010.
Jeffrey Brainard	"The Big Deals in Biofuels," *Chronicle of Higher Education*, April 20, 2007.
Harry De Gorter and David R. Just	"How Green Is My Valley (er, Corn)," *USA Today Magazine*, March 2010.
Diane Greer	"Ethanol By-Product Raises Biogas Output," *BioCycle*, January 2010.
Ben Hewitt	"The Post-Oil Era Begins," *Discover*, January 2009.
Keith Kline, Virginia H. Dale, Russell Lee, and Paul Leiby	"In Defense of Biofuels, Done Right," *Issues in Science and Technology*, Spring 2009.
Charles J. Murray	"Could Car Batteries Back up Our Electrical Grid?," *Design News*, November 9, 2009.
C. Ford Runge and Benjamin Senauer	"How Biofuels Could Starve the Poor," *Foreign Affairs*, May–June 2007.
Jeff Tollefson	"Car Industry: Charging Up the Future," *Nature*, November 26, 2008.
Michael Totty	"Five Technologies That Could Change Everything," *Wall Street Journal*, October 19, 2009.
Michael Totty	"The Long Road to an Alternative-Energy Future," *Wall Street Journal*, February 22, 2010.
Todd Woody	"Jet Green," *Forbes*, August 8, 2011.
Ken Zweibel, James Mason, and Vasilis Fthenakes	"US Plan for 2050," *Scientific American*, January 2008.

OPPOSING
VIEWPOINTS®
SERIES

CHAPTER 4

What Should Be Government's Role in Promoting Renewable Energies?

Chapter Preface

In early 2010, the administration of President Barack Obama unveiled its $28.4 billion fiscal year 2011 budget for the Department of Energy. Some of the fund was slated to contend with nuclear issues (weapons security, the building of two new power plants, etc.), but nearly $500 million was requested to guarantee loans of approximately $40 billion supporting alternative energy development. Perhaps more significantly, the budget called for the stripping of some $40 billion in subsidy money from oil, coal, and gas enterprises, indicating to the nation and the energy producers that the future must lie with clean power.

In his 2011 State of the Union address, the president reiterated the ideas laid out in the 2011 budget. Defending his decrease in subsidies to fossil fuel corporations, Obama quipped, "I don't know if you've noticed, but they're doing just fine on their own. So instead of subsidizing yesterday's energy, let's invest in tomorrow's." However the president's rhetoric was more hopeful than adamant. Congress tossed out the $40 billion subsidy cuts soon after the budget had been proposed, and Obama sought new ways to end the subsidies. In addition, although the president anticipated that the United States could be running on 80 percent clean energy by 2035, he expected that natural gas, clean coal technologies, and nuclear power would remain part of the nation's energy portfolio for some time.

Those who challenge the president's vision most often contend that government could never orchestrate the widespread systemic changes needed to reach his goal. Writing for the Energy Collective website on January 26, 2011, editor and journalist Keith Schneider maintains, "To achieve 80 percent clean energy generation essentially means replacing at least 500 gigawatts of conventional coal-fired generation with cleaner alternatives. In essence, the U.S. would have to nearly completely rebuild its electrical generating infrastructure, which last year had about

940 gigawatts of electrical generating capacity. By 2035, according to DOE projections, electrical generating demand in the U.S. could grow to 1,200 gigawatts." Despite the president's optimism, Schneider states that the United States produces less than one-fourth of its electrical power through wind, solar, hydroelectric, and other renewables, so up-scaling would be a near-impossible task, especially given the political debate that still contests the proper course for the nation.

Supporters of Obama's initiative, however, argue that the government has to take a more forceful hand in weaning the country off nonrenewables. The Center for American Progress put forth a unified statement on February 7, 2011, insisting that "setting a clear and stable goal is essential to organize the American clean energy market, and focus capital investors firmly on innovation." The organization advocates, "The sooner we make a commitment to build a domestic clean energy market, the sooner American innovation, entrepreneurship, venture capital, and advanced manufacturing skills can be fully unleashed; that will be needed to ensure early leadership."

Regardless of what supporters and detractors say, the Obama administration appears determined to push America toward a clean energy future. The authors in the following chapter analyze the administration's aims as well as the proper function of government in mandating energy policy.

"President Obama's 80-percent clean energy standard and our proposed '35 by '35' renewable energy goal, if developed properly, can usher in a new era of American innovation, entrepreneurship, and competitiveness."

US Government Support for Renewable Energies Will Benefit the Country

Richard W. Caperton et al.

In the viewpoint that follows, Richard W. Caperton and colleagues from the Center for American Progress encourage the federal government to impose a viable clean energy standard to boost America's commitment to renewable energies. According to the authors, a clean energy standard will help put America on par with other nations that are already investing in clean technologies, and it will generate business at home. Caperton and his co-authors lay out nine principles that the government should follow in promoting a clean energy standard; these include allowing states to capitalize on their own renewable resources, maintaining environmental safeguards, and establishing short-term goals to encourage continued investment.

Robert W. Caperton, Kate Gordon, Bracken Hendricks, and Daniel J. Weiss, "Helping America Win the Clean Energy Race," Center for American Progress, February 7, 2011. This material was created by the Center for American Progress. www.americanprogress.org.

As you read, consider the following questions:

1. According to Caperton, by what year does President Obama's clean energy standard expect to reach 80 percent of America's energy production?
2. What do the authors claim is happening to America's renewable energy businesses in recent times when the country has not shown a willingness to back these industries?
3. What are the five characteristics that the Center for American Progress believes essential in a clean energy standard?

President Barack Obama laid out a broad agenda for investment, innovation, jobs, and American competitiveness in his 2011 State of the Union. At the heart of the president's plan is an ambitious proposal to transform the nation's energy infrastructure away from the technologies we've been using for over 100 years—inefficient and polluting coal-fired power plants—toward new, clean energy sources.

The president challenged Americans to put our innovative spirit and entrepreneurial prowess to the test, asking us to fuel the engine of our economic recovery with a new generation of clean energy resources with the power to create jobs in U.S.-based industries, launch new businesses, and rewire our cities and rural communities with cutting-edge technology and state-of-the-art infrastructure.

Encapsulating this challenge is President Obama's call for a "clean energy standard" to produce 80 percent of our nation's electricity from cleaner energy sources by 2035. The president harkened back to President John F. Kennedy's response to Soviet space successes by launching a space race that challenged Americans to reach the moon within the decade. Americans rolled up our sleeves and met this challenge in eight years—and in so doing built an entire aerospace industry that has continued to foster American innovation and create jobs and exports to this day.

The race to produce clean energy as a source of economic competitiveness and innovation is at the heart of our generation's new "Sputnik moment." But President Obama's State of the Union address included a cautionary message as well, which citizens, entrepreneurs, and lawmakers must recognize as we prepare to meet the president's clean energy challenge. "The future is ours to win. But to get there, we can't just stand still" he told us. Instead, "clean energy breakthroughs will only translate into clean energy jobs if businesses know there will be a market for what they're selling."

Building a Clean Energy Market

Dramatically increasing the certainty and transparency of market demand for innovative, clean, and efficient technology is the first and most important step in ensuring that the U.S. remains a major player in these rapidly growing global markets. Without clear market signals here at home, domestic investment in clean tech will falter and we will cede potential American jobs and businesses to our global competitors. The sooner we make a commitment to build a domestic clean energy market, the sooner American innovation, entrepreneurship, venture capital, and advanced manufacturing skills can be fully unleashed.

Setting a clear and stable goal is essential to organize the American clean energy market, and focus capital investors firmly on innovation. For this reason, the Center for American Progress [CAP] applauds the president's call for an 80-percent clean energy standard by 2035. In embracing this agenda, however, we emphasize that it is essential that such a policy builds a strong market for innovative clean energy technologies in order to foster the rapid expansion of the emerging American cleantech industry. First and foremost, that requires a specific and separate target to ensure the growth of our cleanest electricity resources including energy efficiency, and wind, solar, geothermal, and other truly renewable electricity sources.

For that reason, we recommend that an 80-percent clean energy standard include a requirement that 35 percent of America's energy needs will be met by truly renewable energy and energy efficiency by 2035. This internal goal of "35 by '35" within the clean energy standard, will ensure the growth of strong markets for technologies such as wind, solar, sustainable biomass, incremental hydroelectric power, and geothermal energy, as well as the most effective solutions for reducing energy demand though energy efficiency. CAP believes strongly that such a target is essential for a strong and effective clean energy standard.

In addition, we offer in this paper five "design principles" that are essential for ensuring that a clean energy standard speeds the coming transformation of our nation's electricity grid to a truly sustainable mix of clean, efficient, and renewable energy, while realizing the jobs and economic promise of these emerging industries. As Congress and the Obama administration work to craft effective clean energy legislation they should ensure that any standard meets the following core principles:

- It must generate new, long-lasting jobs and grow the economy
- It must effectively spur development and deployment of renewable energy and energy efficiency technologies
- It must account for regional diversity in resources and electricity markets
- It must be simple and transparent, and minimize costs
- It must provide a floor not a ceiling for clean energy, strengthening and building on existing state leadership. . . .

Meeting the Investment Challenge

Over the past two years, the American Recovery and Reinvestment Act of 2009 provided substantial investments for clean energy innovation and deployment. The law provided funding for technology innovation at every stage from invention to commercialization to deployment. Case in point: It included funds for the Advanced Research Projects Administration-Energy, or ARPA-E, modeled after the Defense Department's DARPA [Defense Advanced Research Projects Agency] program that invests in commercializing technologies necessary for our national defense. Just as DARPA provided the seed money that eventually led to the Internet, ARPA-E will help discover the clean energy sources that will eventually power our future, by providing money to scientists and fledgling companies doing research on groundbreaking technologies.

The American Recovery and Reinvestment Act also provided substantial tax credits and grants to renewable energy projects that rely on existing technology in wide use already in other countries, but (until the Recovery and Reinvestment Act passed two years ago) not deployed at scale yet in the United States. These programs brought America back into a leadership position on clean energy, and resulted in this country connecting more wind turbines to the grid than any other country during the peak year of 2009.

But these successes cannot continue without a strong signal that the U.S. government is fully committed to building a domestic market for clean energy technologies. Many new business plans were written with the expectation that Congress would pass comprehensive climate and energy legislation that would put a price on carbon pollution that levels the playing field for clean technologies to compete with coal and oil. This effort included a "renewable electricity standard" [RES] proposed by Sen. Jeff Bingaman (D-NM), which passed the Senate Energy Committee with bipartisan support. The RES would have required utilities to generate at least 15 percent of their electricity by wind, solar, and other renewable sources.

Unfortunately Senate Republican leaders blocked any energy legislation in 2010, just as the Recovery and Reinvestment Act funds began to run their course. The result: Clean-tech companies now find themselves in a tight financial position, facing slackening market demand and a tightening supply of private-sector investment capital.

This is no way to build a modern industry. Already we have seen cutting-edge solar power manufacturing companies begin to close their doors, either permanently or to move to other countries with strong and dedicated clean energy markets. Evergreen Solar Inc., for example, recently announced plans to close its Massachusetts plant to put more funds into solar panel manufacturing in China. The company followed on the heels of SpectraWatt Inc. in New York and Solyndra Inc. in California closing some of their facilities. As General Electric Co.'s chairman and chief executive, Jeff Immelt, said at last year's ARPA-E summit, those countries with strong demand for renewable energy products will naturally pull these companies into their borders because "innovation and supply chain strength gets developed where the demand is the greatest."

Similarly, wind manufacturers in Iowa, once a state leader in this industry, are laying off workers as new orders fail to materialize. Leading global financier Deutsche Bank decided to move billions of investment dollars out of the U.S. clean energy market, and into China and Europe as soon as it was clear there would be no comprehensive climate and energy legislation coming out of the 111th Congress. China and our other economic competitors in Asia, Europe, and emerging markets are not waiting for America to regroup.

Other Nations Are Leading the Clean Energy Race

These stories share a common theme: investment dollars leaving the United States to be deployed among our global competitors who have fully embraced the economic and environmental imperative to enter a new era of cleaner, more sustainable and domestic energy. China is the most striking example. In 2009, even as the United States was installing more wind turbines, China, driven by stable long-term demand for its products, became the world's largest manufacturer of wind power systems. It was already the world's largest solar manufacturer and developer of efficient nuclear and coal technologies.

But China isn't alone. Not by a long shot. Germany is not far behind in linking strong clean energy policies to market growth and manufacturing leadership, as the leading global manufacturer of solar inverters—a key part of solar power systems—and has made huge strides in energy storage solutions that will further accelerate the widespread adoption of renewable power. Denmark, Japan, and the United Kingdom are also global clean energy leaders with thriving domestic markets.

All these countries have comprehensive programs in place to spur robust and stable demand for low-carbon energy, which then creates a market for businesses to manufacture and install the technologies to meet that demand. Last June, China announced its plan to meet a renewable energy standard of 20 percent by 2020, matching the European Union's target. Germany has set a target of 60 percent by 2050. The country already gets 16 percent of all its power from renewables, well on its way to meeting this ambitious goal, and some think it may reach 100 percent by 2050. Denmark has gone a step further, actually announcing its intention to become 100 percent independent of fossil fuels by 2050, something that at least one of its islands has already achieved. This occurred in a country that in 1970 was almost completely dependent on foreign fossil fuels.

These countries prove that strong clean energy standards build growing economies. But even more than that, strong clean energy standards are now imperative if we are to compete on the same playing field as China and Europe. America over the course of the 20th century took command of the Industrial Revolution and the communications revolution, and then led the world into the Information Age. It is time for us to lead the clean-tech revolution, too.

Today, others are beating us to the punch, not because we lack the technology and innovation to lead this new revolution, but because we are not providing the market signals needed for our private-sector entrepreneurs to invest over the long haul. This clean energy investment gap is rapidly becoming the greatest threat to America's technology leadership.

First Steps to Reduce Carbon Emissions

Building on the pioneering renewable electricity or portfolio standards already in place in 30 states, a nationwide clean energy standard would provide much-needed certainty to electricity markets, utilities, energy investors, and state power regulators. With meaningful standards in place, these businesses could make smarter long-term planning decisions on engineering, capital budgets, and investment needs. But for a new generation of technology companies to grow up to meet the changing needs of this marketplace, any clean energy standard must be carefully crafted, setting a target that not only phases out older, more inefficient and polluting plants, but also accelerates the growth of diverse domestic renewable energy supplies to meet our changing energy needs.

President Obama proposed an 80-percent clean energy standard by 2035 to achieve these economic goals. We recommend that this program include a separate target for deployment of truly renewable sources, including wind, solar, geothermal, and wave technologies, as well as energy efficiency to reduce demand. A target of meeting 35 percent of our electricity needs by 2035 through energy efficiency and truly renewable energy sources would boost certainty for investors that there will be a market for these sources.

This "35 by '35" provision will provide an overall end goal for the economy and a predictable market for renewable energy and energy efficiency within that emerging demand for clean energy. The remaining 45 percent can be met by a mix of other low-carbon technologies—such as nuclear power, natural gas, and coal with carbon capture and sequestration—as well as renewable energy and energy efficiency.

A National Renewable Portfolio Standard (RPS) Would Save American Consumers $49.1 Billion Each Year

A 20 percent by 2020 federal RPS would decrease consumer energy bills by an average of 1.5 percent per year, and save consumers in every region billions of dollars:

• West South Central	$13.3 billion
• East North Central	$8.4 billion
• California	$6.0 billion
• Mid-Atlantic	$5.7 billion
• Mountain	$5.0 billion
• South Atlantic	$2.9 billion
• Northwest	$2.6 billion
• West North Central	$2.2 billion
• East South Central	$1.6 billion
• New England	$1.4 billion

Lower natural gas prices save consumers $10 to $40 billion.
Renewable generation offsets natural gas combustion. A 1 percent decrease in natural gas demand can reduce the price of natural gas by up to 2.5 percent. Nine of fifteen studies found that a national RPS would save consumers $10 to $40 billion in natural gas expenditures.

Higher RPS targets save utilities 0.4 to 0.6 cents per kWh.
Renewable resources can serve as a "hedge" against the financial risks associated with volatility in the natural gas market. The value of this "hedge benefit" increases as the percent of the RPS mandate increases.

TAKEN FROM: Christopher Cooper and Benjamin Sovacool, *Renewing America: The Case for Federal Leadership on a National Renewable Portfolio Standard*, Report No. 01–07, New York: Network for Energy Choices, June 2007.

Near- and mid-term goals for clean technology deployment and regionally determined targets will also be critical for shaping how real projects get planned, financed, and built in addition to a long term 25 year national standard. An 80-percent clean energy standard will send a clear signal that America is moving toward a new generation of power plants, but without more specific policies within that goal we will not create a vibrant American clean-tech industry.

Here's why. In the near term, the cheapest and easiest solution for reducing the emissions of our existing fleet of power plants will be to run existing natural gas plants more of the time while phasing out our most inefficient, dirtiest coal-fired plants. Over time, more coal-burning generators will be directly replaced, but with natural gas technology, not advanced renewable energy technologies. Although natural gas is one-third to one half cleaner than coal, relying on gas alone is not a recipe for cleaning up our skies or reducing vulnerability to fluctuating fossil-fuel prices. After all, natural gas is very cheap today, but it cost three times as much just two years ago. Price stability will only come from a balanced and more diverse portfolio of investments in new energy technology.

What's more, a new array of natural gas-fired power plants will not power a new, innovation-led renewable energy industry able to rival China or the leading European clean energy producers. What will drive economic innovation and job creating investment, is our "35 by '35" target. This standard should be met by requiring a national target of 25 percent renewable electricity generation alongside a requirement that utilities reduce demand to save energy by 10 percent.

Flexibility should be given to individual states to vary these targets to account for their local energy market characteristics. Regional flexibility within a strong national framework will allow each part of the country to realize its own economic potential while ensuring that the "35 by '35" target is achievable on a national scale. . . .

Building a Stronger America

President Obama's 80-percent clean energy standard and our proposed "35 by '35" renewable energy goal, if developed properly, can usher in a new era of American innovation, entrepreneurship, and competitiveness. This paper outlines key concerns for ensuring that a national clean energy standard builds on innovative policies that have already created more dynamic energy markets in the states and in other countries. Hewing to the design principles outlined here can help American businesses, workers, and consumers navigate the fundamental transitions in energy and technology deployment that our country faces today. Successfully meeting this challenge will improve the competitive footing of the entire U.S. economy.

Today America faces a wide range of energy challenges: to our economic security, our global competitiveness, to homeowners' pocketbooks, and to the health of our communities. President Obama's ambitious but realistic goal of transforming the way we fuel our economy from outdated and inefficient technologies to clean and cutting-edge advanced technologies offers not only a safer and healthier future, but a better economic vision for America moving forward. A new national clean energy standard, if properly designed and executed, will help achieve many of these pressing goals, by boosting investment in profitable American companies and creating hundreds of thousands of jobs for American families, all while improving our environmental security and reducing our dependence on imported energy.

The Energy Independence and Security Act, the most recent clean energy law, had bipartisan support and was signed into law by President George W. Bush in 2007. A politically divided Congress and administration must once again set aside their political differences to meet this national challenge. A national clean energy standard that reflects these principles could go a long way toward building a more vital and growing economy to benefit all Americans.

> *"Renewable subsidies and mandated purchases may benefit a chosen few, but the adverse economic impacts, including job losses, are borne by everyone else."*

US Government Support for Renewable Energies Will Not Benefit the Country

Jonathan A. Lesser

In the following viewpoint, Jonathan A. Lesser argues that supporting renewable energy mandates will adversely impact the US economy. Because Lesser claims that renewable energy has a higher production cost than fossil fuel energy, he insists these costs will be passed on to consumers either through direct pricing or tax-borne subsidies. Dismissing studies that assert that renewable investment will create new jobs, Lesser concludes that the higher price of renewables will actually divert consumer finances away from other sectors of the economy and lead to unaccounted-for job loss in those sectors. Jonathan A. Lesser is the president of Continental Economics, an energy consulting firm. He is also the co-author of Fundamentals of Energy Regulation.

Jonathan A. Lesser, "Renewable Energy and the Fallacy of 'Green' Jobs," *Electricity Journal,* vol. 23, August–September 2010, pp. 45–53. Reproduced with permission from Elsevier.

As you read, consider the following questions:

1. What has been the cost per "green job" in Germany, according to a study cited by Lesser?
2. Why does Lesser claim the hedging benefits of renewable energy sources are "illusory at best"?
3. According to Lesser's model for Pennsylvania, higher electricity costs (due to a 15 percent renewable energy standard) would lead to how many lost jobs each year?

A s the United States economy continues to struggle, many politicians and energy regulators have adopted a "green jobs" mantra. They espouse the view that policies mandating renewable resources will provide both environmental and economic salvation. Moreover, electric utilities that are being forced to purchase green energy at above-market prices have been hesitant to criticize the wobbly economics on which these policies rest, either because they can simply pass through the costs to ratepayers or, more likely, are afraid to challenge regulators who hold sway over the utilities' earnings.

Economists continue to point out that there is no such thing as a free lunch, green or otherwise. And, empirical evidence in other countries, such as Spain and Germany—both of which invested heavily in green energy—shows that the cost of these jobs is extraordinarily high. In Spain, for example, *each green job created led to the loss of two jobs in the rest of the Spanish economy*. In Germany, the cost per green job created has been estimated to be 175,000 € [euro] ($225,000). Moreover, as the authors of the German study note, "proponents of renewable energies often regard the requirement for more workers to produce a given amount of energy as a benefit, failing to recognize that this lowers the output potential of the economy and is hence counterproductive to net job creation." Yet, politicians, perhaps because their own lunches are paid for by others, blithely ignore economists and continue promoting a mythical "green" economy that will soon emerge.

Examining the Overall Economic Impact of Renewables

While ignoring economists—including this author—may be considered a civic virtue, doing so does not invalidate basic economic principles. Quite simply, forcing consumers to buy high-cost electricity from subsidized renewable energy producers will not and cannot improve economic well-being. Subsidizing renewable energy development may improve the environment (although there is no actual evidence of this), create new jobs for renewable energy developers, and even "suppress" electricity and fossil fuel prices by reducing demand. But, when the *entire* economic ledger is tallied, the net impact of renewable energy subsidies will be lower economic growth and fewer jobs overall.

Several economic fallacies underlie green jobs policies. For example, some renewable energy proponents and green jobs advocates fundamentally misrepresent wealth *transfers* as wealth *benefits*. And several recent "green jobs" studies have touted renewables development as a source of unbridled economic growth, but these studies contain errors: the economic models that drive their results fail to address all of the economic impacts. They are cost-benefit analyses, without the "cost" part. No wonder the results are so enthusiastic. . . .

Suspicious Job Growth Claims

Since fall 2009, several high-profile green jobs studies have been published. In November 2009, a report published by the College of Natural Resources at the University of California at Berkeley concluded:

> By aggressively promoting efficiency on the demand side of energy markets, alternative fuel and renewable technology development on the supply side can be combined with carbon pollution reduction to yield economic growth and net job creation. Indeed, a central finding of this research is that *the stronger the federal climate policy, the greater the economic reward.*

The authors conclude that, by adopting a comprehensive energy policy, between 900,000 and 1.9 million new jobs can be created, and per-household income can increase between about $500 and $1,200 per year. However, their conclusion that "the stronger the federal climate policy, the greater the economic reward" is a stunning example of free-lunch economics. The study notes that from 1972 to 2006, energy efficiency programs in California "created 1.5 million additional jobs." However, the authors fail to provide the most important component of their assertion: compared to what? And there is no evidence that the authors considered the impacts on businesses and households from higher electricity prices and taxes to fund energy efficiency programs.

Another national study, by Navigant Consulting, was released in February 2010. It was prepared for the RES Alliance for Jobs, which is a group whose members primarily include renewable generation manufacturers. The premise of this study was to examine the economic impacts of adopting a mandatory national RPS [renewable portfolio standard] of 25 percent of total generation by the year 2025. The report concludes that such a standard "will lead to job growth in all states, especially those currently without state-level renewable electricity standards" and that it will create 274,000 new jobs in the renewables industry.

The Price of Ignoring Hidden Risks and Costs

Left unanalyzed is the number of jobs that this "25% by 2025" mandate will eliminate because of the higher prices for electricity that will result. While such a standard may indeed create 274,000 new jobs by the year 2025, the additional cost of the electricity provided will necessarily reduce available income for other goods and services and investment. Moreover, the report noted that nearer-term renewable standards are required to "mitigate a flattening or decline in industry-supported jobs that will otherwise occur across industries with the expiration of tax incentives and stimulus-related policies." Thus, the report is actually arguing that without continued subsidies and mandates the renewable energy industry will shrink.

The third and most recent study, prepared by Black & Veatch (B&V), is a state-level analysis of implementing a more stringent RPS in Pennsylvania. Unlike the other two reports, which did not provide information regarding the underlying assumptions used to estimate job creation, the B&V study does provide a detailed discussion of modeling assumptions. Moreover, the B&V study estimates the additional cost of implementing the more stringent RPS and concludes that the latter has a higher net present value cost of $1.6 billion, or about $180 million per year on a levelized cost basis.

The B&V study then estimates the cumulative (direct, indirect, and induced) economic impacts of the 15 percent RPS by using the Bureau of Economic Analysis RIMS II model. Although the report sets out some of the key assumptions—including regional purchase coefficients (RPCs)—other assumptions, such as the direct levels of employment in the construction and operation phases that drive the study's estimate of an additional 129,000 job-years between 2009 and 2026, are not identified.

The B&V study also highlights three other "benefits" of the 15 percent renewables policy: (1) provision of a hedge against volatile natural gas prices; (2) reductions in fossil fuel prices; and (3) the suppression of electricity market prices. Regarding the first benefit, the use of renewable resources to hedge natural gas prices is inefficient and expensive. Utilities and wholesale power producers concerned about volatile natural gas prices can hedge their risk exposure to the precise degree they prefer by using highly liquid options contracts, whereas with mandated renewable generation, that liquidity vanishes. Since renewable generation such as wind and solar are not firm resources, their output volatility (both in terms of quantity and timing) must itself be hedged, typically with natural-gas-fired generation. Thus, the

Some Oregonians Balk at State-Imposed "Green Energy" Mandates

It would be wise to learn from previous failures and realize that the renewable portfolio standards will be extremely costly and most likely unachievable. If Oregonians value and can afford renewable energy, there is an option. Ratepayers can support renewable energy through voluntary programs. In the end mandates force all ratepayers to pay the cost of expensive renewable energy whether ratepayers value it or not. Not only does this system destroy choice for ratepayers, but it also puts undue financial burden on citizens and businesses in the state.

Torey Holderith and Todd Wynn,
Renewable Energy Failure: Why Government
Mandates Don't Work and What They Will
Do to Our Economy, *Portland, OR: Cascade
Policy Institute, December 2010.*

hedging benefits of renewable resources are illusory at best. The second "benefit," reductions in fossil fuel prices, confuses income transfers with benefits. . . . Moreover, there is no empirical evidence that increased reliance on renewable generation reduces fossil fuel prices. Finally, we have the price "suppression" benefit. Again, the benefit misconstrues income transfers for economic benefits. Moreover, the report ignores the additional costs imposed by having to cycle generators on and off to account for the unpredictable nature of renewable generation availability. Such cycling increases operating costs of these units and reduces their fuel efficiency.

Estimating the Economic Impacts
of Higher Electricity Prices

All of the studies mentioned in the previous section ignore the economic impacts of higher electricity prices that result from mandates to purchase above-market-cost renewable generation. To examine those impacts, I prepared a simple analysis of the state of Pennsylvania using the IMPLAN model [an economic modeling system developed by M16, Inc.].

To estimate the overall economic impacts of the higher wholesale electric prices, I assume that consumers would not, initially, reduce their electricity consumption in response to the higher electric prices they faced. (In other words, price elasticity of demand is zero.) Because consumer income is assumed to be fixed in the short run, this implies consumers must reduce their expenditures on all other goods and services (including savings and investment) by an equivalent amount.

Similarly, I assume that Pennsylvania businesses would react to the increased price of electricity by reducing total output, such that their aggregate production expenses remained unchanged. . . . [This model] also assumes that businesses would not be able to simply pass along their increased production costs to consumers.

Using the employment multipliers and RPCs from the IMPLAN model for Pennsylvania, I calculate weighted average output and employment multipliers over all sectors except electricity. The IMPLAN data implies a weighted-average RPC of about 0.71 for all sectors of the Pennsylvania economy. Thus, using the $180 million annual levelized cost value from the B&V report, the direct reduction in purchases in all other sectors of the Pennsylvania economy would be $128 million, and the total reduction in purchases would be about $236 million, which reflects an output multiplier of 1.84.

To determine the employment impacts of this reduction of in-state expenditures, I calculated the average employment level per million dollars of output. With an average of 6.4 employees per million dollars of output, a $180 million reduction in expenditures translates into over 800 jobs lost per year. Then, by applying the estimated weighted average jobs multiplier of 2.78, higher electricity costs translate into over 2,300 lost jobs each year. Thus, while the RPS standard would obviously create jobs in renewable energy sectors, it would destroy them throughout the rest of the Pennsylvania economy.

Subsidies Reduce Economic Well-being

Proponents of stringent mandates for renewable generation tend to emphasize different "benefits" of such policies: reductions in greenhouse gases, energy "independence," and most recently, with the U.S. economy in recession, green jobs (whatever those may be). Yet, empirical evidence in other countries, such as Spain and Germany, shows that the cost of these jobs is extraordinarily high. And, a straightforward analysis of adverse economic impacts, including the loss of several thousand jobs each year because of higher electric prices, shows that the promised economic benefits of renewable energy come with a stiff price—on everyone else.

The simple economic fact is that mandated subsidies for renewable generation (and states define what is and is not "renewable" in various ways) will necessarily reduce economic well-being, as all subsidies do. Renewable subsidies and mandated purchases may benefit a chosen few, but the adverse economic impacts, including job losses, are borne by everyone else. Ultimately, if the goal is just jobs, whether green, red, or blue, then to paraphrase Keynes, "there are holes to be dug, and holes to be filled in."

| "If governments remove subsidies for fossil fuels and increase investments in renewable energy to make them cost competitive, then the Copenhagen Accord can still be upheld."

Renewable Energies Need Government Subsidies to Succeed

Stephen Kurczy

In the following viewpoint, staff reporter for the Christian Science Monitor *Stephen Kurczy reports on the importance of government support for renewable energy in the United States. He writes that if government subsidies are removed from fossil fuels and investments are made in renewable energy technologies the goals of the Copenhagen Accord can be met. Renewable energy can play a significant role in reducing carbon-dioxide emissions and can diversify energy options, but government support and subsidies are required for it to be successful.*

As you read, consider the following questions:

1. As stated in the article, what is the Copenhagen Accord's goal?

Stephen Kurczy, "Global Temperature to Rise 3.5 Degrees C. by 2035: International Energy Agency," *Christian Science Monitor*, November 11, 2010. Reproduced by permission from Christian Science Monitor. www.csmonitor.com.

2. How many nations signed the Copenhagen Accord, according to this viewpoint?

3. According to this author, how much money does the International Energy Agency estimate must be spent to meet the Copenhagen Accord pledges?

Global temperatures are projected rise 3.5 degrees C. [celsius] over the next 25 years, the International Energy Agency said Tuesday, meaning that governments worldwide will have failed in their pledge to hold global temperature at a 2-degree increase.

But there's hope yet, says Fatih Birol, the chief economist for the Paris-based International Energy Agency (IEA).

If governments remove subsidies for fossil fuels and increase investments in renewable energy to make them cost competitive, then the Copenhagen Accord[1] can still be upheld. The voice of guarded optimism comes just ahead of a summit starting Nov. 29 [2010] in Cancún, Mexico, for another round of climate talks.

"Renewable energies need substantial subsidies from governments," Dr. Birol said in a telephone interview. "The important task [for governments] is to decide whether they will support energy renewables in the future. It could be bad news for energy security and climate change if they don't."

Renewable Energy Plays a Central Role

None of that may be surprising, considering the 28-nation Copenhagen Accord signed in December 2009 was not legally binding and also fell short of recommendations from the UN-sponsored Intergovernmental Panel on Climate Change for how to prevent temperatures from rising more than 2 degrees C. Yet if global warming is going to be curtailed, then governments must support the development and use of renewable energy.

"Renewable energy can play a central role in reducing carbon-dioxide emissions and diversifying energy supplies, but only if

Shipments of Solar Collectors (2000–09)

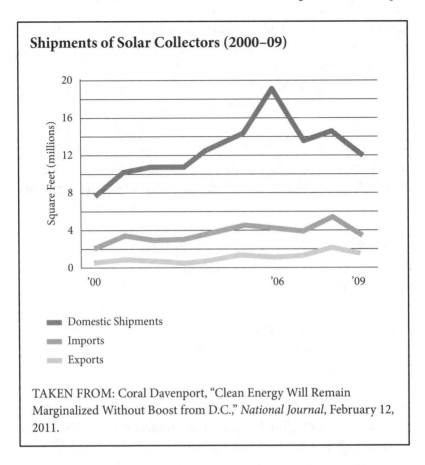

■■ Domestic Shipments

■ Imports

Exports

TAKEN FROM: Coral Davenport, "Clean Energy Will Remain Marginalized Without Boost from D.C.," *National Journal*, February 12, 2011.

strong and sustained support is made available," IEA executive director Nobuo Tanaka said in a statement upon Tuesday's release of the 2010 World Energy Outlook.

The IEA projects global energy demand to surge 36 percent over the next 25 years. As that happens, use of modern renewable energy sources will triple as their share in total primary energy demand increases from 7 percent to 14 percent, the IEA said.

According to current government commitments and policies, the IEA projects government intervention in support of renewables (electricity from renewables and biofuels) will increase from $57 billion in 2009 to $205 billion (in 2009 dollars) by 2035. Still, these current government policies "are collectively inadequate to meet the Copenhagen Accord's overall goal of holding the global temperature increase to below 2 degrees C.," according to the report.

As carbon dioxide emissions rise 21 percent to 35 billion tons, temperatures will rise 3.5 degrees C.

To keep temperatures from rising more than 2 degrees C., the share of renewables among total energy use must reach to 38 percent by 2035, governments must end their subsidies on fossil fuels, and global demand for coal, oil, and gas must plateau before 2020.

The longer the world waits to tackle the issue the more expensive it will become. The IEA estimates the price tag of meeting the Copenhagen Accord pledges at $11.6 trillion through 2030, which is a $1 trillion increase from the IEA's projection one year ago.

But the world has never been quick to adopt new energy policies, as *Monitor* correspondent Douglas Fox pointed out in his cover story on the future of energy.

"Energy revolutions have usually been slow, starchy, conservative affairs, not overnight explosions; and the next one promises to be, too—never before has humanity replaced 15 trillion watts of worldwide energy production," writes Mr. Fox. "Our success in making it happen quickly enough to stave off climate change will depend every bit as much on strategic use of fossil fuels now as it does on flashy new technologies in the future."

Note

1. An international agreement to reduce emissions thought to cause climate change.

> *"Energy subsidies undermine the working of the free market, and they make rational approaches to long-term energy challenges and climate change impossible."*

Eliminating All Energy Subsidies Will Benefit Renewable Energies

Jeffrey Leonard

In the viewpoint that follows, Jeffrey Leonard argues that government subsidies for energy interests in the United States have only served to waste taxpayers' money and stifle free-market progress in the energy sector. Leonard maintains that subsidies may have been important in giving energy startups a way into the crowded marketplace, but he believes all producers should now be capable of existing on their own merits. According to Leonard, all subsidies should be eliminated so that renewable, nuclear, coal, oil, and natural gas energies can compete on a level playing field, forcing each to innovate and offer consumers better prices to stay in business. While Leonard agrees that the end of subsidies may force some renewable energy companies to fail, the market will eventually favor greater participation of renewables as fossil-fuel resources decline

Jeffrey Leonard, "Get the Energy Sector off the Dole," *Washington Monthly*, vol. 43, January–February 2011, pp. 36–41. Reproduced by permission.

and their carbon emissions become a heavier burden in a world grappling with the consequences of climate change. Jeffrey Leonard is the CEO of the Global Environment Fund, an investment firm seeking to find cost-effective solutions to environmental and energy issues. He is also the chairman of the Washington Monthly *board of directors.*

As you read, consider the following questions:

1. What percent of energy subsidies in the United States is given to fossil fuels, as Leonard states?
2. Why does Leonard believe "benign neglect" would be the best strategy for Washington to adopt in the energy market?
3. What market trends does Leonard say will encourage the development of cleaner energy solutions?

Last September [2010], President [Barack] Obama promised that the cornerstone of his legislative program for 2011 would be to set an energy policy "that helps us grow at the same time as it deals with climate change in a serious way."

Today [Winter 2010], the president might seem to stand a better chance of refreezing the melting Arctic ice caps. After all, he's up against a House Republican majority rife with members who openly deny that humans contribute to global warming, as well as members of his own party who are beholden to domestic fossil fuel industries. In November, West Virginia's new Democratic senator, Joe Manchin, boasted to his constituents that he had secured Harry Reid's assurance "that cap and trade is dead."

But not all is lost. If President Obama wants to set us on a path to a sustainable energy future—and a green one, too—he should propose a very simple solution to the current mess: eliminate *all* energy subsidies. Yes, eliminate them all—for oil, coal, gas, nuclear, ethanol, even for wind and solar. It will be better for national security, the balance of payments, the budget deficit, and even, believe it or not, the environment. Indeed, because wind, solar, and other green energy sources get only the tiniest sliver of the overall subsidy pie, they'll have a competitive advantage in the long term if all subsidies, including the huge ones for fossil fuels, are eliminated. And with anti-pork Tea Partiers loose in Washington and deficit cutting in the air, it's not as politically inconceivable as you might think.

The History of Energy Subsidies

Energy subsidies are the sordid legacy of more than sixty years of politics as usual in Washington, and they cost us somewhere around $20 billion a year. To put that sum in perspective, that's more than the State Department's entire budget. It's also enough to send half a million Americans to college each year with all expenses paid. Energy subsidies undermine the working of the free market, and they make rational approaches to long-term energy challenges and climate change impossible. They are not an aid to energy independence or environmental stewardship. They are an impediment.

Energy subsidies take many forms. Some of them are direct outlays of taxpayer dollars, like payments to corn producers for ethanol. Most are in the form of tax benefits, such as the deduction for "intangible drilling costs" (labor, repairs, hauling, you name it) in oil exploration—a notoriously abused provision of the tax code. The sheer number of subsidies is part of what makes them so hard to track.

But one thing about them is easy to summarise: they are heavily tilted toward fossil fuels. Government statistics show that about 70 percent of all federal energy subsidies goes toward oil, natural gas, and coal. Fifteen percent goes to ethanol, the only renewable source of energy that consistently gets bipartisan support in Congress (think farm lobby and Iowa). Large hydro-power companies—TVA, Bonneville Power, and others—soak up another 10 percent. That leaves the greenest renewables—wind, solar, and geothermal—to subsist on the crumbs that are left.

None of these estimates account for continuing support to the nuclear industry, estimated to be about $1 to $2 billion, much of it to promote research and development efforts on new nuclear technologies and waste disposal methods. There are plenty of hidden subsidies, too. We place a cap on liability for accidents (like the BP oil spill). We offer the nuclear industry large loan guarantees. And, of course, we maintain an immense military embroiled in the Middle East and elsewhere as it tries to secure access to energy resources around the globe.

What do we taxpayers get in return? Not much. Certainly there's no evidence that subsidies do anything significant to increase our domestic energy supply. A recent study by the U.S. Energy Information Agency found that subsidies for domestic energy production doubled between 1999 and 2007, but despite all the extra money the amount of energy supplied by domestic sources stayed the same. . . .

Subsidies Help Dictate the Nation's Energy Future

Today, a whole new round of government-promised subsidies is enabling the energy industry to make multibillion-dollar investments—in ethanol refineries, nuclear power facilities, and "clean coal" plants. The danger with these large-scale and highly capital-intensive "white elephant" projects is that the decisions made today will drive energy supply considerations for the next forty years. The very industries supporting such projects admit that they cannot survive in the market without government support. But, once built, these boondoggles create political interests demanding still more subsidies while limiting our nation's flexibility to shift to cleaner and more cost-efficient energy sources.

As an investor in clean and green energy, I will confess that some of our companies have benefited from increased sales of equipment and services thanks to federal incentives to step up investment activity in solar and wind power in recent years. The primary jumpstart was the new tax credits that were built into the Energy Act of 2005 and renewed, haltingly, on an annual basis by Congress since then. I find myself concluding, however, that even subsidies for the truly green renewable sources can lead to perverse energy outcomes. For example, the entrance of the green renewable industry into the energy subsidy race over the past few years has in many places created the energy equivalent of suburban sprawl—a patchwork of wind and solar farms being deployed helter-skelter across the landscape. Thus, in some instances, wind projects have been launched without due attention to the additional infrastructure expenses that will be necessary to build new transmission lines, leaving new wind facilities stranded or underutilized. Texas, for example, has found that it must create at least $3 billion worth of transmission lines to get electricity from its wind projects to its cities, and concluded, ironically, that in some instances transmission line corridors must incorporate plans for new coal-fired power plants to justify the investment.

So we can waste money and distort the market by subsidizing all of these forms of energy. Or we can just call it quits on the waste. Disarm completely. Kill all the subsidies—yours and mine.

Let the Free Market Decide

Liberals and environmentalists may fear that they have no cards left to play except pushing for gradually increasing subsidies for their favored clean energy solutions. After all, they have struggled to get Congress to address what they consider to be the heart of the global warming problem: the failure of the market to factor in pollution and other externalities that result from our use of fossil fuels. The whole point of the cap-and-trade bill was to remedy that shortcoming, which would have had the effect of making green energy sources more competitive. That's why the collapse of cap and trade has left many environmentalists despondent. It is also why they are now pressing President Obama to use the regulatory power of the EPA [US Environmental

Protection Agency] to set limits on carbon emissions. But let's be honest: neither cap and trade nor carbon taxes are coming back anytime soon. And Obama is going to face a political firestorm in Congress and around the country if he moves aggressively through EPA regulatory fiat.

What the green lobby may underestimate is the degree to which the "free market," given the current natural direction of the energy sector, would ultimately support the cause of clean energy in the absence of subsidies. Hence a "benign neglect" approach by Washington to the energy industry would be the best strategy for now. Emphasizing the elimination of existing subsidies and the creation of a level playing field would benefit green energy sources by enabling them to fit into rational long-term energy supply strategies pursued by public utilities, while also allowing the whole energy sector to respond better to price signals and consumer demands.

Major changes in the picture of domestic energy supply make it possible to sweep away decades of accumulated subsidies without seriously threatening the affordability of energy. In the mid-1900s, the dominant fuels and sources of energy in America—for all sectors of the economy—were petroleum and coal. The rationale for subsidizing these fuels was simple: they were the backbone of the economy, and adequate supplies needed to be assured. The good news is that this rationale no longer applies; the U.S. energy market, if left to its own devices, without distortions or subsidies, will continue to provide plentiful and affordable power while gradually evolving away from oil and coal as the primary energy sources. This changeover to what will be cleaner energy solutions will accelerate considerably in coming years, thanks to several major trends.

Tapping Natural Gas Reserves Will Benefit Renewables

The first trend, a real game changer, is the discovery in recent years that America is sitting on many decades' worth of exploitable natural gas. Natural gas emits half the carbon dioxide of coal. Although its extraction poses threats to underground water supplies in some places, these can be managed with proper regulation and are in any event much less serious than the environmental threats posed by coal mining. Gas is also more cheaply and safely transported. It can be moved to power plants through underground pipelines, unlike coal, which requires heavy trucks and trains to struggle over mountain ranges. And it is every bit as abundant as coal, if not more so, and as widely dispersed geographically. Since the late 1980s, natural gas has been the fuel of choice for the majority of new electricity-generating plants constructed in the United States. Over the next forty years, nearly all of America's existing coal-fired power plants will reach the end of their useful lives, and a significant portion of them will probably be replaced by cleaner-burning natural gas facilities, especially if the subsidies that buoy the coal industry today are allowed to expire. Now that adequate supplies are assured for the future, a lot of investors are betting that natural gas will gradually replace coal as the dominant fuel in the electricity-generation sector. This trend by itself will significantly lower America's carbon footprint by 2050.

Natural-gas-fueled electric plants will also foster increased use of wind and solar power. Both these renewable energy sources require a backup source, because the wind blows intermittently and the sun doesn't always shine. A coal plant must be kept burning once it's been fired up, so coal-fired electric plants make a poor intermittent source. Gas-fired plants, by contrast, are virtually the only economical sources of electricity that can be powered up and powered down to support lulls in other sources of power.

Another encouraging market trend involves nuclear power. While Washington has been hurling loan guarantees and other subsidies at the industry in order to spur the building of a new generation of reactors, only a few new projects, if any, are going to move forward. The reason is simple arithmetic. When the huge construction costs of new nuclear power plants are factored into the price of the electricity they produce, they can't compete with power from natural-gas-fired plants. That arithmetic won't change unless Washington throws even more subsidies to the nuclear industry (something many Republicans are keen to do).

But the surprising good news is that America's existing nuclear plants, which were built at exorbitant cost decades ago, are now largely paid off. Today, these plants supply 20 percent of the nation's electricity, all of it carbon free and priced competitively. Thanks to gains in plant utilization at existing nuclear installations—brought about through improvements in maintenance and safety—the nuclear industry has increased its output by 40 percent since 1990, the equivalent of adding twenty nine new 1,000-megawatt reactors. This is a lot of unexpected new electricity supply for the country; by way of comparison, at the end of 2009 the U.S. had in total about 35,000 megawatts of installed wind power and about 500 megawatts of solar photovoltaic panels providing electricity. . . .

State Mandates Spur Growth in Renewables

A third positive trend is the increasing competitiveness of solar, wind, and geothermal power to provide diversification and decentralized power generation, and to enable utilities to meet consumer demands and state mandates for green power. Nearly half of all states now have renewable portfolio standards (RPS) requiring their utilities to procure a certain percentage of electricity from renewable sources in coming years, with California leading the way by requiring that 33 percent of electricity come from renewables by 2030. RPS mandates, along with consumer and industry demand for and local government procurement of green electricity, are gradually becoming more important drivers of the wind and solar industries than tax subsidies.

But let's face facts. The renewable industries will mature as commercially viable on their own only in future years, as more natural gas generation is deployed on the grid, transmission grids are extended and interconnected, and energy storage technologies become more available. The government tax credits were valuable to support the industry in its infancy, but the solar and wind industries can, and will need to, become cost competitive. In the past few years, the prices of solar photovoltaic modules have fallen in the United States by more than 50 percent, and the efficiency of large wind turbines has increased dramatically. This provides great hope that, with a level playing field, and if they do not get "addicted" to subsidies like so many other energy industries are, solar and wind will be able to compete and grow to generate some 20 to 25 percent of America's electricity in the next few decades.

A fourth positive market trend, at least from an energy-efficiency and environmental standpoint, is the future price of oil. Right now, because of the economic slump, petroleum prices are moderate. But analysts and the energy futures market are anticipating that in 2011 oil prices will begin to climb again as worldwide demand works back toward 2006–2007 levels. Regardless of short term fluctuations, virtually all international studies of the petroleum industry show substantial demand-supply imbalances during this coming decade, particularly as China and India continue to add tens of millions of new cars to their motorways each year. Sooner or later, prices at the pump will rise considerably and permanently.

American consumers will feel the pain. But as was evident during the last (albeit short-term) run-up in petroleum prices, which drove gasoline prices over four dollars a gallon in 2008, Americans will respond to higher prices with countless adjustments—in the cars they buy and in their daily routines—that in turn will move the whole economy toward more efficient energy use.

The rising price of oil will hasten yet another market clean energy trend that is already apparent: the growing dependence by every sector of the economy on electricity and, in particular, the nascent move toward electrification of transportation.

The much ballyhooed new crop of electric cars, like the Nissan Leaf and the Chevy Volt, are the popular face of this trend, but these are but precursors of a market that is still some years away. Meanwhile, a more salient development is the return of electric-powered rail transit. Today, metro areas around the country are building and expanding light rail lines, a movement that will almost certainly accelerate. It could well be followed by the eventual electrification of heavily trafficked freight and passenger rail corridors. Gasoline-powered cars will be the mode of choice for most Americans for many years to come, but not forever.

Government's Vital Role in the Energy Arena

Taken together, these market trends—cheaper natural gas; more expensive oil; the gradual turnover of old, polluting, inefficient power plants and their replacement by natural gas or cleaner-generating technologies; the extended life of existing nuclear facilities; and the slow but steady electrification of transportation—will gradually turn America's economy toward reducing greenhouse gas emissions while supplying us with abundant and affordable energy. These trends will also buy us time to develop the more innovative energy sources of the future.

Government has a legitimate and vital role to play in dramatically accelerating this evolution. It should invest heavily in long-term research and development to hasten the progress of new energy technologies. It should stiffen regulations on coal use and all fossil fuels so that the fuel's environmental and health costs are born by industry and reflected in its price. It should make sure that natural gas produced from hydraulic fracturing techniques is environmentally responsible. And eventually, when the political climate is right, it should impose a tax on carbon.

What government *shouldn't* be doing is subsidizing and protecting incumbent energy producers. All that will do is slow the transformation to a cleaner energy future. In my rounds in Washington recently, I have heard persons representing, separately, the nuclear, ethanol, coal, and green renewable industries float the suggestion that the government set a floor on the price of natural gas because the low prices of gas are making their existing and planned projects uneconomical and uncompetitive. Energy lobbying firms are surely being paid right now to work up the talking points on this harebrained idea. . . .

A New Energy Landscape

There is no question that the elimination of energy subsidies across the board would bring disruptive change to the energy landscape. Oil producers would keep profiting handsomely but mourn the elimination of their deeply embedded—and beloved—government largess. But they would probably start to invest a lot more of their available capital in energy industries and technologies of the future. Nuclear energy advocates and ethanol producers—the recipients of the lion's share of "new energy" subsidies awarded in recent years, and poised to receive hundreds of billions of new subsidies in coming years—would see their so-called private funding sources shrivel overnight. And renewable energy interests, newly nurtured on the mother's milk of Washington cash, would have to scramble to cut costs rapidly to ensure continued consumer demand. Some players in the renewable energy industries would be less competitive, and eventually would go out of business, but others would take their place—and do much better in honest competition. The winner, in spite of its loss of subsidies, would be natural gas. It is the cleanest and most intrinsically competitive energy source for electricity production and as a direct fuel for heating homes and commercial spaces.

The real question to ask is not whether some energy companies, and indeed whole industries focused on certain "protected" or government-favored technologies or fuels, would survive in their current form if we did slash energy subsidies. Imagine where the American economy would be today if the government had decided to protect and continue to subsidize steam engines or whale oil as sources of energy in past eras. The important question is whether the elimination of energy subsidies would constitute good long-term energy policy for America. Never in my lifetime has it been more important to ask this question.

Periodical Bibliography

The following articles have been selected to supplement the diverse views presented in this chapter.

Glen Andersen	"Climate for Change," *State Legislatures*, December 2009.
Corina Cerovski-Darriau	"Policy: A Tale of Two Years," *Earth*, December 2009.
Coral Davenport	"Climate Change Fight Moves to States," *National Journal*, February 24, 2011.
James Fallows	"Dirty Coal, Clean Future," *Atlantic Monthly*, December 2010.
Thomas L. Friedman	"We're Gonna Be Sorry," *New York Times*, July 25, 2010.
Mike Hall	"The US Needs a Feed-in Tariff," *Power Engineering*, October 2010.
Ryan Lizza	"As the World Burns," *New Yorker*, October 11, 2010.
Beth Lowery	"Past, Present and Future of Alternative Fuels," *Vital Speeches of the Day*, May 2006.
Christian Parenti	"The Big Green Buy," *Nature*, August 2, 2010.
Bradford Plumer	"Climate Control," *Audubon*, March–April 2010.
Kenneth T. Walsh	"Changing America's Energy Ways," *US News & World Report*, April 2009.
Susan Ward	"Renewable Energy: The Carrot and the Stick," *Composites Technology*, February 2011.

For Further Discussion

Chapter 1

1. How does Greenpeace envision renewable energies as a major factor in mitigating climate change? On what assumptions does Greenpeace base its arguments? Why does Jason Harrow believe that such optimistic models are faulty? After examining both opinions, with which viewpoint do you agree most? Explain what arguments swayed your decision.

2. Jorge Madrid, Bracken Hendricks, and Kate Gordon claim that innovation in the field of renewable energies will lead to decreasing costs for consumers. David W. Kreutzer and colleagues, however, contend that prices for renewables are still very high in comparison to fossil fuel resources, and thus increasing their use will raise prices for consumers. Such arguments entail a prediction of the future state of energy production and the influence of government mandates. Focusing on this part of their viewpoints, whose vision of the future do you think seems more likely? Explain why you have come to this conclusion.

3. Bob Marshall contends that renewable energy production sites—such as solar arrays and wind farms—require more land to create the same amount of energy generated by a relatively compact coal plant. How does Amory B. Lovins refute this notion that renewables will waste precious land and negatively impact wildlife that could otherwise utilize environments taken up by renewable energy sites? Do you think Lovins's assessment of the situation is reasonable, or are there weaknesses to his prediction that wind farms and solar cells will not clutter up precious real estate? Explain your answer.

Chapter 2

1. Tim Dickinson asserts that in order to fully embrace the benefits of renewable energy, some environmental concerns

may have to be sacrificed to make room for the large-scale solar arrays and wind farms that will be needed. Dickinson insists that environmentalists should not hold up renewable energy projects due to wildlife or ecosystem concerns because the need to arrest climate change and to end fossil fuel pollution are greater concerns for the entire planet. Do you think Dickinson's claims are correct? Which issue should take priority in your opinion? Explain your answer using quotes from this viewpoint.

2. Some advocates for renewable energies insist the world can make a complete transition to clean energy in the foreseeable future. The World Wildlife Fund, Ecofys, and Office for Metropolitan Architecture make such a claim in their viewpoint, noting that a mixed portfolio of renewables can satisfy all the various energy needs of the planet. Ted Trainer, on the other hand, maintains that renewables simply cannot provide the power to run the large-scale, capitalist society that has dominated the globe. Using the evidence in these viewpoints and any other articles you find, give your opinion on whether renewable energies could ever provide enough power to make fossil-fuel resources obsolete.

3. In his viewpoint, Charles Forsberg believes that nuclear power will play an important role in supplementing renewable energies with another "carbon-free" resource. Some critics argue that nuclear power is not "clean" and therefore should not be part of a future based on renewables. Explain your opinion on whether nuclear energy should be or will be a facet of the world's energy portfolio if the transition to renewables is successful.

Chapter 3

1. Danny Chivers makes the commonplace claim that biofuels are currently an impractical part of a renewable energy future because they require too much cropland to produce, and their

manufacture may not be as "carbon free" as expected. After reading his viewpoint and the viewpoint by Rachel Ehrenberg, give your review of the usefulness of biofuels in the world's energy mix. Use example or quotes from these viewpoints and any other articles you find to support your answer.

2. The American Coalition for Ethanol claims that ethanol production can supplant gasoline in powering automobiles. The coalition asserts that ethanol crops are not hogging precious land and that the energy required to make ethanol is decreasing, making the product more affordable and practical. James Eaves and Stephen Eaves, however, refute these notions, adding that ethanol crops are susceptible to weather shocks and therefore cannot guarantee consistent fuel production. Whose arguments do you find more believable? Explain what convinced you to take one side over the other.

3. After reading the viewpoints by James Kliesch and Robert Bryce, make a list of the obstacles to the widespread implementation of electric automobiles. Once you have compiled your list, explain if and how each impediment might be overcome in time. By the end of your assessment, make a claim whether you think electric vehicles are worth investing in or whether they will never match up to their combustion-engine counterparts.

Chapter 4

1. One of the major issues concerning US government support for renewable energies is whether such backing will lead to job creation in the country. Richard W. Caperton and his colleagues differ with Jonathan A. Lesser on this subject. Explain how each envisions the impact of government support for renewables on job creation. Then decide whose opinion you favor and explain why.

2. After reading Stephen Kurczy's viewpoint, explain why he believes government subsidies for renewable energy are

necessary. Then explain why Jeffrey Leonard disagrees with government subsidies. Provide your own assessment of whether subsidies will or will not benefit renewable energy production in the United States. In forming your answer, consider the progress of renewables in Europe and the fact that many European governments heavily subsidize these technologies. Should the United States follow the European model or are there other concerns that you think should take precedence in the United States?

Organizations to Contact

The editors have compiled the following list of organizations concerned with the issues debated in this book. The descriptions are derived from materials provided by the organizations. All have publications or information available for interested readers. The list was compiled on the date of publication of the present volume; the information provided here may change. Be aware that many organizations take several weeks or longer to respond to inquiries, so allow as much time as possible.

American Enterprise Institute for Public Policy Research (AEI)
1150 Seventeenth Street, NW
Washington, DC 20036
(202) 862-5800 • fax (202) 862-7177
website: www.aei.org

AEI is a nonpartisan public policy institute dedicated to conducting research in the following areas: economic policy, foreign and defense policy, health policy, legal and constitutional studies, political and public opinion studies, and social and cultural studies. While it does not participate in any direct policy advocacy, its research is addressed to members of the government as well as individuals in academia, business, journalism, and the general citizenry. AEI has sponsored numerous events concerning the adoption of renewable energy sources such as "Power Hungry: The Myths of 'Green' Energy and the Real Fuels of the Future," and "Toward a Low-Cost, Clean Energy Policy." Additionally, articles assessing individual types of renewable energy sources and these energies' impact on the economy and jobs can be accessed on the AEI website.

Center for American Progress (CAP)
1333 H Street, NW, 10th Floor

Washington, DC 20005
(202) 682-1611 • fax (202) 682-1867
website: www.americanprogress.org

CAP is a progressive think tank whose stated goal is "improving the lives of Americans through progressive ideals and action." CAP develops policies in five areas—domestic issues, the economy, national security, energy and the environment, and the media and progressive values. The organization's energy policies focus on protecting the environment, boosting global prosperity, and creating sustainable sources of clean energy. Articles such as "How to Shape the Clean Energy Future of the United States," "Clean Energy Development Done Right," and "In Defense of Clean Energy" are available on the CAP website.

Greenpeace International
702 H Street, NW, Suite 300
Washington, DC 20001
(202) 462-1177 • fax (202) 462-4507
e-mail: greenpeace.usa@wdc.greenpeace.org
website: www.greenpeace.org

Founded by activists in 1971, Greenpeace is an environmental organization that organizes and coordinates environmental activism worldwide, produces scientific reports on environmental issues, and advocates for environmental policy change. Greenpeace views renewable energy sources as essential to halting global warming and ensuring environmental conservation. Numerous articles and reports can be read on the Greenpeace website covering a wide range of renewable energy technologies and their impact on global warming and the environment.

Heritage Foundation
214 Massachusetts Ave., NE
Washington, DC 20002-4999
(202) 546-4400

e-mail: info@heritage.org
website: www.heritage.org

The Heritage Foundation is a conservative think tank that works to advance the principles of free enterprise, limited government, individual freedom, traditional American values, and a strong national defense within the American political system. The foundation's scholars conduct research on current issues and provide their findings to policy makers in order to influence the adoption of policy consistent with their ideology. In general the organization views renewable energy as unsustainable without government subsidy and therefore rejects it, arguing that the free market will determine when and if renewable energy is a viable option. "The Department of Energy Should Not Be the Green Banker," "Capability, Not Politics, Should Drive DOD Energy Research," and "Alternative Fuels as Military Strategy," along with other articles on renewable energy can all be read online.

Institute for Local Self-Reliance (ILSR)
2001 S Street, NW, Suite 570
Washington, DC 20009
(202) 898-1610
e-mail: info@ilsr.org
website: www.ilsr.org

ILSR seeks to help citizens make their communities environmentally sound while still meeting the needs of those who live there through community development programs that engage community members, activists, policy makers, and entrepreneurs. Much of the organization's work focuses on renewable energy with the Energy Self-Reliant States project dedicated entirely to helping states identify the best method of energy generation in a region and then implement a plan to get that energy to the residents of the area. Articles such as "Why Tax Credits Make Lousy Renewable Energy Policy," "What Renewable Energy Policy Works Best? Feed-in Tariffs," and

"Smaller Generation Incites Largest Renewable Energy Gains" can all be read online.

Intergovernmental Panel on Climate Change (IPCC)

c/o World Meteorological Organization
7bis Avenue de la Paix, C.P. 2300
Geneva 2 CH-1211 Switzerland
+41 22-730-8208/54/84 • fax +41 22-730-8025/13
e-mail: IPCC-Sec@wmo.int
website: www.ipcc.ch

IPCC was founded in 1988 by the United Nations Environment Programme and the World Meteorological Organization as an international body dedicated to studying, understanding, and determining the impact of climate change. As such, scientists worldwide voluntarily provide research and participate in IPCC projects to further these aims. While the organization's main focus is studying climate change, it has examined the use of renewable energy sources as an option to halt continued global warming and recently published the landmark study *Special Report on Renewable Energy Sources and Climate Change Mitigation.* This report and others can be accessed on the IPCC website.

International Energy Agency (IEA)

9 rue de la Fédération 75739
Paris Cedex 15 France
+33 14-057-6500 • fax +33 14-057-6509
e-mail: info@iea.org
website: www.iea.org

IEA was founded following the 1973/74 oil crisis to enable nations to coordinate their efforts in the event of any future disruptions to the oil supply and maintain the needed levels of fuel. In the years since, the IEA's focus has shifted toward energy security, economic development, environmental awareness, and engagement worldwide, all with the overarching goal of ensuring steady energy supplies for both member countries and others world-wide. With regard to renewable energies, the IEA analyzes energy technologies and their integration into existing supply and market systems. The *OPEN Energy Technology Bulletin* provides up-to-date information about renewable energy technologies and the *IEA Energy Technology Essentials* provides detailed information about individual technologies. Additional reports about these technologies can also be found on the organization's website.

National Renewable Energy Laboratory (NREL)
1617 Cole Blvd.
Golden, CO 80401-3305
(303) 275-3000
website: www.nrel.gov

As the principal research laboratory for the US Department of Energy's Office of Energy Efficiency and Renewable Energy, NREL is in charge of researching and developing renewable energy and energy efficiency for the country. The lab's efforts begin with scientific innovation, then move to finding ways this innovation can be used in generating electricity or as fuel, and conclude with finding practical ways to deliver this technology to the citizens of the country. NREL researches all renewable energy sources ranging from biomass to solar to wind, among others, with information about specific projects and findings available online.

Natural Resources Defense Council (NRDC)
40 West 20th Street
New York, NY 10011
(212) 727-2700 • fax (212) 727-1773
e-mail: nrdcinfo@nrdc.org
website: www.nrdc.org

With more than one million members, the NRDC is one of the largest and most active environmental organizations in the

United States. Its efforts focus on protecting wildlife and the wild places worldwide and conserving the environment for all the planet's inhabitants. The NRDC has identified renewable energy to be one of the most important weapons against climate change and has also noted its importance to both the US economy and job creation. Publications such as "Renewable Energy for America," "Stop Dirty Fuels," and state-level guides on the use of renewable energy sources can be accessed on the NRDC website.

Reason Foundation
3415 S. Sepulveda Blvd., Suite 400
Los Angeles, CA 90034
(310) 391-2245 • fax (310) 391-4395
website: www.reason.org

The Reason Foundation is a libertarian organization that sees principles such as liberty, free markets, and the rule of law as essential to the advancement of a free society. These ideals form the basis for the foundation's research, engagement with policy makers, and public education efforts. Reason's coverage of renewable energy has focused mainly on the policy and economic implications with articles such as "No Biofuels Bailout," "The Green Jobs Delusion," and "Wind Turbines Are Beautiful . . . but a Tad Expensive."

Renewable Energy Policy Project (REPP)
1612 K Street, NW, Suite 202
Washington, DC 20006
(202) 293-2898 • fax (202) 293-5857
website: www.repp.org

REPP has been working since its founding in 1995 to bring renewable energy to the market more quickly by providing current research to policy makers concerning the connection between policy and market and environmental concerns. Information separated by energy source can be accessed on the organization's website. The REPP library online also provides an extensive archive of the project's papers, including state-level analysis of renewables and reports on emerging issues in renewable technologies.

Sierra Club
85 Second Street, 2nd Floor
San Francisco, CA 94105
(415) 977-5500 • fax (415) 977-5799
e-mail: information@sierraclub.org
website: www.sierraclub.org

The Sierra Club is a grassroots environmental organization that has been working for more than one hundred years to promote and aid in the conservation of America's natural landscapes. More recently, the organization has focused on finding renewable energy solutions to halt climate change and preserve natural resources and environments. The Sierra Club website provides an overview of renewable energy sources as well as articles discussing related issues such as clean energy at the community level and government decisions regarding new energy options.

Union of Concerned Scientists (UCS)
2 Brattle Square
Cambridge, MA 02138-3780
(617) 547-5552 • fax (617) 864-9405
website: www.ucsusa.org

UCS is a science-based nonprofit organization comprised of both citizens and scientists dedicated to promoting the adoption of solutions at the government, corporate, and individual levels to the problems facing society today. Through its research and education efforts, UCS seeks to make people aware of the gravity of problems such as global warming and provide options for how to address these issues. The union promotes a multi-resource approach to renewable energy that encourages the employment of varied sources of energy to meet the demands of consumers to-day. Information on the renewable energy sources available and how they can be implemented in meaningful ways can be found on the UCS website.

US Department of Energy (DOE)
1000 Independence Ave., SW
Washington, DC 20585
(202) 586-5000
e-mail: the.secretary@hq.doe.gov
website: www.energy.gov

The DOE is the US government agency charged with ensuring the energy future of the country, providing scientific and technological leadership, promoting nuclear security, and resolving environmental problems stemming from the Cold War. Within the department, the Office of Energy Efficiency and Renewable Energy (EERE) is specifically tasked with investing in renewable energy technologies to provide the country with sustainable energy options that do not harm the environment and help decrease the country's need for foreign oil. Information about these technologies and the government's projects to advance them can be found on the EERE website at www.eere.energy.gov.

Bibliography of Books

Frances Beinecke — *Clean Energy Common Sense: An American Call to Action on Global Climate Change.* Lanham, MD: Rowman and Littlefield, 2010.

Lester Russell Brown — *World on the Edge: How to Prevent Environmental and Economic Collapse.* New York: Norton, 2011.

Robert Bryce — *Power Hungry: The Myths of "Green" Energy and the Real Fuels of the Future.* New York: Public Affairs, 2010.

Gwyneth Cravens — *Power to Save the World: The Truth About Nuclear Energy.* New York: Knopf, 2007.

Brian Dumaine — *The Plot to Save the Planet: How Visionary Entrepreneurs and Corporate Titans Are Creating Real Solutions to Global Warming.* New York: Crown Business, 2008.

Andres R. Edwards — *The Sustainability Revolution: Portrait of a Paradigm Shift.* Gabriola, British Columbia, Canada: New Society, 2005.

Joan Fitzgerald — *Emerald Cities: Urban Sustainability and Economic Development.* New York: Oxford University Press, 2010.

Paul Gilding

The Great Disruption: Why the Climate Crisis Will Bring on the End of Shopping and the Birth of a Brave New World. New York: Bloomsbury, 2011.

Steve Hallett and John Wright

Life Without Oil: Why We Must Shift to a New Energy Future. Amherst, NY: Prometheus, 2011.

Richard Heinberg and Daniel Lerch, eds.

The Post Carbon Reader: Managing the 21st Century's Sustainability Crises. Berkeley: University of California Press, 2010.

David Holmgren

Future Scenarios: How Communities Can Adapt to Peak Oil and Climate Change. White River Junction, VT: Chelsea Green, 2009.

Roy Innis

Energy Keepers Energy Killers: The New Civil Rights Battle. Bellevue, WA: Merril, 2008.

Bob Johnstone

Switching to Solar: What We Can Learn from Germany's Success in Harnessing Clean Energy. Amherst, NY: Prometheus, 2011.

Van Jones

The Green-Collar Economy: How One Solution Can Fix Our Two Biggest Problems. New York: HarperOne, 2008.

David J.C. MacKay

Sustainable Energy—Without the Hot Air. Cambridge, England: UIT, 2009.

James Mahaffey   *Atomic Awakening: A New Look at the History and Future of Nuclear Power*. New York: Pegasus Books, 2009.

Chris Martenson   *The Crash Course: The Unsustainable Future of Our Economy, Energy, and Environment*. Hoboken, NJ: Wiley, 2011.

Leonardo Maugeri   *Beyond the Age of Oil: The Myths, Realities, and Future of Fossil Fuels and Their Alternatives*. Santa Barbara, CA: Praeger, 2010.

Gerald McNerney   *Clean Energy Nation: Freeing America from the Tyranny of Fossil Fuels*. New York: AMACOM, 2012.

Craig Morris   *Energy Switch: Proven Solutions for a Renewable Future*. Gabriola Island, British Columbia, Canada: New Society, 2006.

Auden Schendler   *Getting Green Done: Hard Truths from the Front Lines of the Sustainability Revolution*. New York: Public Affairs, 2009.

Vaclav Smil   *Energy Myths and Realities: Bringing Science to the Energy Policy Debate*. Washington, DC: AEI, 2010.

F.E. Trainer   *Renewable Energy Cannot Sustain a Consumer Society*. London: Springer, 2007.

William Tucker

Terrestrial Energy: How Nuclear Power Will Lead the Green Revolution and End America's Energy Odyssey. Savage, MD: Bartleby, 2008.

Charles Weiss and William B. Bonvillian

Structuring an Energy Technology Revolution. Cambridge, MA: MIT Press, 2009.

Index

$\mathcal{D}$ays to
$\mathcal{R}$emember

Photography: Daniel Fortin
Graphic Design: Hélène Boudreau for Zapp
Astrology Illustrations: Evelyn Butt
Gemstone Photography: Nathalie Dumouchel

© 1995 Tormont Publications Inc.
   338 Saint Antoine St. East
   Montreal, Canada H2Y 1A3
   Tel.: (514) 954-1441
   Fax: (514) 954-5086

ISBN 2-89429-830-7
Printed in U.S.A.

Days to Remember

Birthdays

Anniversaries

Special Days

TORMONT

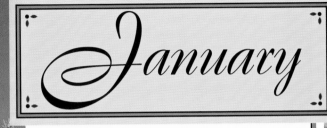

January

And now there came
both mist and snow,

And it grew wondrous cold:

And ice, mast-high,
came floating by,

As green as emerald.

Samuel Taylor Coleridge

January

"Now the New Year reviving old
   Desires,
The thoughtful Soul to Solitude
   retires . . ."

Edward Fitzgerald

1
New Year's Day

1863 Baron Pierre de Coubertin, French creator of the present day Olympics

1879 E M Forster, British author of *A Room with a View*

1920 J D Salinger, American author of *Catcher in the Rye*

2

1920 Isaac Asimov, Russian-born American biochemist and science-fiction writer

1938 David Bailey, British photographer

3

1888 J R R Tolkien, British fantasy novelist, author of *Lord of the Rings*

1945 Victoria Principal, American actress

4

1809 Louis Braille, blind French organist and professor, inventor of the writing system for the blind

1914 Jane Wyman, American actress

5

1931 Robert Duvall, American actor

1938 Juan Carlos I, king of Spain

1946 Diane Keaton, American actress

6
Epiphany

1412 Joan of Arc

1822 Heinrich Schliemann, German discoverer of Troy

7

". . . on this whirligig of Time
We circle with the seasons."

Alfred, Lord Tennyson

January

8

1935 Elvis Presley, American "King of rock 'n roll"

1937 Shirley Bassey, Welsh-born singer

1947 David Bowie, British musician and actor

9

1908 Simone de Beauvoir, French author of *The Second Sex*

1913 Richard Nixon, 37th US president

1941 Joan Baez, American folk singer

10

1918 The vote for women supported by the US House of Representatives

1945 Rod Stewart, Scottish singer and musician

11

1896 William Stephenson, the man called "Intrepid," Canadian WWII spy

12

1628 Charles Perrault, French collector of fairy tales

1876 Jack London, American author of *Call of the Wild*

13

1884 Sophie Tucker, Russian-born American singer

1919 Robert Stack, American actor

14

1875 Albert Schweitzer, French philosopher, musician and missionary doctor

1941 Faye Dunaway, American actress

January

15
1622 Molière, French playwright

1929 Martin Luther King, American civil rights campaigner

16
1853 André Michelin, French tire manufacturer

1909 Ethel Merman, American songstress and actress

17
1706 Benjamin Franklin, American scientist and politician

1928 Vidal Sassoon, British hairdresser

1942 Muhammad Ali, American boxing champion

18
1882 A A Milne, British creator of *Winnie-the-Pooh*

1904 Cary Grant, British-born American actor

1913 Danny Kaye, American film and stage actor

19
1809 Edgar Allan Poe, American writer

1839 Paul Cézanne, French painter

1943 Janis Joplin, American rock 'n roll singer

20
1896 George Burns, American comedian

1910 Joy Adamson, German-born conservationist and writer

1920 Frederico Fellini, Italian cinematographer

21
1905 Christian Dior, French couturier

1940 Jack Nicklaus, American golf champion

1941 Placido Domingo, Spanish-born opera singer

January

22
1788 Lord Byron, British poet

1940 John Hurt, British actor

23
1783 Stendhal, French author of *The Red and The Black*

1832 Édouard Manet, French painter

24
1945 Neil Diamond, American singer-songwriter

1961 Nastassja Kinski, German-born actress

25
1759 Robert Burns, Scottish poet

1882 Virginia Woolf, British writer

26
1925 Paul Newman, American actor

1928 Eartha Kitt, American singer and actress

27
1756 Wolfgang Amadeus Mozart, Austrian composer

1832 Lewis Carroll (Charles Lutwidge Dodgson) British author of *Alice in Wonderland*

28
1873 Colette (Gabrielle Sidonie), French novelist

1912 Jackson Pollock, American painter

1948 Mikhail Baryshnikov, Russian-born ballet dancer

January

29

1879 W C Fields, American comedian

1939 Germaine Greer, Australian feminist, author of *The Female Eunuch*

1941 Tom Selleck, American actor

30

1860 Anton Chekhov, Russian playwright

1931 Gene Hackman, American actor

1937 Vanessa Redgrave, British actress

31

1797 Franz Schubert, Austrian composer

1885 Anna Pavlova, Russian prima ballerina

1903 Tallulah Bankhead, American actress

Sometimes hath the brightest day a cloud;
And after summer evermore succeeds
Barren winter, with his wrathful nipping cold:
So cares and joys abound, as seasons fleet.

William Shakespeare

February

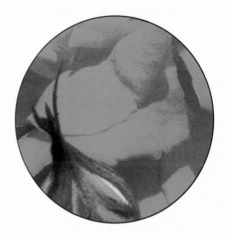

I dreamed that, as I wandered
by the way,

Bare Winter suddenly was
changed to Spring,

And gentle odours led
my steps astray . . .

Percy Bysshe Shelley

February

"This time, like all times, is a very good one, if we but know what to do with it."

Ralph Waldo Emerson

1

1901 Clark Gable, American actor

1918 Muriel Spark, Scottish author

1931 Boris Yeltsin, Russian politician

2

Groundhog Day

1861 Salomon Guggenheim, American collector

1882 James Joyce, Irish writer

1946 Farrah Fawcett, American actress

3

1809 Felix Mendelssohn, German composer and musician

1874 Gertrude Stein, American writer

4

1902 Charles Lindberg, the first pilot to cross the Atlantic solo

1948 Alice Cooper, American pop singer

5

1945 Bob Marley, Jamaican reggae musician

1947 Charlotte Rampling, British actress

6

1911 Ronald Reagan, actor and 40th US president

1912 François Truffaut, French cinematographer

1920 Zsa Zsa Gabor, Hungarian-born actress

7

1812 Charles Dickens, British writer

1885 Sinclair Lewis, American writer

February

8

1828 Jules Verne, French author and father of science-fiction

1925 Jack Lemmon, American actor

1931 James Dean, American actor

9

1941 Carole King, American singer and songwriter

1945 Mia Farrow, American actress

10

1890 Boris Pasternak, Russian author of *Dr. Zhivago*

1898 Bertold Brecht, German writer

11

1847 Thomas Alva Edison, American scientist and inventor

1934 Mary Quant, British fashion designer

1936 Burt Reynolds, American actor

12

1809 Charles Darwin, British evolutionist

1809 Abraham Lincoln, 16th US president

13

1903 Georges Simenon, Belgian author of the Maigret mysteries

1933 Kim Novak, American actress

1950 Peter Gabriel, British musician

14
Saint Valentine's Day

1894 Jack Benny, American comedian

1944 Alan Parker, British film director

February

15
1564 Galileo, Italian scientist and astronomer

1812 Charles Tiffany, American jeweller

1882 John Barrymore, American actor

16
1926 John Schlessinger, British film director

1959 John McEnroe, American tennis player

17
1930 Ruth Rendell, British novelist

1934 Alan Bates, British actor

18
1898 Enzo Ferrari, Italian car manufacturer

1933 Yoko Ono, Japanese artist and wife of John Lennon

1954 John Travolta, American actor

19
1473 Nicolas Copernicus, Polish astronomer

1917 Carson McCullers, American author

1924 Lee Marvin, American actor

20
1694 Voltaire, French philosopher and writer

1927 Sidney Poitier, American actor

1966 Cindy Crawford, American supermodel

21
1903 Anaïs Nin, French writer

1934 Nina Simone, American jazz singer

February

22

1732 George Washington, the first US president

1900 Luis Buñuel, Spanish cinematographer

23

1633 Samuel Pepys, British diarist

1685 George Frederick Handel, German composer

24

1932 Michel Legrand, French composer and conductor

1955 Alain Prost, French racecar driver

25

1873 Enrico Caruso, Italian opera singer

1841 Pierre Auguste Renoir, French painter

1943 George Harrison, British singer-songwriter, member of *The Beatles*

26

1802 Victor Hugo, French writer

1932 Johnny Cash, American country singer

27

1902 John Steinbeck, American novelist

1932 Elizabeth Taylor, British-born American actress

28/29

1913 Vincente Minnelli, American film director (28)

1792 Rossini, Italian composer (29)

March

Large streams from little
fountains flow,
Tall oaks from little
acorns grow.

David Everett

March

"How the March sun feels like May!"

Robert Browning

1

1810 Frederick Chopin, Polish composer

1904 Glenn Miller, American trombonist and musician

1927 Harry Belafonte, American singer and actor

2

1931 Mikhail Gorbachev, Russian politician

1943 George Benson, American singer

3

1847 Alexander Graham Bell, inventor of the telephone

1911 Jean Harlow, American actress

4

1678 Antonio Vivaldi, Italian composer

1931 Miriam Makeba, South African singer

5

1751 James Madison, fourth US president

1908 Rex Harrison, British actor

6

1475 Michelangelo, Italian artist, epitome of the Renaissance man

1619 Cyrano de Bergerac, French duelist

1806 Elizabeth Barrett Browning, British poet

7

1872 Piet Mondrian, Dutch abstract painter

1875 Maurice Ravel, French composer of *Bolero*

1960 Ivan Lendl, Czech tennis player

March

8

International Women's Day

1859 Kenneth Grahame, Scottish author of *The Wind in the Willows*

1921 Cyd Charisse, American actress and dancer

9

1892 Vita Sackville-West, British writer and gardener

1913 André Courrèges, French couturier

10

1876 The first telephone call made by Alexander Graham Bell

11

1898 Dorothy Gish, American silent film actress

1916 Harold Wilson, British prime minister

12

1890 Vaslav Nijinsky, Russian dancer and choreographer

1922 Jack Kerouac, American writer

1946 Liza Minnelli, American singer and entertainer

13

1930 American astronomer Clyde Tombaugh announced the discovery of the planet Pluto

14

1879 Albert Einstein, American physicist

1933 Michael Caine, British actor

March

15
1941 Mike Love, American singer and member of *The Beach Boys*

16
1926 Jerry Lewis, American actor

1940 Bernardo Bertolucci, Italian cinematographer

17
Saint Patrick's Day

1834 Gottlieb Daimler, German car inventor

1917 Nat "King" Cole, American singer and pianist

1938 Rudolf Nureyev, Russian dancer and choreographer

18
1932 John Updike, American author

1963 Vanessa Williams, American singer and actress

19
1813 David Livingstone, Scottish missionary and explorer

1936 Ursula Andress, Swiss actress

1955 Bruce Willis, American actor

20
1823 Henrik Ibsen, Norwegian writer

1958 Holly Hunter, American actress

21
1685 Johann Sebastian Bach, German composer

1944 Timothy Dalton, Welsh actor

March

22

1930 Stephen Sondheim, American composer and songwriter

1931 William Shatner, Canadian actor, "Captain Kirk" in *Star Trek*

1948 Andrew Lloyd Webber, British composer

23

1887 Juan Gris, Spanish painter

1908 Joan Crawford, American actress

24

1834 William Morris, British painter, writer and craftsman

1930 Steve McQueen, American actor

25

1921 Simone Signoret, German-born French actress

1942 Aretha Franklin, American singer

1947 Elton John, British musician

26

1874 Robert Frost, American poet

1911 Tennessee Williams, American writer

1944 Diana Ross, American singer and actress

27

1898 Gloria Swanson, American actress

1924 Sarah Vaughan, American jazz singer

28

1483 Raphael, Italian painter

1849 Maxim Gorky, Russian writer

1954 Reba McEntire, American country singer

March

29
1886 *Coca-Cola* first made in the US

1918 Pearl Bailey, American jazz singer

30
1853 Vincent van Gogh, Dutch painter

1937 Warren Beatty, American actor

1945 Eric Clapton, British guitarist and lyricist

31
1596 René Descartes, French philosopher and mathematician

1732 Franz Joseph Haydn, Austrian composer

1935 Richard Chamberlain, American actor

Who has seen the wind?

Neither you nor I.

But when the trees bow down their heads,

The wind is passing by.

Christina Rossetti

April

I wandered lonely as a cloud

That floats on high o'er vales
and hills,

When all at once I saw
a crowd,

A host, of golden daffodils;

Beside the lake, beneath
the trees,

Fluttering and dancing in
the breeze.

William Wordsworth

April

"Grow old along with me!
The best is yet to be."
Robert Browning

1

April Fool's Day

1873 Sergei Rachmaninov, Russian composer

1929 Milan Kundera, Czech writer

1938 Ali MacGraw, American actress

2

1805 Hans Christian Andersen, Danish writer of fairy tales

1840 Émile Zola, French novelist

1914 Sir Alec Guinness, British actor

3

1924 Marlon Brando, American actor

1924 Doris Day, American singer and actress

1961 Eddie Murphy, American comedian

4

1914 Marguerite Duras, French writer

1932 Anthony Perkins, American actor

5

1900 Spencer Tracy, American actor

1908 Bette Davis, American actress

1916 Gregory Peck, American actor

6

1874 Harry Houdini, American escape artist

1929 André Previn, American conductor and composer

7

World Health Day

1770 William Wordsworth, British poet

1915 Billie Holiday, American jazz singer

1939 Francis Ford Coppola, American movie director

April

8
1893 Mary Pickford, Canadian-born American actress

1912 Sonja Henie, Norwegian figure skating champion

1929 Jacques Brel, Belgian singer

9
1821 Charles Baudelaire, French writer

1933 Jean-Paul Belmondo, French actor

10
1847 Joseph Pulitzer, American journalist, founder of the Pulitzer Prize in journalism and literature

1932 Omar Sharif, Egyptian actor

1941 Paul Theroux, American writer

11
1932 Joel Grey, American singer and actor

12
"Beauty is in the eye of the beholder."

Margaret Wolfe Hungerford

13
1866 Butch Cassidy, American outlaw

1906 Samuel Beckett, Irish playwright

14
1904 Sir John Gielgud, British actor and theater impresario

1940 Julie Christie, British actress

April

15
1843 Henry James, American author

1894 Bessie Smith, American blues singer

16
1889 Charlie Chaplin, British-born actor and director

1921 Peter Ustinov, British playwright and actor

17
1894 Nikita Khrushchev, Soviet politician

1916 Mrs. Sirimavo Bandaranaike, the world's first woman prime minister, Sri Lanka

18
1480 Lucrezia Borgia, Italian patron of the arts

1946 Hayley Mills, British actress

19
1933 Jayne Mansfield, American actress

1935 Dudley Moore, British actor and musician

20
1889 Adolph Hitler, German dictator

1893 Joán Miró, Spanish artist

1941 Ryan O'Neal, American actor

21
1816 Charlotte Brontë, British poet and novelist

1926 Elizabeth II, queen of England

April

22
1724 Immanuel Kant, German philosopher

1922 Charlie Mingus, American jazz innovator and bandleader

1937 Jack Nicholson, American actor and movie director

23
1564 William Shakespeare, British writer, actor and playwright

1928 Shirely Temple, American child star

1936 Roy Orbison, American singer-songwriter

24
1815 Anthony Trollope, British author

1934 Shirley MacLaine, American actress and dancer

1942 Barbra Streisand, American singer, actress and director

25
1599 Oliver Cromwell, British dictator

1918 Ella Fitzgerald, American jazz singer

1939 Al Pacino, American actor

26
1452 Leonardo da Vinci, Italian artist and scientist

1785 John James Audubon, American naturalist and artist

1936 Carol Burnett, American comedienne

27
1759 Mary Wollstonecraft, British feminist

1791 Samuel Morse, American inventor of the Morse code

1932 Anouk Aimée, French actress

28
1878 Lionel Barrymore, American actor

1941 Ann-Margret, Swedish-born American actress and singer

April

29

1863 William Randolph Hearst, American newspaper baron

1889 Duke Ellington, American jazz musician

1957 Michelle Pfeiffer, American actress

30

1909 Juliana, Queen of the Netherlands

1944 Jill Clayburgh, American actress

Thou wast that all to me, love,
For which my soul did pine —
A green isle in the sea, love,
A fountain and a shrine,
All wreathed with fairy fruits and flowers,
And all the flowers were mine.

Edgar Allan Poe

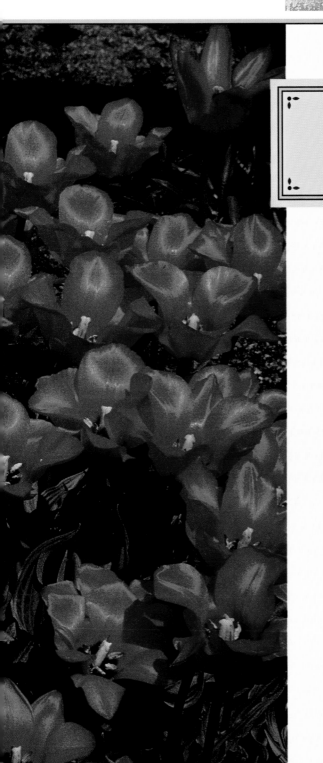

May

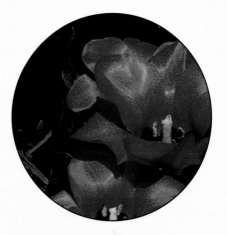

And a bird overhead
sang Follow,

And a bird to the right
sang Here;

And the arch of the leaves
was hollow,

And the meaning of May
was clear.

Algernon Charles Swinburne

May

"Sweet April showers
Do spring May flowers."
Thomas Tusser

1

1929 Joseph Heller, American writer

1931 The Empire State Building opened in New York

2

1729 Catherine the Great, empress of Russia

1903 Dr. Benjamin Spock, American childcare specialist

1904 Bing Crosby, American singer and actor

3

1469 Machiavelli, Italian author of *The Prince*

1874 François Coty, Corsican perfume creator

1898 Golda Meir, Israeli prime minister

4

1852 Alice Liddell, Lewis Carroll's muse for *Alice in Wonderland*

1929 Audrey Hepburn, American actress

5

1818 Karl Marx, German political theorist

1943 Michael Palin, British comedian and actor

6

1856 Sigmund Freud, Austrian psychiatrist

1895 Rudolph Valentino, Italian-born American silent screen idol

1915 Orson Welles, American actor and film director

7

1812 Robert Browning, British poet

1833 Johannes Brahms, German composer and musician

1840 Peter Ilyich Tchaikovsky, Russian composer

May

8
World Red Cross Day

1926 Sir David Attenborough, British naturalist and broadcaster

1940 Peter Benchley, American author of *Jaws*

9

1860 J M Barrie, Scottish author of *Peter Pan*

1920 Richard Adams, British author of *Watership Down*

1946 Candice Bergen, American actress

10

1899 Fred Astaire, American dancer and actor

1933 Barbara Taylor Bradford, British writer

1946 Donovan, Scottish musician

11

1888 Irving Berlin, American composer

1893 Martha Graham, American dancer

1904 Salvador Dali, Spanish artist

12

1820 Florence Nightingale, British nursing pioneer

1828 Dante Gabriel Rossetti, British painter and poet

13

1842 Sir Arthur Sullivan, British composer of operettas

1907 Daphne du Maurier, British author of *Rebecca*

1950 Stevie Wonder, American musician

14

1727 Thomas Gainsborough, British painter

1936 Bobby Darin, American singer

May

15

1856 Frank Baum, American author of *The Wonderful Wizard of Oz*

1909 James Mason, British actor

16

1905 Henry Fonda, American actor

1919 Liberace, American pianist and performer

1966 Janet Jackson, American pop singer

17

1936 Dennis Hopper, American actor

1955 Grace Jones, Jamaican-born American actress and singer

18

1912 Perry Como, American singer

1919 Margot Fonteyn, British prima ballerina

1920 John Paul II, the Polish pope

19

1890 Ho Chi Minh, Vietnamese politician

1926 Malcolm X, American black militant leader

20

1908 Jimmy Stewart, American actor

1945 Cher, American singer-songwriter and actress

21

1844 Henri Rousseau, French painter

1921 Andrei Sakharov, Soviet physicist and Nobel Peace prize winner in 1975

May

22

1813 Richard Wagner, German composer
1859 Sir Arthur Conan Doyle, Scottish creator of Sherlock Holmes
1907 Sir Laurence Olivier, British actor

23

1883 Douglas Fairbanks, American actor

1933 Joan Collins, British actress

1951 Anatoly Karpov, Russian chess champion

24

1819 Queen Victoria of England

1941 Bob Dylan, American folk singer

25

1926 Miles Davis, American jazz trumpeter

1930 Sonia Rykiel, fashion designer

26

1886 Al Jolson, American singer and entertainer

1907 John Wayne, American actor

1920 Peggy Lee, American singer-songwriter and actress

27

1878 Isadora Duncan, American dancer

1911 Vincent Price, American actor

1923 Henry Kissinger, American politician

28

1908 Ian Fleming, British creator of James Bond

1934 The Dionne Quintuplets: Emilie, Yvonne, Cecile, Marie and Annette

May

29

1903 Bob Hope, American comedian

1917 John F Kennedy, 35th US president

1953 Sir Edmund Hillary and Sherpa Tenzing reached Everest's summit

30

1846 Peter Carl Fabergé, Russian jeweller

1909 Benny Goodman, American bandleader

31

1819 Walt Whitman, American poet

1930 Clint Eastwood, American actor and director

1965 Brooke Shields, American model and actress

There are twelve months in all the year,

As I hear many men say,

But the merriest month in all the year

Is the merry month of May.

**Ballad of Robin Hood
and the Widow's Three Sons**

June

And what is so rare
as a day in June?

Then, if ever,
come perfect days;

Then Heaven tries earth
if it be in tune,

And over it softly
her warm ear lays.

James Russell Lowell

June

"A thing of beauty is a joy forever."
John Keats

1
1926 Marilyn Monroe, American actress

1934 Pat Boone, American actor and singer

2
1740 Marquis de Sade, French writer

1840 Thomas Hardy, British author of *Tess of the D'Urbervilles*

3
1906 Josephine Baker, American singer and dancer

1925 Tony Curtis, American actor

1926 Allen Ginsburg, American poet

4
1908 Rosalind Russell, American actress

5
International Day of the Environment

1898 Federico García Lorca, Spanish poet and playwright

1939 Margaret Drabble, British author

6
1799 Aleksandr Pushkin, Russian writer

1956 Bjorn Borg, Swedish tennis player

7
1848 Paul Gauguin, French painter

1940 Tom Jones, Welsh singer

1960 Prince, American singer

June

8
1810 Robert Schumann, German composer

1869 Frank Lloyd Wright, American architect

1933 Joan Rivers, American comedienne

9
1893 Cole Porter, American composer and songwriter

1961 Michael J Fox, Canadian actor

10
1915 Saul Bellow, American writer

1922 Judy Garland, American singer and actress

11
1776 John Constable, British painter

1864 Richard Strauss, German composer

1910 Jacques Yves Cousteau, French oceanographer and filmmaker

12
1924 George Bush, 41st US president

1929 Anne Frank, German-born Jewish diarist

13
1865 William Butler Yeats, Irish poet

1893 Dorothy L Sayers, British mystery writer

14
1928 Che Guevara, Cuban revolutionary

1969 Steffi Graf, German tennis player

June

15
World Children's Day

1843 Edvard Grieg, Norwegian composer

1941 Harry Nilsson, American singer and songwriter

16

1890 Stan Laurel, thin member of the comic duo, "Laurel & Hardy"

17

1882 Igor Stravinsky, Russian composer

1946 Barry Manilow, American singer and composer

18

1942 Paul McCartney, British musician, member of *The Beatles*

1952 Isabella Rossellini, Italian-born model and actress

19

1896 Wallis Simpson, Duchess of Windsor

1947 Salman Rushdie, British author of *The Satanic Verses*

1954 Kathleen Turner, American actress

20

1819 Jacques Offenbach, French composer

1909 Errol Flynn, Australian-born American actor

1949 Lionel Richie, American singer-songwriter

21

1905 Jean-Paul Sartre, French Existentialist philosopher

1935 Françoise Sagan, French writer, author of *Bonjour Tristesse*

1953 Benazir Bhutto, prime minister of Pakistan

June

22

1936 Kris Kristofferson, American singer and actor

1949 Meryl Streep, American actress

23

1763 Joséphine, wife of Napoleon

1927 Bob Fosse, American choreographer and director

24

Saint John the Baptist's Day

1895 Jack Dempsey, American boxer

1947 Mick Fleetwood, British member of *Fleetwood Mac*

25

1903 George Orwell, British writer

1945 Carly Simon, American singer-songwriter

1963 George Michael, British pop singer

26

1892 Pearl S Buck, American writer

1904 Peter Lorre, Hungarian-born American actor

27

1880 Helen Keller, American blind and deaf writer and lecturer

28

1577 Peter Paul Rubens, Flemish painter

1712 Jean-Jacques Rousseau, French philosopher

1902 Richard Rodgers, American composer and songwriter

June

29

1900 Antoine de Saint-Exupéry, French pilot and author of *The Little Prince*

30

1917 Lena Horne, American singer

1966 Mike Tyson, American boxer

When June is come, then all the day
I'll sit with my love in the scented hay:
And watch the sunshot palaces high,
That the white clouds build in the breezy sky.

Robert Bridges

July

. . . the hour
Of splendor in the grass,
of glory in the flower.

William Wordsworth

July

"The human heart has hidden treasures,
In secret kept, in silence sealed."
Charlotte Brontë

1
Canada Day

1804 George Sand (Aurore Dupin), French writer

1961 Diana, princess of Wales

1961 Carl Lewis, American track and field champion

2

1877 Herman Hesse, German-born Swiss writer

3

1883 Franz Kafka, Austrian-Czech writer

1927 Ken Russell, British filmmaker

1937 Tom Stoppard, Czech-born British dramatist

4
Independence Day (US)

1804 Nathaniel Hawthorne, American author of *The Scarlet Letter*

1918 Ann Landers, American advice columnist

1927 Neil Simon, American playwright

5

1810 P T Barnum, American showman

1889 Jean Cocteau, French writer and movie director

6

1925 Bill Haley, American rock 'n roll musician

1935 Dalai Lama, 14th religious leader of Tibet

1946 Sylvester Stallone, American actor and director

7

1887 Marc Chagall, Russian-born French painter

1922 Pierre Cardin, French fashion designer

1940 Ringo Starr, British drummer for *The Beatles*

July

8

1839 John D Rockefeller, American billionaire

1951 Angelica Houston, American actress

9

1901 Barbara Cartland, British romance writer

1937 David Hockney, British painter

10

1830 Camille Pissaro, French artist

1834 James Whistler, American painter

1871 Marcel Proust, French novelist

11

1767 John Quincy Adams, sixth US president

1915 Yul Brynner, American actor

12

1817 Henry David Thoreau, American writer and naturalist

1884 Amedeo Modigliani, Italian artist

1937 Bill Cosby, American comedian

13

1942 Harrison Ford, American actor

14

Bastille Day (France)

1912 Woody Guthrie, American folk singer

1918 Ingmar Bergman, Swedish film writer-director

July

15
1606 Rembrandt, Flemish painter

1919 Iris Murdoch, British writer

1946 Linda Rondstadt, American singer

16
1872 Roald Amundsen, Norwegian adventurer, the first European to arrive at the South Pole in 1911

1911 Ginger Rogers, American dancer and actress

17
1899 James Cagney, American actor

1917 Phyllis Diller, American comedienne

1935 Donald Sutherland, Canadian actor

18
1918 Nelson Mandela, South African politician

1955 Disneyland opened in California

19

20
1834 Edgar Degas, French painter

1919 Sir Edmund Hillary, New Zealand mountain climber, the first to scale Everest

1938 Diana Rigg, British actress

1969 First moon landing

21
1899 Ernest Hemingway, American writer

July

22

1822 Gregor Mendel, Austrian botanist and geneticist

23

1888 Raymond Chandler, American mystery writer

24

1783 Simón Bolívar, South American revolutionary

1802 Alexandre Dumas (Père), French author of *The Three Musketeers*

1898 Amelia Earhart, American aviatrix

25

1978 Louise Brown, the first test-tube baby

26

1856 George Bernard Shaw, British writer

1894 Aldous Huxley, British writer

1943 Mick Jagger, lead singer of *The Rolling Stones*

27

1824 Alexandre Dumas (Fils), French author of *La Dame aux Camélias*

28

1866 Beatrix Potter, British children's writer, creator of *Peter Rabbit*

1929 Jacqueline Bouvier Kennedy Onassis

July

29

1883 Benito Mussolini, Italian dictator

30

1818 Emily Brontë, British author of *Wuthering Heights*

1863 Henry Ford, American car manufacturer

1947 Arnold Schwarzenegger, Austrian-born American actor

31

1944 Geraldine Chaplin, American actress

Shall I compare thee to a summer's day?

Thou art more lovely and temperate:

Rough winds do shake the darling buds of May

And summer's lease hath all too short a date.

William Shakespeare

August

. . . the Glory of the Garden
lies in more
than meets the eye.

Rudyard Kipling

August

1

1819 Herman Melville, American author of *Moby Dick*

1936 Yves Saint-Laurent, French fashion designer

2

1905 Myrna Loy, American movie actress

1924 James Baldwin, American writer

1932 Peter O'Toole, Irish actor

3

1887 Rupert Brooke, British WWI poet

1920 P D James, British mystery writer

1926 Tony Bennett, American singer

4

1792 Percy Bysshe Shelley, British poet

1900 Queen Elizabeth, the Queen Mother

5

1850 Guy de Maupassant, French novelist

1930 Neil Armstrong, the first astronaut on the moon

6

1809 Alfred, Lord Tennyson, British poet

1911 Lucille Ball, American comedienne

1917 Robert Mitchum, American actor

7

1876 Mata Hari, Dutch dancer and spy

1936 Roland Kirk, American jazz musician

August

8

1937 Dustin Hoffman, American actor

1957 Melanie Griffith, American actress

1963 Whitney Houston, American singer

9

"Dry August and warm
Doth harvest no harm."

Thomas Tusser

10

1928 Eddie Fisher, American actor and singer

11

1897 Enid Blyton, British children's writer

1921 Alex Haley, American author of *Roots*

12

1881 Cecil B De Mille, American film producer and director

13

1860 Annie Oakley, American sharpshooter

1899 Alfred Hitchcock, British-born American filmmaker

1927 Fidel Castro, Cuban revolutionary leader

14

1864 John Galsworthy, British writer of *The Forsyte Saga*

1947 Danielle Steele, American novelist

August

15
1769 Napoleon Bonaparte, emperor of France

1912 Julia Child, American cook

1925 Oscar Peterson, Canadian jazz pianist

16
1913 Menachem Begin, Israeli prime minister

1958 Madonna, American pop singer

17
1786 Davy Crockett, American frontiersman

1892 Mae West, American actress

1943 Robert de Niro, American actor

18
1922 Shelley Winters, American actress

1933 Roman Polanski, Polish filmmaker

1937 Robert Redford, American actor and film director

19
1883 "Coco" Chanel, French fashion designer

1902 Ogden Nash, American humorist and lyricist

20
"All the live murmur of a summer's day."

Matthew Arnold

21
1904 Count Basie, American jazz pianist

1930 Princess Margaret, younger sister of Queen Elizabeth II

August

22

1862 Claude Debussy, French composer

1893 Dorothy Parker, American satirical writer

1908 Henri Cartier-Bresson, French photographer

23

1912 Gene Kelly, American dancer and actor

1949 Shelley Long, American actress

24

1899 Jorge Luis Borges, Argentinean author

25

1905 Clara Bow, American actress

1918 Leonard Bernstein, American composer-conductor

1930 Sean Connery, Scottish actor

26

1740 Joseph Michel Montgolfier, French hot air balloon inventor

27

1910 Mother Teresa of Calcutta, Yugoslavian-born missionary

28

1749 Goethe, German poet and dramatist

1828 Leo Tolstoy, Russian author

August

29

1915 Ingrid Bergman, Swedish-born American actress

1949 Richard Gere, American actor

1958 Michael Jackson, American singer

30

1748 Jacques Louis David, French painter

1797 Mary Wollstonecraft Shelley, British author of *Frankenstein*

31

1870 Maria Montessori, Italian educator

1945 Van Morrison, Irish-born singer

To see a World in a grain of sand,
And a Heaven in a wild flower,
Hold Infinity in the palm of your hand,
And Eternity in an hour.

William Blake

September

The Bird of Time
has but a little way

To fly — and Lo!
the Bird is on the Wing.

Edward Fitzgerald

September

1

1908 Estée Lauder, American make-up manufacturer

1939 Lily Tomlin, American comedienne

1958 Gloria Estefan, Cuban-born American singer

2

1952 Jimmy Connors, American tennis player

3

1875 Ferdinand Porsche, automobile manufacturer

1913 Alan Ladd, American actor

4

1905 Mary Renault, British writer

1920 Liz Claiborne, American designer

5

1847 Jesse James, American outlaw

1929 Bob Newhart, American comedian

1940 Raquel Welch, American actress

6

1942 Britt Ekland, Swedish actress

1947 Roger Waters, British musician, member of *Pink Floyd*

7

1533 Elizabeth I of England

1860 "Grandma" Moses, American painter

1936 Buddy Holly, American pop singer

September

8

1841 Antonin Dvořák, Czech composer

1925 Peter Sellers, British comedian and actor

9

1900 James Hilton, British writer

1941 Otis Redding, American singer-songwriter

10

"All Nature wears one universal grin."

Henry Fielding

11

1862 O Henry, American author

1885 D H Lawrence, British author of *Lady Chatterly's Lover*

12

1888 Maurice Chevalier, French singer and actor

1913 Jesse Owens, American track and field athelete

13

1905 Claudette Colbert, American actress

1925 Mel Torme, American singer and musician

1944 Jacqueline Bisset, British actress

14

1867 Charles Dana Gibson, American artist, originator of the "Gibson Girl"

September

15
1890 Agatha Christie, British mystery writer

1945 Jessye Norman, American opera singer

16
1924 Lauren Bacall, American actress

1925 Charlie Byrd, American jazz musician

1925 B B King, American blues guitarist

17
1931 Anne Bancroft, American actress

18
1709 Dr. Samuel Johnson, dictionary editor

1905 Greta Garbo, Swedish-born American actress

1933 Bob Dylan, American singer-songwriter

19
1911 Sir William Golding, British author of *Lord of the Flies*

1948 Jeremy Irons, British actor

1949 Twiggy, British model, actress and 60s trendsetter

20
1885 Jelly Roll Morton, jazz musician

1934 Sophia Loren, Italian actress

21
1866 H G Wells, British writer

1931 Larry Hagman, American actor

1934 Leonard Cohen, Canadian singer and writer

September

22

23
1931 Fay Weldon, British writer

1932 Ray Charles, American singer and musician

1943 Julio Iglesias, Spanish singer

1949 Bruce Springsteen, American singer-songwriter

24
1896 F Scott Fitzgerald, American writer

1936 Jim Henson, American co-creator of *The Muppets*

25
1897 William Faulkner, American writer

1932 Barbara Walters, American TV journalist

1944 Michael Douglas, American actor

26
1888 T S Eliot, American-born poet

1898 George Gershwin, American composer

1948 Olivia Newton-John, British-born singer

27
1947 Cheryl Tiegs, American model

28
1923 Marcello Mastroianni, Italian actor

1934 Brigitte Bardot, French film star

September

29

1518 Tintoretto, Italian painter

1935 Jerry Lee Lewis, American musician

1943 Lech Walesa, Polish politician

30

1921 Deborah Kerr, Scottish-born actress

1924 Truman Capote, American writer

1931 Angie Dickinson, American actress

Tears, idle tears, I know not what they mean,
Tears from the depth of some divine despair
Rise in the heart and gather to the eyes,
In looking on the happy autumn fields,
And thinking of the days that are no more.

Alfred, Lord Tennyson

October

The swallows are making
them ready to fly,

Wheeling out on a windy sky:

Goodbye, Summer, goodbye,
goodbye.

G J Whyte-Melville

October

1

1920 Walter Matthau, American actor

1924 Jimmy Carter, 39th US president

1935 Julie Andrews, British singer, star of *The Sound of Music*

2

1869 Mahatma Gandhi, Hindu nationalist leader and pacifist

1890 Groucho Marx, American comedian

1951 Sting, British singer, lyricist and actor

3

1916 James Herriott, British veterinarian and author

1925 Gore Vidal, American writer

1941 Chubby Checker, American singer

4

1895 Buster Keaton, American actor and movie director

1924 Charlton Heston, American actor

5

1936 Vaclav Havel, Czech playwright and president

1954 Bob Geldof, Irish musician

6

1887 Le Corbusier, French architect

7

1931 Reverend Desmond Tutu, South African civil rights campaigner

1955 Yo Yo Ma, Chinese cellist

1957 Jayne Torvill, British figure skating champion (with Christopher Dean)

October

8

"In seed time learn, in harvest teach, in winter enjoy."
William Blake

9

1940 John Lennon, British singer-songwriter and member of *The Beatles*

10

1813 Giuseppe Verdi, Italian opera composer

1900 Helen Hayes, American actress

1930 Harold Pinter, British playwright

11

1884 Eleanor Roosevelt, American writer and social activist

1919 Art Blakey, American jazz drummer and bandleader

1928 Ennio Morricone, Italian composer of movie soundtracks

12

1492 Columbus discovered the New World

1935 Luciano Pavarotti, Italian opera singer

13

1921 Yves Montand, French singer and actor

1925 Margaret Thatcher, British politician

1941 Paul Simon, American musician and songwriter

14

1894 e e cummings, American poet

1928 Roger Moore, British actor

1941 Anne Rice, American author

1946 Susan Sarandon, American actress

October

15

1908 John Kenneth Galbraith, Canadian economist

1920 Mario Puzo, American author of *The Godfather*

16

1854 Oscar Wilde, Irish-born writer and satirist

1925 Angela Lansbury, British-born American actress

17

1885 Isak Dinesen, Danish author of *Out of Africa*

1918 Rita Hayworth, American actress

18

1926 Chuck Berry, American singer

1956 Martina Navratilova, Czech-born American tennis player

19

1931 John Le Carré, British writer

1944 Peter Tosh, Jamaican reggae musician

20

1632 Christopher Wren, British architect of St. Paul's Cathedral

1884 Bela Lugosi, Hungarian actor who played *Dracula*

21

1833 Alfred Nobel, Swedish industrial scientist, established the Nobel Prizes

1917 Dizzy Gillespie, American jazz trumpeter and bandleader

October

22
- **1811** Franz Liszt, Hungarian pianist and composer
- **1844** Sarah Bernhardt, French actress
- **1943** Catherine Deneuve, French actress

23
- **1925** Johnny Carson, American talk show host
- **1940** Pelé, Brazilian soccer player

24
United Nations Day
- **1930** The Big Bopper (John P. Richardson), American singer and songwriter

25
- **1825** Johann Strauss the Younger, Austrian composer
- **1881** Pablo Picasso, Spanish artist
- **1967** Julia Roberts, American actress

26
- **1916** François Mitterand, French president
- **1942** Bob Hoskins, British actor
- **1947** Hillary Rodham Clinton, American lawyer

27
- **1914** Dylan Thomas, Welsh writer
- **1932** Sylvia Plath, American poet and author of *The Bell Jar*
- **1939** John Cleese, British comedian, writer, and director

28
- **1903** Evelyn Waugh, British writer
- **1927** Cleo Laine, British singer

October

29

1948 Richard Dreyfuss, American actor

1971 Winona Ryder, American actress

30

1885 Ezra Pound, American poet

1932 Louis Malle, French filmmaker

31
Halloween

1632 Jan Vermeer, Dutch painter

1795 John Keats, British poet

The one red leaf, the last of its clan,
That dances as often as dance it can,
Hanging so light, and hanging so high,
On the topmost twig that looks up at the sky.

Samuel Taylor Coleridge

November

Season of mists and mellow
fruitfulness,

Close bosom-friend of
the maturing sun;

Conspiring with him
to load and bless

With fruit the vines that
round the thatch-eaves run.

John Keats

November

"If winter comes, can spring be far behind?"

Percy Bysshe Shelley

1

1500 Benvenuto Cellini, Italian Renaissance sculptor

1871 Stephen Crane, American author of *The Red Badge of Courage*

2

1734 Daniel Boone, American pioneer

1755 Marie Antoinette, the last queen of France

1913 Burt Lancaster, American actor

3

1801 Vincenzo Bellini, Italian composer

1921 Charles Bronson, American actor

4

1879 Will Rogers, American actor and humorist

1916 Walter Cronkite, American journalist and TV anchorman

1944 Loretta Swit, American actress

5

1912 Roy Rogers, "King of the Cowboys," American actor

1913 Vivien Leigh, British actress

1963 Tatum O'Neal, American actress

6

1854 John Philip Sousa, American composer and conductor

1948 Glenn Frey, American musician, member of *The Eagles*

7

1867 Marie Curie, Polish-born French scientist

1913 Albert Camus, French Existentialist writer

1943 Joni Mitchell, Canadian singer-songwriter

November

8

1847 Bram Stoker, Irish creator of *Dracula*

1900 Margaret Mitchell, American author of *Gone With the Wind*

9

1909 Katherine Hepburn, American actress

1913 Hedy Lamarr, American actress

10

1483 Martin Luther, German church reformer

1925 Richard Burton, British actor

11

Remembrance Day/Veterans' Day (US)

1821 Fyodor Dostoyevsky, Russian novelist

1922 Kurt Vonnegut, American writer

1962 Demi Moore, American actress

12

1840 Auguste Rodin, French sculptor

1929 Princess Grace of Monaco, former American actress

1945 Neil Young, Canadian musician

13

1850 Robert Louis Stevenson, Scottish writer

1950 Whoopi Goldberg, American actress

14

1840 Claude Monet, French painter

1948 Prince Charles, the prince of Wales

November

15

1932 Petula Clark, British singer-actress

16

"Flowers are lovely; love is
    flower-like;
Friendship is a sheltering tree."
Samuel Taylor Coleridge

17

1925 Rock Hudson, American actor

1942 Martin Scorsese, American film director

18

1836 Sir W S Gilbert, collaborated with Sullivan in writing light operas

1939 Margaret Atwood, Canadian author

19

1917 Indira Gandhi, the first woman prime minister of India

1905 Tommy Dorsey, American trombone player and bandleader

1963 Jodie Foster, American actress and director

20

1908 Alistair Cooke, English writer and broadcaster

1925 Robert Kennedy, American senator

21

1898 René Magritte, Belgian painter

1945 Goldie Hawn, American actress

November

22

1890 Charles de Gaulle, French president

1958 Jamie Lee Curtis, American actress

1943 Billy Jean King, American tennis player

23

1887 Boris Karloff, British-born American actor known for *Frankenstein*

24

1864 Toulouse-Lautrec, French artist

1868 Scott Joplin, American ragtime pianist and composer

25

1844 Karl Benz, German inventor of the automobile

1914 Joe Di Maggio, American baseball star

26

1922 Charles Schulz, American cartoonist, creator of *Peanuts*

1939 Tina Turner, American singer

27

1942 Jimi Hendrix, American guitarist and singer

28

1757 William Blake, British poet

1907 Alberto Moravia, Italian author

November

29

1832 Louisa May Alcott,
American author of *Little Women*

1898 C S Lewis, British author of
The Narnia Chronicles

30

1835 Mark Twain, American writer
and satirist

1874 Sir Winston Churchill, British
politician

1874 L M Montgomery, Canadian
author of *Anne of Green Gables*

How do I love thee? Let me count the ways.

I love thee to the depth and breadth and height

My soul can reach, when feeling out of sight

For the ends of being and ideal grace.

I love thee with the breath, smiles, tears, of all my life

And if, God choose,

I shall but love thee better after death.

Elizabeth Barrett Browning

December

We live in deeds, not years;
in thoughts, not breaths;

In feelings, not in figures
on a dial.

We should count time
by heart-throbs.

Philip James Bailey

December

1

1935 Woody Allen, American humorist and filmmaker

1945 Bette Midler, American singer and entertainer

2

1859 Georges Seurat, French painter

1923 Maria Callas, American-born Greek opera singer

3

1857 Joseph Conrad, Polish-born author of *Heart of Darkness*

1930 Jean-Luc Godard, French filmmaker

4

1866 Wassily Kandinsky, Russian-born French abstract painter

1892 Francisco Franco, Spanish dictator

5

1901 Walt Disney, American filmmaker specializing in animation

1935 Little Richard, American rock 'n roll singer

1946 José Carreras, Spanish opera singer

6

1896 Ira Gershwin, American songwriter of popular musicals

1920 Dave Brubeck, American jazz musician

7

December

8

1865 Jean Sibelius, Finnish composer
1925 Sammy Davis Jr, American entertainer
1943 Jim Morrison, American rock singer (*The Doors*)

9

1909 Douglas Fairbanks, Jr. American actor

1918 Kirk Douglas, American actor

1957 Donny Osmond, American pop singer

10

1830 Emily Dickinson, American poet

1914 Dorothy Lamour, American actress

11

1803 Hector Berlioz, French composer

1918 Alexandr Solzhenitsyn, Russian author

12

1821 Gustave Flaubert, French author of *Madame Bovary*

1915 Frank Sinatra, American singer and entertainer

1941 Dionne Warwick, American singer

13

1925 Dick van Dyke, American actor

1929 Christopher Plummer, Canadian actor

14

1503 Nostradamus, French astrologer

1935 Lee Remick, American actress

December

15

1832 Alexandre Gustave Eiffel, French engineer, creator of the Paris landmark

1892 John Paul Getty, American millionaire

16

1775 Jane Austen, British author

1889 Noël Coward, British playwright

1901 Margaret Mead, American anthropologist and author

17

1770 Ludwig von Beethoven, German composer

1903 The Wright Brothers' first flight

18

1879 Paul Klee, Swiss artist

1916 Betty Grable, American actress

1947 Steven Spielberg, American film director

19

1902 Sir Ralph Richardson, British actor

1915 Édith Piaf, French singer and actress

20

"The supreme happiness of life is the conviction that we are loved."

Victor Hugo

21

1937 Jane Fonda, American actress

1940 Frank Zappa, American singer-composer

1954 Chris Evert, American tennis player

December

22

1858 Giacomo Puccini, Italian opera composer

1907 Dame Peggy Ashcroft, British actress

23

1908 Yousuf Karsh, Turkish-Armenian portrait photographer

24

Christmas Eve

1905 Howard Hughes, American tycoon

1922 Ava Gardner, American actress

25

Christmas Day

1899 Humphrey Bogart, American actor

1918 Anwar Sadat, Egyptian president who initiated peace with Israel

1949 Sissy Spacek, American actress

26

Boxing Day

1891 Henry Miller, American author

1893 Mao Tse-tung, Chinese communist leader

27

1822 Louis Pasteur, French scientist

1904 Marlene Dietrich, German-born actress and singer

1948 Gérard Depardieu, French actor

28

1905 Earl "Fatha" Hines, American jazz pianist

1934 Maggie Smith, British actress

1956 Nigel Kennedy, British violinist

December

29

1800 Charles Goodyear, American chemist

1937 Mary Tyler Moore, American actress

30

1865 Rudyard Kipling, British author

1928 Bo Didley, American jazz musician

31

New Year's Eve

1869 Henri Matisse, French painter

1937 Anthony Hopkins, British actor

1943 Ben Kingsley, British actor

Thereby to see the minutes how they run,

How many make the hour full complete;

How many hours bring about the day;

How many days will finish up the year . . .

William Shakespeare

Chinese Astrology

*A*ccording
to an ancient legend,
one day Buddha decided to reor-
ganize the Chinese empire. He sum-
moned all the animals to a meeting on New
Year's Day, but only twelve came. The quick-
witted Rat arrived first, followed by the hardworking Ox. Next came the powerful Tiger and the
prudent Hare. Soon the bewitching Dragon and
the resourceful Snake appeared, followed by the
capable Horse and the kindly Sheep. The fun-loving
Monkey and the proud Rooster joined them, and then
came the faithful Dog and the trustworthy Pig.

As a reward, Buddha named a year for each
animal, in order of their arrival. From that day
forward, the years of the Chinese calendar
took on the characteristics of the animals
for which they were named, and
people born in a particular year
had personality traits
to match.

Rat

5 February 1924 – 24 January 1925
24 January 1936 – 10 February 1937
10 February 1948 – 28 January 1949
28 January 1960 – 14 February 1961
15 February 1972 – 2 February 1973
2 February 1984 – 19 February 1985
19 February 1996 – 7 February 1997
6 February 2008 – 25 January 2009

*R*at people have natural charm, a quick mind, and an outgoing nature that attracts friends. However, their friendships aren't always lasting, because they have a tendency to spread gossip. Although they may lose their tempers over small things, Rats are usually able to hide their emotions and give the impression of being calm and controlled.

Rats are thrifty, sometimes even grasping, because they feel an enormous need for security. Their ambition and determination bring them success in the business world, provided they feel supported and encouraged. They are successful in many fields, whether at work or play.

Women Rats have an aura that is partly femme fatale, partly business executive. At the same time, they want a dependable emotional relationship with a partner they can trust. Because of their thrifty nature, they find it hard to be generous.

Men Rats are often misunderstood and sometimes difficult to live or work with. They waste a lot of energy brooding over things they consider unsatisfactory. They like to feel useful, and have impeccable manners.

Ox

25 January 1925 – 12 February 1926
11 February 1937 – 30 January 1938
29 January 1949 – 16 February 1950
15 February 1961 – 4 February 1962
3 February 1973 – 22 January 1974
20 February 1985 – 8 February 1986
8 February 1997 – 28 January 1998
26 January 2009 – 13 February 2010

*O*x people are emotionally well balanced and serene, which makes for stable relationships. They are completely dependable, extremely hardworking, resolute individuals who can overcome difficulties and achieve the goals that they have set for themselves.

Ox people show great judgment in choosing their friends. Once they decide to trust you, they become firm friends whose help and wise advice are much appreciated. However, don't ever take advantage of an Ox, or you'll find yourself with a sworn enemy.

Ox people are homebodies who make excellent parents, wonderful lovers, and sensitive, reliable partners.

The loyal and trusting nature of Ox women makes them vulnerable. They prefer to keep to a familiar circle of family and friends rather than move out into the world. For them, affection and responsibility go hand in hand. They always give the best of themselves, and expect the same in return.

Ox men are loners. They enjoy taking command, and deserve the important posts that they hold. However, their zeal at work may affect their private lives.

Tiger

13 February 1926 – 1 February 1927
31 January 1938 – 18 February 1939
17 February 1950 – 5 February 1951
5 February 1962 – 24 January 1963
23 January 1974 – 10 February 1975
9 February 1986 – 28 January 1987
29 January 1990 – 15 February 1999
14 February 2010 – 2 February 2011

*T*igers are natural leaders. They are energetic and enthusiastic, qualities that enable them to fill key positions at work and in the community. Sometimes they are self-centered and stubborn, unwilling to submit to authority. As a result, they often rebel against people who are older or occupy more important posts. This characteristic may also enable them to lead the way in fighting oppression or working for social change.

Tigers can be loners. It's often hard to make them fit in. They prize their independence and freedom, and are often unstable and impatient. On the other hand, taking on challenges allows them to develop their full potential.

Women Tigers have sensual natures and captivating personalities. They are fiercely passionate in love, but their need for independence and freedom can be exasperating.

Men Tigers are extremely interesting people, but refuse to let others invade their territory. Although they can be authoritarian at times, they also like to charm and are attracted by women who appear helpless.

Hare

2 February 1927 – 22 January 1928
19 February 1939 – 7 February 1940
6 February 1951 – 26 January 1952
25 January 1963 – 12 February 1964
11 February 1975 – 30 January 1976
29 January 1987 – 16 February 1988
16 February 1999 – 3 February 2000
3 February 2011 – 22 January 2012

*H*ares are highly sensitive, intuitive people who seek friendship. They value emotional relationships that give them a sense of well-being and security. They are tactful and discreet friends or partners, well-intentioned and amiable by nature. Above all, they seek harmony in their relationships and will back off at the first sign of discord.

Because they are naturally reserved, Hares are interested in stable, enduring relationships. A real home, with a tranquil and welcoming atmosphere, is very important to them. They are extremely lucky at games of chance, but their natural discipline and prudence keeps them from going overboard.

Hare women demand a great deal of affectionate behavior from family and friends. They blossom in a setting where there is money, a home, and lots of leisure time. They are well-groomed and elegant, and love getting dressed up.

Hare men make good husbands, indulgent fathers, and wonderful friends. They don't like competitive situations, and may avoid them by becoming distant or preoccupied. Often, they are dreamy people.

Dragon

3 February 1916 – 22 January 1917
23 January 1928 – 9 February 1929
8 February 1940 – 26 January 1941
27 January 1952 – 13 February 1953
13 February 1964 – 1 February 1965
31 January 1976 – 17 February 1977
17 February 1988 – 5 February 1989
4 February 2000 – 24 January 2001

*D*ragon people always seem larger than life — like movie stars on a giant screen. They always stand out in a crowd — and the crowd can't help being impressed! They have sparkling, strong-willed personalities with plenty of charisma. People are easily attracted to Dragons, who are enterprising and dynamic, and almost always rise to the top in their chosen field — often in politics, business, or the entertainment world. However, they are sometimes rather full of themselves and inconsiderate of others. They may at times be disloyal or unfaithful, but their irresistible charm usually convinces people to give them a second chance.

Dragon women may seem very sophisticated and cosmopolitan, but they're also very down-to-earth, warm, and understanding. Their vitality and glamor sometimes make them intimidating and tactless.

Dragon men are hard to understand. They love being the center of attention, and enjoy a good laugh. However, they won't tolerate being ruled by a woman. They have a short attention span, and prefer challenges that call for action.

Snake

23 January 1917 – 10 February 1918
10 February 1929 – 29 January 1930
27 January 1941 – 14 February 1942
14 February 1953 – 2 February 1954
 2 February 1965 – 20 January 1966
18 February 1977 – 6 February 1978
 6 February 1989 – 26 January 1990
25 January 2001 – 12 February 2002

*S*nake people have an infallible instinct for making the best of things. They possess a special kind of creativity, and are particularly resourceful — and successful — when it comes to taking on projects that seem doomed to failure. As a result, they often do well in business. They are skilful, ingenious, and able to demonstrate their competence without stooping to petty rivalry.

Snakes are great romantics, attentive to the well-being and happiness of those they love. However, they may become morose or bitter if they don't receive the same loving attention from those close to them.

Snake women are extremely attractive. They love parties, expensive clothes, jewels, and other luxury items. At the same time, they are practical people who like to help others, but hate fuss and bother. They are faithful partners, although inclined to jealousy.

Snake men are handsome, elegant people who have their lives well under control. They like paying attention to others. If they are discontented, they don't show it — but they may simply move on!

Horse *milk*

11 February 1918 – 31 January 1919
30 January 1930 – 16 February 1931
15 February 1942 – 4 February 1943
 3 February 1954 – 23 January 1955
21 January 1966 – 8 February 1967
 7 February 1978 – 27 January 1979
27 January 1990 – 14 February 1991
13 February 2002 – 1 February 2003

*H*orse people inspire friendship and are very supportive companions, but their impetuous nature sometimes leads them to lash out at others. They are strong, vigorous, have lots of stamina, and can work hard and tirelessly. However, their excessive enthusiasm can sometimes make them hot-headed and stubborn.

Horse people are enormously fun-loving. Leisure activities and especially travel form part of their lifestyle. They are good at combining pleasure and business, and don't spend money lavishly or needlessly. However, when they fall in love, they tend to lose their heads and become highly unrealistic.

Horse women are good at technical or artistic activities. They are extremely determined, practical-minded, and straightforward people who like to have their own way — a trait that can make their love lives difficult, to say the least.

Horse men shy away from love, even if they need it. They are practical, hardworking people, affectionate but possessive, and tend to rule over others in their immediate circle while insisting on loyalty and devotion.

Sheep

1 February 1919 – 19 February 1920
17 February 1931 – 5 February 1932
5 February 1943 – 24 January 1944
24 January 1955 – 11 February 1956
9 February 1967 – 29 January 1968
28 January 1979 – 15 February 1980
15 February 1991 – 3 February 1992
2 February 2003 – 21 January 2004

*S*heep people are noted for their kindliness and devotion. They are naturally artistic, with a distinct preference for the applied arts. They excel in this field, being inclined to follow conventional styles rather than develop one of their own. They are generally trusting, passive, easily led, and model their behavior and opinions on those around them.

These generally peaceful and gentle people have an easy-going manner that inspires confidence. Their tact and delicacy makes them good diplomats. However, Sheep can sometimes give way to violent bursts of anger. If they are badly advised or left to themselves, they may become irresponsible and detached from reality.

Women sheep are fascinating people, and particularly good at finding exactly the sort of mate they want. They are sensual and generous, but need to feel deeply loved in an enduring relationship.

Men Sheep are lovable people, but not very good about assuming day to day responsibilities. They make better lovers than husbands. When they do marry, they are quite happy to let their wives rule the roost.

Monkey _Ed_

20 February 1920 – 7 February 1921
6 February 1932 – 25 January 1933
25 January 1944 – 12 February 1945
12 February 1956 – 30 January 1957
30 January 1968 – 16 February 1969
16 February 1980 – 4 February 1981
4 February 1992 – 22 January 1993
22 January 2004 – 9 February 2005

_M_onkey people are highly talented, adaptable, and intelligent. They are wily and shrewd, and make excellent negotiators. As a result, they are successful in business. On the other hand, their cleverness and natural wit make them wonderful comedians or mimics.

Because of their playful, amusing personalities, Monkeys are wonderful companions. However, it isn't always possible to count on them. Sometimes they are deceitful or mischievous in their relationships with others. For this reason, they feel the need to play the field before getting involved in a deep and stable relationship.

Monkey women are whimsical and possess a disarming innocence that is most attractive. They have a great capacity for adapting to situations, and remain faithful to one man as long as he holds their interest.

Monkey men are charming, love to clown around, and seem to laugh or cry more than other people. They don't take themselves too seriously, which is perhaps the key to their eternal youthfulness.

Rooster _- mom_

8 February 1921 – 27 January 1922
26 January 1933 – 13 February 1934
13 February 1945 – 1 February 1946
31 January 1957 – 17 February 1958
17 February 1969 – 5 February 1970
5 February 1981 – 24 January 1982
23 January 1993 – 9 February 1994
10 February 2005 – 29 January 2006

_R_ooster people are proud, and at times a little haughty. They tend to overwork, are efficient and independent, but take on more than they can handle, and this puts them in difficult and often disappointing situations. Occasionally, they are rather bossy in their demands on less competent colleagues.

Roosters are honest, sincere people. However, their frankness sometimes borders on rudeness that can break up friendships. Their forthright and independent personalities make them excellent explorers, because they love adventure and traveling into the unknown.

Rooster women fuss a lot over those close to them. However, they consider their own activities important as well, and usually manage to fit everything in. At the first hint of inefficiency, they become bossy and find fault. On the other hand, they themselves need approval and recognition.

Rooster men are subject to rapid mood-swings. In general, they are very gregarious. They are great charmers and know how to make the most of their strong points.

Dog

28 January 1922 – 15 February 1923
14 February 1934 – 3 February 1935
 2 February 1946 – 21 January 1947
18 February 1958 – 7 February 1959
 6 February 1970 – 26 January 1971
25 January 1982 – 12 February 1983
10 February 1994 – 30 January 1995
30 January 2006 – 17 February 2007

*D*og people are exceptionally loyal and willing workers. They always do the job assigned, and carry out their responsibilities to the best of their ability. They aren't much interested in new or original ideas. Conservative by nature, they are slow to adapt to change — a characteristic that sometimes makes those around them impatient.

Dog people like to be have close relationships. They are sympathetic by nature, indulgent, and discreet, qualities that gain them many friends. On the other hand, if they find you unsympathetic they can become sarcastic or aggressive. Dogs appreciate encouragement enormously, as they tend to lack self-confidence.

Dog women consider themselves ambitious, although what they really want is power. They need a great deal of reassurance — plenty of words of comfort and lots of warm hugs and caresses.

Dog men tend to be wary. They become irritated at too much interference, but are always grateful when people show confidence in them and provide encouragement.

Pig

16 February 1923 – 4 February 1924
 4 February 1935 – 23 January 1936
22 January 1947 – 9 February 1948
 8 February 1959 – 27 January 1960
27 January 1971 – 15 January 1972
13 February 1983 – 1 February 1984
31 January 1995 – 18 February 1996
18 February 2007 – 5 February 2008

*P*ig people are models of tolerance and understanding. They are attentive to the well-being of the people around them, and particularly devoted and selfless in relations with their families. They are good and compassionate listeners as well as being generous and indulgent in their relationships, and this earns them firm friendships that usually last a lifetime.

Pigs are conscientious, with a strong sense of responsibility that makes them diligent, reliable workers. They make a point of always trying to do their best and prove their ability, because they are anxious to succeed on their personal merits.

Pig women are supportive companions, kind, dependable, and undemanding. However, they run the risk of regretting that they have not been more self-assertive. In return, they need a loyal and protective partner.

Pig men are charming. They are good at coaxing others, and are attracted by kindness. These engaging, loving, and open personalities have a tender and confiding heart, with an occasional tendency to become very depressed.

Signs of the Zodiac

*A*strology probably originated with the shepherds of ancient Chaldea, who observed the night sky as they watched over their flocks. The points of light in the dark heavens seemed to be arranged in patterns that depicted mythical or living things — the Ram, the Hunter, the Virgin, and so on — and these became the signs of the Zodiac.

The wise men of Babylon, the capital of Chaldea, noticed that people born at the same period of the year showed similar character traits. These astrologers would "cast a horoscope"— in other words, interpret the influence of heavenly bodies on human behavior and earthly events, especially in relation to the position or "ascendancy" of stars and planets at the time of one's birth. Different periods in the year were endowed with qualities corresponding to the twelve signs of the Zodiac.

Aries

21 March – 19 April

People born under the sign of Aries (the Ram) are spontaneous, enthusiastic individuals. They are simple, direct, loyal, and have good judgment. They like to be active, and prefer to take the initiative rather than work at a routine job. They are enterprising and would rather attack problems directly than try to avoid them.

Rams tend to act on impulse rather than think things out. Sometimes they are torn between tenderness and violence, generosity and anger. At other times, their enthusiasm may make them unrealistic. Although passionate in friendship and love, Rams attach great importance to their independence and tend to impose their tastes and opinions on others.

Ram women have dynamic, spontaneous personalities. Their likes and dislikes are immediate, and tact is not their strong point. They are generous and brave, and often come to the defense of the oppressed.

Ram men have the enthusiasm of a youngster. They need a life filled with action, risk, and adventure, all of which keep them in a state of constant, youthful effervescence.

Taurus

20 April – 20 May

People born under the sign of Taurus (the Bull) need material and emotional security. Possessions are the outward sign of their social success. They have a methodical, well-reasoned approach to their lives and work, and plan for the long term. Although they have difficulty getting started, nothing can stop them once they're on their way.

They have a natural charm, often accompanied by a soft-spoken and friendly manner. They know how to listen and to give good advice. They make tender and affectionate lovers and express their fondness in generous ways. They have a highly-developed sense of family and tradition, and want their relationships to be peaceful and harmonious.

Taurus women are very sentimental. They are physically attractive, make faithful and tender lovers, but are possessive and don't want to share the loved one. Their stubbornness and inability to break up a relationship sometimes prolongs difficult situations.

Taurus men are charming lovers, but demanding. They won't stand for people breaking their word. They love nature and the countryside, and therefore enjoy outdoor activities.

Gemini

21 May – 20 June

People born under the sign of Gemini (the Twins) have an amazing faculty for adapting to different situations. They are outgoing, witty, and young at heart. They love talking, meeting people, and improvising. They are articulate and intelligent, but tend to know a little about a lot.

In their love lives, Gemini people look for a lively yet enriching intellectual relationship. However, they tend to flit from one lover to another rather than settling down, and this can prevent them from becoming seriously involved. Their dual, often contradictory nature can make them feel misunderstood. Although they may be totally sincere, their focus tends to shift constantly. Intellectual Gemini may be capable of great duplicity.

Gemini women possess a refined charm, and can express their feelings easily. What they want most is to be loved. Consequently, they can be outrageous flirts in order to prove how attractive they are.

Gemini men are witty and charming, but tend to collect conquests. Their passion for change can easily become instability.

Cancer

21 June – 22 July

People born under the sign of Cancer (the Crab), have a hard exterior that hides a tender, affectionate nature. These highly emotional, intuitive, and hypersensitive people are great worriers. They often view the past with nostalgia.

Their moods change frequently, but anything that touches their hearts is given immediate attention. They have an instinctive urge for parenthood, and are very protective of their families.

They make affectionate and sensitive partners who seek Love with a capital L. Once a stable relationship has been established, their goal is to create a home and start a family.

Cancer women are outstanding mothers. They adore their children, spoil them, and tend to fret over them. On the other hand, they themselves need a great deal of tenderness and constant proofs of love.

Cancer men have a gentle, vulnerable temperament. They sometimes feel the need to be mothered. They look for reassuring, intimate relationships, hoping that this will provide the stability and sense of well-being that they seek.

Leo

23 July – 22 August

People born under the sign of Leo (the Lion) are generous, warmhearted, and blessed with a sunny disposition. They are extremely creative and live life to the full. These good planners and organizers accomplish a lot in a day. The notion of leisure is foreign to Leos. They take their recreation seriously and perfect their skills to an almost professional level.

Leos make sensitive partners, but they are easily hurt, because they idealize their emotional relationships. They ask a lot and give a lot, but are disappointed if others don't meet their expectations. They usually like to dominate a relationship and make the decisions. They have an overwhelming need to be emotionally involved and to feel fulfilled.

Leo women love being wooed by an ardent partner who wines and dines them. They like luxury and comfort, and seek beauty in all things. They are passionate and noble-hearted.

Leo men have an inborn sense of responsibility. They are loyal, fair-minded, and courageous, and can surpass themselves when rising to great challenges.

Virgo

23 August – 22 September

Those born under the sign of Virgo (the Virgin), are rather modest, unassertive people. They are great perfectionists and very reliable, but they sometimes allow themselves to be swamped by small details. These practical, logical-minded people tend to be critical and inflexible. They are very articulate, and enjoy discussions where there is an exchange of ideas and opinions.

Because they usually think with their heads rather than their hearts, Virgo people have difficulty becoming emotionally involved. When they do, they are obliging and kind to loved ones. Paradoxically, they often put on a show of great assurance, or appear reserved and distant, in order to hide their modest, unassertive nature.

Virgo women dream of romantic love but hesitate to let themselves go. They like daily routine, and involve themselves almost exclusively in activities where a sense of logic and detail are important.

Virgo men are hardworking and practical, but can lack self-confidence. They are loyal and methodical by nature, but feel the need to be supervised.

Libra

23 September – 22 October

People born under the sign of Libra (the Scales) look for equilibrium first and foremost. They are thoughtful, sensitive people who will make any sacrifice to achieve peace and harmony. They tend to see all sides of a question, and for this reason may have difficulty making decisions. They don't adjust well to major changes. They have an inborn sense of beauty, and love the arts in all forms, beautiful surroundings, and good food.

Their ideal of a perfect love relationship involves balance and harmony. They don't rush into things. When times are difficult, reason and common sense prevail, and emotions are put aside for the time being. Their ultimate goal is to establish an environment in which there is no conflict or rupture.

Libra women are pure romantics. Their relationship with their partner is enormously important to them. They can be conciliatory in order to foster harmony.

Libra men are friendly, fond of society, peace-loving, and very generous. They are masters of the art of self-control, and generally want to please.

Scorpio

23 October – 21 November

People born under the sign of Scorpio (the Scorpion) are strong-willed and passionate. They hate social obligations and interruptions, and don't take kindly to authority unless they hold their superiors in high esteem. They have the reputation of being sex symbols, but this erotic power is symptomatic of their need to get to the heart of things.

Scorpios are generally anxious, hypersensitive people who are subject to periods of emotional stress. They tend to be guided by intuition rather than logic. They don't talk about themselves much, and this gives them a fascinating air of mystery. They are rather cold at first meeting, but can suddenly become very friendly — they either adore people or detest them.

Scorpio women are often divided between passionate love and violent aversion. They can hurt others with sharp words or actions, then tend the wound they've just inflicted.

Scorpio men are powerful, determined people who will go to great lengths to protect their individuality. They hate being emotionally dependent, although they can be jealous and resentful of others.

Sagittarius

22 November – 21 December

The chivalrous spirit of Sagittarius (the Archer) makes for enthusiastic people who seek an absolute ideal. They are jovial, honest, and open-hearted, with a spiritual quality that is illuminating for themselves and others. They like challenges and are always pursuing new objectives, although they don't always manage to achieve their goals. Their natural joy in living sometimes makes them careless or thoughtless.

Sagittarius people look for sincere feelings in friends and lovers, based on similarity of tastes, but won't stand for infringements on their personal freedom. They are often conventional in love, because they need to believe in enduring relationships. They detest emotional complications. In crisis situations, they have difficulty in readjusting their outlook.

Sagittarius women feel a marked attraction for the exotic in friends and lovers. They love life, and possess a freshness and candor that is reflected in their natural exuberance and sense of humor.

Sagittarius men hate to be in constricting situations. They are sincere and spontaneous lovers with a healthy and joyful sensuality.

Capricorn

22 December – 19 January

People born under the sign of Capricorn (the Goat), are calm and clearheaded observers of what goes on around them. Their outlook is conventional, and they have a strong, almost stubborn need for stability and permanence. They are very patient, and their projects are well planned and well executed. This makes them appear rather calculating. Capricorns feel they should know everything, and lose confidence in themselves when they don't achieve the success they counted on. They are contradictory people, and can be both impulsive and reserved, whimsical and enigmatic.

Capricorns have difficulty expressing their feelings, a disability that they hide under a stoic, rather brusque exterior. They sometimes alternate between an apparent dryness and melodramatic demonstrativeness.

Capricorn women have a highly original sense of humor that contrasts with their tendency to nag. They are determined and tenacious.

Capricorn men feel more at ease when they have lots of emotional and physical space. They like solitude, fear emotional involvement, and don't allow their feelings to come to the fore until they are established in life.